THE TRAJECTORY OF HOLOCAUST MEMORY

The Trajectory of Holocaust Memory: The Crisis of Testimony in Theory and Practice re-considers survivor testimony, moving from a subject-object reading of the past to a subject-subject encounter in the present. It explores how testimony evolves in relationship to the life of eyewitnesses across time.

This book breaks new ground based on three principles. The first draws on Martin Buber's "I-Thou" concept, transforming the object of history into an encounter between subjects. The second employs the Jungian concept of identity, whereby the individual (internal identity) and the persona (external identity) reframe testimony as an extension of the individual. They are a living subject, rather than merely a persona or narrative. The third principle draws on Daniel Kahneman's concept of the experiencing self, which relives events as they occurred, and the remembering self, which reflects on their meaning in sum. Taken together, these principles comprise a new literacy of testimony that enables the surviving victim and the listener to enter a relationship of trust.

Designed for readers of Holocaust history and literature, this book defines the modalities of memory, witness, and testimony. It shows how encountering the individual who lived through the past changes how testimony is understood, and therefore what it can come to mean.

Stephen D. Smith is Executive Director Emeritus, USC Shoah Foundation, and USC Visiting Professor of Religion. His published titles include *Never Again Yet Again* (2009), *The Holocaust and the Christian World* (2020), and *The Routledge Handbook of Religion, Mass Atrocity and Genocide* (2021).

THE TRAJECTORY OF HOLOCAUST MEMORY

The Crisis of Testimony in
Theory and Practice

Stephen D. Smith

LONDON AND NEW YORK

Designed cover image: Nimrod 'Zigi' Ariav gives testimony to USC Shoah Foundation's Visual History Archive in Tel Aviv, 2016 (photo courtesy of Stephen D. Smith).

First published 2023
by Routledge
4 Park Square, Milton Park, Abingdon, Oxon OX14 4RN

and by Routledge
605 Third Avenue, New York, NY 10158

Routledge is an imprint of the Taylor & Francis Group, an informa business

© 2023 Stephen D. Smith

The right of Stephen D. Smith to be identified as author of this work has been asserted in accordance with sections 77 and 78 of the Copyright, Designs and Patents Act 1988.

All rights reserved. No part of this book may be reprinted or reproduced or utilised in any form or by any electronic, mechanical, or other means, now known or hereafter invented, including photocopying and recording, or in any information storage or retrieval system, without permission in writing from the publishers.

Trademark notice: Product or corporate names may be trademarks or registered trademarks, and are used only for identification and explanation without intent to infringe.

British Library Cataloguing-in-Publication Data
A catalogue record for this book is available from the British Library

Library of Congress Cataloging-in-Publication Data
A catalog record has been requested for this book

ISBN: 978-0-367-70617-3 (hbk)
ISBN: 978-0-367-70618-0 (pbk)
ISBN: 978-1-003-14722-0 (ebk)

DOI: 10.4324/9781003147220

Typeset in Bembo
by Apex CoVantage, LLC

To Isabel Wollaston with enduring gratitude.

CONTENTS

Acknowledgments ix
Preface xi
Foreword xii

PART I
The Crisis of Witness 1

1   Name, Date, Place 3
    The First Testimony 3
    The Trajectory of Holocaust Memory 9

2   What It Means, and What It Doesn't 20
    The Hanging Scene 20
    Witness and the Many Forms of the Present 26
    Rehumanizing the Past 35
    Limits of Collective Conscience 38
    The Crisis of Witness 42
    The Mandate 45
    Resolving the Dilemma 47

3   The Constrained Witness 54
    Limits of Language 58
    Who Is a Holocaust Witness? 66
    The Impossibility of Forgetfulness 73

4 All That Is Real (and Some That Is Not) 79
   Sabina's Missing Face 79
   Being-for-Itself or Something-Others? 83
   Testimony and Its Many Forms 87
   Past in the Present 91
   Witness as Authentication 93
   Marvelous But Fallacious 98
   Returns to Auschwitz 104
   The Value of Rutabagas 107
   (False) Testimony 112

PART II
The Origins of Holocaust Witness 125

5 Witness within the Storm 127
   An Audience of Strangers 127
   Historiographical Defiance 136

6 They Were Not Silenced 143
   The Need to Talk 143
   The Awakening 151
   No Traveler Returns 156
   Dos Polyishe Yidntum 160
   To Tell the World 163
   That's How It Was 169
   The Boy Who Drew Auschwitz 171
   The Theory and Practice of Hell 174
   Ka-Tzetnik 135633 176

PART III
Trajectories Beyond the Final Word 187

7 Deep Inside, I'm Still There 189
   The Holocaust Man 189
   Reasons to Speak 193
   Scraps of Memory 197
   Listen Then Listen Again 200
   The Ossification of Witness 203
   The Keyhole and the Clothesline 211
   (Non)Closure 212

Index 223

ACKNOWLEDGMENTS

This book is the culmination of many years of research and practice. Hundreds of people have offered thousands of hours of their time as colleagues, friends, and partners in the pursuit of Holocaust education, remembrance, and research. To everyone who has helped me along the way, thank you.

The survivors of the Holocaust who have given me specific insights and guidance personally over the years include Zigi Ariav, Celina Beniaz, Yehuda Bacon, Susi Bechoffer, Edith Birken, Naomi Blake, Ella Blumenthal, Dolly Botton, Julio Botton, Elisabeth Citrom, George Citrom, Bat-Sheva Dagan, Lily Ebert, Dr. Edith Eva Eger, Max Eisen, Riane Eisler, Aaron Elster, Gisella Feldman, Renee Firestone, Steven Frank, John Fransman, Hedi Fried, Fritzie Fritzschal, Dario Gabbai, Thomas Geve, Waldemar Ginsburg, Ibi Ginburg, Richard Glazar, Ely Gotz, Leon Greenman, Bernard Grunberg, Pinchas Gutter, Roman Halter, Kitty Hart-Moxon, Ben Helfgott, Arek Hersh, Richard Horowitz, Eric Kandel, Denise Kandel, Miriam Katin, Joshua Kaufmann, Ruben Katz, Roman Kent, Eva Kor, Anita Lasker-Wallfisch, Sonia Lax, Michael Lee, Ben Lesser, Miriam Lichterman, Paula Lebovics, Trudy Levy, Ella Lingens-Reiner, Edith Maniker, Philip Maisel, Steven Mendelson, Joanna Milan, Daisy Miller, Ed Mosberg, Paul Oppenheimer, Rudi Oppenheimer, Eve Oppenheimer, Joseph Perl, Samuel Pisar, Sam Pivnik, Nathan Pivnik, Susan Pollak, Renee Salt, Trudy Silman, Max Schindler, Rose Schindler, Eva Schloss, Sid Shachnow, Sara Shapiro, Martin Stern, Andrew Stevens, Dana Schwartz, Gina Schwarzmann, Mala Tribich, Gina Turgel, Marian Turski, Lisa Vincent, Victoria Vincent, Erna Viterbi, Sonia Warshawski, Max Webb, George Weiss, Dr. Ruth Westheimer, Simon Wiesenthal, Frieda Wineman, and Simon Winston. May those of you who are still the guardians of memory find strength and for those who have left us, I hope this book represents what you have taught me.

Isabel Wollaston, my patient and supportive Ph.D. mentor: thank you. Without you I would not be here, and I certainly would not have had the skills to write this book. You will always be my mentor.

Jonathan Webber, I not only owe you for being willing to examine my Ph.D. in 2000, which began my own journey into memory and witness. I have also long admired your lifelong personal and academic commitment to help us all better understand Holocaust memorial culture. Thank you for your beautiful Foreword.

Henry Greenspan, I thought I was doing something unique in the late 1990s. Then in 1998 you published "On Listening to Holocaust Survivors." To this day, you and I share a common understanding of the need to deeply respect the source. Thank you for your heart, soul, and mind.

Robert Langham and the Routledge history team, thank you for believing that oral history and memory are an integral part of the ways in which we think about the past.

Andrew Schrock, thank you for your perceptive and skillful guidance throughout this project.

Yasmin, Natalia, Stephanie, and Aaron, you stuck with me during my early years of research. Many of the people listed are like extended family to you—extra grandparents—who smothered you with affection. Thank you for allowing me to follow what I needed to pursue. Stephanie, I owe you for pushing me to finally start publishing my research!

James you are always my journeyman.

Heather, your willingness to ask questions and preserve conversations for future generations represents the best application of my theory of testimony. You dreamed that up out of your own brilliance, without knowledge of my theory. You know how to listen with your heart and are brilliant on your own accord. Thank you for being with me every step, every day.

Mum, your wisdom is sorely missed. Dad, you have always supported and believed in me. I know you always will.

PREFACE

The great Jewish rabbinical sage Hillel is reported to have once described the Golden Rule of Classical Judaism to a new convert:

> That which is hateful to you do not do to another. That is the entire Torah, the rest is its interpretation.
>
> *(Talmud, Shabbat 31a)*

In that same spirit, the entirety of this book can be summed up in a single line: "listen to the surviving victims of the Holocaust with all your heart." That is the entire book; the rest is its interpretation.

Stephen D. Smith
Los Angeles, February 2022

FOREWORD

Following the liberation of the Nazi death camps by the Allied armies towards the end of the Second World War, some might have wondered whether the world would ever have first-hand testimony of what transpired. Such concerns turned out to be warrantless. The British Army filmed what they found when they liberated Bergen-Belsen in April 1945, as did the Red Army when they liberated Auschwitz three months earlier. Mountains of documents were brought to the war crimes trials. Recorded audio and audio-visual personal testimonies of surviving victims of the Holocaust now total at least 200,000 hours, stored in archives around the world. If this vast amount of testimony could be viewed or listened to non-stop, it would take more than 20 years to experience it all. Still now the voices of the witnesses continue to amass in the visual arts, performing arts, memoirs, fiction, poetry, documentaries, narrative films, memorials, museums, commemorations, tours, education programs, social media channels, conferences, and speeches. Their voices are not identical, as each person has something different to say. To make sense of this extraordinarily large amount of material we need an experienced guide.

Dr. Stephen D. Smith is particularly well-qualified to fulfil such a task, as the reader of this volume will rapidly discover. His co-founding (with his parents and brother) the UK's first Holocaust education and memorial center in 1995 was followed by his personal involvement in other important UK initiatives (notably his chairmanship of the UK Holocaust Memorial Day Trust which foregrounds survivor testimony). He rose to prominence in the field, becoming a leading member of the British delegation to the Intergovernmental Task Force on Holocaust Education, Remembrance and Research (now the International Holocaust Remembrance Alliance) when it was founded in 1998. Dr. Smith then served as advisor to the Swedish Prime Minister at the Stockholm Forum (attended by delegations from 46 countries) in 2000. He was then invited by Steven Spielberg in 2009 to take on the role of executive director of USC Shoah Foundation in Los Angeles. In that capacity he became the chief custodian of over 50,000 audio-visual survivor testimonies now held in an archive purpose-built by the Foundation at the University of Southern California (USC). A few years later he became the university's inaugural UNESCO Chair in Genocide Education.

In this excellent, deeply fascinating book, Dr. Smith takes us through his experiences in encountering these testimonies and their authors. He approaches the subject with considerable compassion, sensitivity, and humility, although at the same time he is certainly able to maintain critical distance. For example, he demonstrates how survivors (whom he consistently calls surviving victims) may disagree on the meaning and purpose of giving testimony. At the same time, he avoids being judgmental about omissions or lapses of memory. In fact, he shows how such features need to be understood as part of testimony.

Dr. Smith has a passionate, hands-on approach to commitment and leadership in this field. In this book we are introduced to his abilities as an experienced interviewer of survivors, a difficult task that requires mastery of innumerable intricacies and nuances, not to mention the emotionally challenging difficulties of continually encountering recollections of real-world atrocity and the raw pain that comes through testimony. He is enormously well-read, constantly in dialog with a wide range of relevant scholarly and philosophical approaches—he has 250 titles of secondary literature listed in his bibliography, which is a useful resource in itself. No less important to his ethnographic approach is his broad grasp of relevant comparative material gained as project director for the creation of the Kigali Genocide Memorial Centre in Rwanda and as a trustee of the South Africa Holocaust and Genocide Foundation. His deep experience has brought respect for the suffering and pain of those who have trusted him to present their testimony to the world and safeguard what they have to say.

Early in this book Dr. Smith introduces us to a distinction made by the eminent American psychologist Daniel Kahneman between the experiencing self (what the individual went through at the time) and the remembering self (how that person reflects on the experience at a later date); the surviving victim of the Holocaust lives with both modalities. Because of the overwhelming pain it may have caused, a survivor giving testimony may succumb to loss, guilt, nostalgia, memorializing, mythologization, and battles with the forgotten past. Interpreting testimony is far from straightforward. And yet, perhaps the real aim of this work of Holocaust memory is to keep watch over "absent memory"—the silence of the majority of victims who did not survive, testimony that has been left unsaid and can never be said. In a very real sense, testimony brings a mandate to speak on behalf of the dead to preserve and transmit their memory to future generations. For some, the fulfilment of that mandate happened within days of liberation. For others, it took over 50 years. For some it is yet to happen. For others it never will.

One needs to understand that each act of testimony represents the struggle to bring the world of the past into that of the present. We need testimony for it to be better understood, if never completely so, by those who did not live through it. Survivors testify because they were witnesses, not because they understand their experience; there is a difference between recounting the events and comprehending them. They usually do not have sufficient time, language, or space to explain the nuances of their conclusions. Language struggles to convey the meaning of abnormal experiences; feeling "thirst" or "hunger" in Auschwitz meant something qualitatively different from everyday thirst or hunger. Their experiences produce a partially formed and largely unexplored narrative that brings them and their listeners together only at limited points. Testimony is thus inherently fragmentary because a complete narration of the events is simply not possible. In short, it needs to be decoded through a suitable commentary. That is what Dr. Smith consistently puts his skill and his knowledge to addressing throughout this book.

For example, he highlights how Paul Oppenheimer explicitly refers in his memoirs to his own "accumulated knowledge," gathered through visits to museums, books by other surviving victims, and lectures by historians. For some, Oppenheimer's search for meaning leaves his narrative open to criticism that he "borrowed" the memories and research of others, creating a form of assisted memory that became a patchwork mosaic. Sensitively, however, Dr. Smith shows that no single surviving victim's narrative can represent the experience of another's, let alone represent history as a whole. One needs multiple narratives and sources.

What is one to make of the common assertion by surviving victims (and indeed also by their descendants) that "the Ukrainians were worse than the Germans?" It was the Germans, not the Ukrainians, who were the architects of the genocide of the Jews. On this point he comments that such witnesses will most likely have encountered Ukrainians more often and in more brutal circumstances, and therefore have the right to that opinion in the context of their own testimonies. Survivors lacked wider information at the time; they can report only what they saw. Dr. Smith suggests that it is our role as readers to understand why they have drawn those generalized opinions (often also said about Poles). He cites the survivor Nathan Alterman, who clarified that "I wasn't scared of the Germans, I was scared of the Ukrainians." His anger towards the Ukrainians was based on the fear he had lived with as a young person knowing how to evade Germans, but being afraid of his own neighbors. Crucially, testimony documents experience, not historical fact.

The life history methodology, as used by the USC Shoah Foundation, starts with detailed, hard data that the interviewee provides prior to the interview. The data can include up to 40 pages of information on specific names, dates, places, family, ghettos, camps, and other personal details, which contributes to the sense of the interview being a documentation session. However, once the interview begins, the mode becomes that of storytelling. The interviewer is not fact-checking or seeking specific historical details. Rather, the interviewees are encouraged to tell their own story in their own words.

Dr. Smith mastered this technique long before he joined USC. Encouraging eyewitnesses to speak in their own words was how Claude Lanzmann presented them in his epic documentary film *Shoah* (1985). Dr. Smith includes an extended discussion of this film, focusing on Szymon Srebrnik and Michael Podchlebnik, both among the very few survivors of the Chełmno death camp in occupied Poland. Podchlebnik had the job of unloading corpses from the vans, inside which victims had been gassed to death. In his testimony he describes the Tuesday when he unloaded the bodies of his own wife and children. It was "unspeakable in every sense of the word," as Dr. Smith says. He then goes on to comment, basing himself on the Hebrew writer and Holocaust survivor Aharon Appelfeld, that the intensity of this experience—the depth of its personal, social, historical, philosophical, spiritual meaning, and consequences—are pains that sit uncomfortably with a narrative retelling.

Testimonies, in other words, are what Dr. Smith calls "human documents." Like all memories, they are not fixed in time and place; they are not carved in stone. Unlike historical records, testimonies change over time based on the identity of the surviving victim at the moment in time being recalled, and the consequence of that moment on his or her own life. Hence, testimonies can evolve by taking on new features, as we learned from Paul Oppenheimer. Testimony is also replete with omissions, whether from a conscious decision to shape the memory to make it more pronounceable, palatable, or comprehensible in the present, or simply because of forgetfulness over time. Hence, as he says, it is always necessary to read, contrast, and juxtapose testimonies. It is best to encounter the same surviving victims more than once in face-to-face meetings. With knowledge of their story, it then becomes possible to understand the audio-visual testimonies at the level of facial expressions and body language during the pauses, silences, and moments of uncertainty. Survivors grapple with their memories when recalling the emotionally difficult moments, even if they end up saying little or nothing about the most traumatic episodes they experienced. Dr. Smith describes two interesting cases in some detail, both of survivors born in Poland, Pinchas Gutter and Kitty Hart-Moxon. Kitty wrote two memoirs and made four documentaries on location at former Holocaust sites.

What he learns from approaching testimonies as human documents is that they are all essentially provisional—they should not be treated as having a formal, finished quality. On the contrary, a testimony is one individual's partial insight, or a fragment of their experience. They are just one among tens of thousands of others who similarly shared their experiences, and represent millions more who could not. But his repeated encounters with survivors over several decades have built trusting relationships. Through evolving conversations with them, he enters into their perspective of the events they witnessed, resisting treating what they have to say as objective statements about historical realities. The same is true for our understanding of the diaries written during the war itself. Several of these survived and were translated and published. Twenty-five years ago, Dr. Smith writes, he read the notebooks of Adam Czerniaków (president of the Jewish Council in the Warsaw Ghetto); they detail his daily activities, which "at times appear mundane." He reread them not to learn about the history of the ghetto, but rather to understand

Czerniaków, who committed suicide when the start of the deportations to Treblinka was announced by the Germans:

> I discovered that I was much more able to understand his decision to take his own life. . . . Seeing the text from the author's point of view changed the text itself, because I understood the perspective of the individual in a different way. Czerniaków was no longer an object of history to me—he had become a subject facing an impossible struggle to save his people.

His experience encountering the diaries of Adam Czerniaków undoubtedly influenced Dr. Smith's approach to the vast archive at USC. Later in the book, he says that he typically watches testimony twice: the first time to take in the historical information provided, the second time to try to understand the individual ("who they are, not just what they say"). For example, the first time he listened to Mala Tribich's testimony he heard her say that she could not remember her deportation on a cattle wagon, even though she remembered being marched to the station and people watching. Her lapse was unusual, since being in the cattle wagons was an experience that many surviving victims typically say remained vivid in their minds. Here is his comment on this:

> The second time I watched the segment, it became clear to me what really troubled her. When she recalled the journey in the cattle wagon, she was not bothered by being unable to describe the physical conditions, but the psychological impact of the spectators observing their misery. What follows that passage is a brief comment about the bystanders. She wonders aloud about "what they [were] thinking and why they were watching." Mala was more troubled by the attitudes of the bystander than the abuse of the perpetrator. A passage that appeared to be about her *forgetfulness* of the journey in the cattle wagon is about her *remembering* the social and emotional humiliation she then felt.

This sensitive comment is a helpful indication of why this excellent book is worthy of careful reading.

As part of his responsibilities overseeing the USC Shoah Foundation, Dr. Smith routinely had to make decisions about how testimonies should be represented in education materials, films, and other media. He was also responsible for the mission and scope of the Foundation, including the collection of testimonies of survivors of genocides other than the Holocaust. He considered whether it was appropriate to use archived testimonies to teach tolerance or Holocaust history. In this context, he raised two vital questions: why witnesses decided to share their life experiences at all and what messages the testimonies might contain for future generations.

The response to those questions turned out to be massive. Over 30,000 witnesses confirmed that they chose to share their memories of their struggle to survive the Holocaust in order to educate. Now, future generations can learn about what they had endured, commemorate the dead, warn humanity of its capacity for genocide, and maintain hope for peace, harmony, and a better world. In this way, surviving witnesses offer us guidance for a better life, telling us to be kind, generous, respectful, and tolerant. One strong example of their generosity is found in the testimony of the Austrian Jew George Papanek, whom Dr. Smith quotes at length:

> I do think that there is something to be learned from these experiences. And the most important to me . . . is to take seriously what's happening now—[just] because the Nazis are gone, doesn't mean that evil is gone in this world. And there are many forms. And whoever you are, and wherever you are, you can find it. And it is very important to be part of the world in which you live, to be . . . engaged . . . in the world, and trying to do what is available to do that's useful. . . . The old saying . . . think globally, act locally is true. We all have opportunities to make a difference. And enough of us can create a critical mass so that the world can be a better place. There's no doubt about that in my mind. . . . I think the effort is worth it. . . . And I hope that we will continue to make this struggle and try to see that the world becomes better.

Encountering such testimony, it is perhaps little wonder that Stephen D. Smith has put decades of effort into nurturing close personal contact with survivors. He has had extensive conversations with them, and ensured that their messages reach the world. In a number of cases, he has even published their testimony through the UK National Holocaust Memorial Centre that he co-founded. Agreeing to be interviewed, and indeed seeing their story in print, has unquestionably been an important part of their ongoing healing process. This is especially true for those who, in the first years after the war, found a world unwilling to listen to the atrocities they had experienced and had considerable difficulty getting their memoirs published.

Recognizing that the inability to speak about the past is one of many symptoms of trauma, psychotherapists have worked with surviving victims, even later in their lives, to help them find their own voice. Their hope was that such therapy would dissipate the bad memories and "disrupted narratives" that have continued to haunt their lives, bringing only confusion and despair. There are now survivors who offer life lessons within their testimony derived both from their experiences and their professional expertise as therapists. Viktor Frankl is the most well-known case, but Dr. Smith quotes one of the USC Shoah Foundation interviewees, Edith Eva Eger, who was born in Kosice, Czechoslovakia, in 1927. "No one can take away from you what you have in your mind," he quotes her from an interview in 1995. Her mother had told her that as they sat in the cattle wagon. It was a piece of advice that became her North Star during and after the Holocaust. In sharp contrast to the French communist Charlotte Delbo, for whom the experience of Auschwitz was "useless knowledge," Edith put "loss, torture, starvation and the constant threat of death" to work as "tools for survival and freedom." She turned the "uselessness" of Auschwitz into a guide for living.

On the other hand, Dr. Smith remains aware that the desire for shorthand versions of the Holocaust brings creeping mythologization and closure that threaten to reduce the Holocaust to myths and legends (what he calls the "ossification of witness"). The language of dualism frequently found in testimony—about overcoming despair with hope, failure with heroism, silence with speaking, and darkness with light—creates a quasi-theological mythology focusing on "meanings." When the Holocaust becomes an incomprehensible mythologized world reduced and contained by dualistic narratives, we are no longer challenged by it. Testimony therefore always needs to be read in the context of what the testifier actually lived through.

In a particularly thoughtful section towards the end of this book, Dr. Smith strongly argues that testimony should not create fixed redemptive legends of a mythologized past. Rather, its daily details give us insight into human nature. These details can be ambiguous, contradictory, or may not conform to convenient patterns of human behavior. But such details give us the opportunity to continue to struggle with their implications rather than draw simplified conclusions. Ossification forces simplification over complexity, and certainty over ambiguity. It occurs when an expected outcome—survival, love, or redemption—is demanded of testimony, even when the narrative depicts death, hate, and deprivation. Ossification is a demand made by the kind of listener who seeks easy answers, rather than one who is prepared to grapple with unanswerable questions. Testimonial narratives, when taken together, are counter-mythological. They struggle with the mundane, the ordinariness, and the confusion, and the traumatic, disruptive, confusing, and ambiguous nature of events. They convey nuances at a personal level, even if they may at times fall into tropes and over-simplify. But because they each add to what we know, they also surprise us with unexpected experiences and new insights. Because they contradict one another, there can be no single narrative. Testimonies are plural and complex, so their interpretations will be similarly numerous and unpredictable. Shouldn't these facets of testimony also shape how we interpret them?

In fact, as he says with his characteristic modesty, there is no conclusion to the story, only a question: will testimony become an object of the past, or will it remain a dynamic subject in an ongoing dialogue about that past? He suggests that our duty is to pursue comprehension, while recognizing the fundamentally incomprehensible nature of the Holocaust. Narratives of survival are about human experience at the extreme, with all their paradoxes, ambivalences, and ironies. They will be best understood if they are allowed to tell, piece by piece, fragment by fragment, about broken lives. We should not expect testimony to provide answers. Rather, it should help us learn to confront the questions that fuel further inquiry, thereby sustaining a cycle of discourse. Dr. Smith suggests this cycle is reminiscent of how rabbinic Judaism's codification of the Talmud remains a dynamic and ongoing interpretative process. We remain in present-day debate with the scholars of ancient times, many centuries after their lives ended.

This is not a book written for beginners—although, as he states in the Preface, it can be summed up in a single line: "listen to surviving victims with all your heart."

That is the entire book, he says, and the rest is its interpretation. Because it is only a matter of time before a cacophony of interpretations—by historians, literary critics, poets, novelists, and others—will be all that we have. In the meantime, read and re-read this book, and take its lessons to heart!

Jonathan Webber
Emeritus UNESCO Chair in Jewish and Interfaith Studies,
University of Birmingham
Emeritus Professor, Institute of European Studies,
Jagiellonian University, Kraków, Poland

PART I
The Crisis of Witness

It is possible that there is no other memory than the memory of wounds.
—*Czeslaw Miłosz*

1
NAME, DATE, PLACE

The First Testimony

On April 24, 1945, Hela Goldstein stood with her back to a mass grave containing hundreds of corpses at Bergen-Belsen. She had encountered a British Movietone news crew that was covering the horrific discovery of the camp (British Movietone 1945). For 93 seconds, she spoke to the camera and described the day of her liberation. In so doing, Hela Goldstein unwittingly gave what is likely the first ever audio-visual testimony about the Holocaust, standing beside a mass grave, speaking to her former SS captors.

Bergen-Belsen had been liberated nine days earlier, when Lt. Derrick Sington first entered the camp with his loud hailer vehicle to inform the inmates that the British had taken control (Sington 1946). He was one of the first witnesses to the extent of the diseased and dying, which he relayed in his 1946 book, *Belsen Uncovered*. The corpses, which Sington estimated at 10,000, were strewn across the landscape. Bodies were stacked in piles and lying motionless in deserted barracks, alongside approximately 40,000 survivors. Sington's initial estimates were low. Other estimates place the number of people who were liberated that day between 57,500 and 60,000 (Lipscomb 1945). Many deaths followed the liberation, which in the hospital block alone were recorded at 13% of survivors (Lipscomb 1945). Over 23,200 corpses were buried in a series of 14 mass graves in the four weeks following liberation (Belsen n.d.). The Army Film and Photographic Unit (AFPU) and British Pathé (1945) filmed the scene. Their silent images and photographs depicted starving survivors in the first days of liberation, as well as the debris of death that Belsen came to visually represent.

After a chaotic start, by April 24 the British had procured resources to feed the surviving victims.[1] They set up a hospital for 15,000 patients in a former Panzer Training School (Sington 1946, 43; Berney 2015, 18) and dug ten mass graves to

DOI: 10.4324/9781003147220-3

bury the rotting corpses (Berney 2015, 15). In filmed reels of the burial, former camp guards are seen loading trucks with skeletal human remains and ferrying them to the graveside. There they are unloaded, then unceremoniously dragged and thrown into open pits. British troops are seen trying to keep order. Film director Sidney Bernstein had arrived at the camp from London that day. With Movietone's experienced newsreel commentator Paul Wyland, they had organized a series of on-camera interviews (Shephard 2005). Bernstein relayed in a later interview that the scene that met his eyes was so incredible, one day he thought it would not be believed. For this reason, Bernstein and Wyland decided that there should be witnesses to the filming, so went to the local towns to bring German civilians to watch. As Bernstein stated in the 1985 documentary *A Painful Reminder*:

> I wanted to record that all the local bigwigs and municipal *burgomeisters* and the like who lived within a reasonable range saw what was being done burying these tragic figures.
> (Blake 1985, 15:54–16:20)

On site at Belsen, he instructed his camera crew to film what they saw. He hoped that the footage would document the outcome of Nazi ideology and counter the denial that he suspected would follow. Instructions had been given to Paul Wyland from London to produce evidence that could not be dismissed as "atrocity propaganda" (Shephard 2005, 72). Bernstein took the unusual step to procure a microphone from Pathé News[2] (Smith and Cerrotti 2021, 22:13) to ensure that the sounds of the camp and the voices of the interviewees were captured in perpetuity. To ensure that perpetrators identified themselves at the scene of their crimes, the microphone was set up in front of the mass grave. Former guards were asked to stand, then state their name and rank in front of the evidence of their crimes. The camera lens was directed toward the perpetrators, with the mass grave filled with corpses in clear view behind.

Eighteen minutes and 35 seconds of footage was compiled on the British Movietone reels (British Movietone 1945), which show the scenes described earlier. During the filming, a young woman, presumably a surviving victim of the camp, can be seen shouting at the former SS guards in Polish, "*Czekajcie, a nasze młode lata wam się zapłaci. Czekajcie!*" which translates as, "[Just] wait. You will pay for [wasting] our youth. [Just] wait!"[3] Eleven minutes, 25 seconds into the reel, the same young woman is seen standing behind the microphone, poised to speak, the mass grave clearly in view behind her.

Over the next 95 seconds the young woman, who identified herself as Hela Goldstein, described her liberation from Bergen-Belsen nine days prior:

> Today is the 24th of April 1945. My Name is Hela Goldstein. I am talking about my experiences, that what I have survived in the camp Birkenwalde.[4] I arrived here under horrible circumstances. We were 1500 in one room.

FIGURE 1.1 Hela Goldstein at the microphone in Bergen-Belsen April 24, 1945. The index card describing the photograph stated: "Hela Goldstein a Polish inmate tells the world her crime: being born of Jewish blood meant four years in concentration camp"

Source: Photo BU4264 used with permission of Imperial War Museums.

We were very dirty and very crowded and there was no food and no water for us. That was just not living. We thought already we will not survive this. And five minutes before they—our comrades the English—came into our camp, the criminal people wanted to take us, and they undressed us totally naked and took everything away and just wanted to leave us there. But God was with us, and he helped us, and we became free after five minutes. And that what I have to tell [you] here was the last, the last that I had to survive. Thanks.[5]

When she volunteered to speak, Hela established enduring principles about Holocaust witnesses even before the Second World War was formally over. The first principle was that surviving victims would self-identify, thereby becoming narrators of their own experience rather than leaving it to others to describe it for them. Second, they would use the tools of new media, which in 1945 was the professional on-location movie camera to which Goldstein spoke. Third, survivors would intentionally use the channels at their disposal to reach to a mass audience.

The reels and photos taken at Belsen, for example, received massive publicity in British and American press (Kushner 1997, 183). Fourth, having just survived the anonymity of ignominious incarceration, for Hela to speak her name and tell her story was a form of narrative revenge; she had a name, and she had a story, she was also speaking directly to the SS who the British had lined up directly in front of her. Witnesses emerged as a form of resistance to Nazis' attempt to remove all trace of Jewish life. Surviving, then testifying, defeated the Nazi's original intent of death and obfuscation.

We have come to expect on-the-spot eyewitnesses to describe unfolding news stories for public consumption on 24-hour news channels. This was not the case for visual media in in 1945, although radio had been broadcast from the site at Bergen-Belsen almost immediately, as evidenced by BBC correspondent Patrick Gordon Walker's interview with Hetty Verolme (née Werkendam) (Cook 2018). When Russian and American film units collected visual images at other sites of mass incarceration, their visual focus was on war heroes arriving, corpses piled high, and skeletal survivors paraded naked in front of the world's cameras. Heroes were lauded and victims objectified. Depersonalization made it more difficult for the surviving victims' trauma to generate empathy (Alexander 2002, 8).

The dehumanization of the victims on film had previously been evidenced when German propaganda units used starved and diseased Jewish victims to show their depravity. Yael Hersonski's documentary *Film Unfinished* (2010) reconstructs the German propaganda footage compiled in the Warsaw Ghetto, where they had filmed orphaned and dying children, a man sifting through garbage, a man in rags dancing like a street bear, and lifeless corpses wheeled through the street. Immobile faces, like mug shots for police identification, were a prominent device in the stylistic armory of antisemitic film (Böser 2013, 48). Their propaganda dehumanized victims, turning them into voiceless objects, thereby accelerating the Jewish genocide. The victims in their silent films had no names, no voices, and no futures.

The British film unit that was filming at Bergen-Belsen was *also* filming for propaganda purposes. Bernstein had served under Eisenhower as Chief of the Film Section at the Supreme Headquarters Allied Expeditionary Forces (SHAEF) and was familiar with the latest techniques in psychological warfare. Nevertheless, their filming at Belsen was a rare rehumanizing change from the dehumanizing antisemitic propaganda that went before it. Propaganda or not, someone in the British Movietone team at Bergen-Belsen that day decided to invite the surviving victim who had been screaming at her former SS captors to speak at the microphone. They allowed Hela Goldstein to state her name, possibly for the first time in several years. They returned her identity and her voice to her as she stood beside a mass grave in Belsen. At that moment, the medium of audio-visual Holocaust testimony was born.

The history of Holocaust testimony does extend further back, through the written word. Later in this book we will examine how escapees from 1930s Nazi Germany and victims in the ghettos and concentration camps were real-time authors of their own histories long before the Second World War had ended. What sets Hela

FIGURE 1.2 In a frame from the film *The True Glory*, British Army Film and Photographic Unit cameraman and photographer, Sgt Mike Lewis, is caught on camera as he films the burial of the dead following the liberation of the concentration camp at Bergen-Belsen

Source: Photo FLM1232 used with permission of Imperial War Museums.

Goldstein apart is that she was among the first to speak in public at the point when it was certain her life was no longer under the direct threat of genocidal murder. She was speaking less than a week before the German Führer, Adolf Hitler—who had promised a "Thousand Year Reich" and initiated the "Final Solution of the Jewish Question"—committed suicide in his Berlin bunker. It was a defining moment of transition; the threat of the continued genocide of the Jews was formally over, and those who survived could speak freely.

Hela Goldstein began her testimony with a very simple opening line; "Today is the twenty-fourth [of] April, 1945. My name is Hela Goldstein. I am talking about my experiences." Unbeknownst to her, this was the opening salvo in what would become a war of narrative retaliation, in which the names, experiences, and presence of survivors would come to be witness for those that did not. When she stated her name, Hela reversed the anonymizing, dehumanizing prisoner numbering system that had been mandated for all inmates (USHMM 2019). By providing the date, she established the temporal moment of the interview, creating a moment when she was able to become *subject* of her own narrative, rather than the *object* of another's. When she stood by the mass grave, the significance of the authentic historical place was in frame. It visually juxtaposed her survival with the mass atrocity vividly represented behind her. She was about to overcome the fact that the dehumanized victims possessed no meaning (Waller 2002, 245) by giving voice, and thereby meaning, to her own experience.

In those 93 seconds, Hela also inadvertently provided a glimpse of the tools for first-person historical research: data and *metadata*. Her narrative and the image of her standing and speaking at that visually identifiable spot is the testimonial source, the data. The date, the place, and the name by which she identified herself in her remarks produced metadata-in-waiting. To this day, we use metadata such as name, time, and place as the basic roadmap to navigate large testimonial databases of complex source material.

Upon hearing her name—Hela Goldstein—on the Movietone reel, it was possible for me to search for her in the USC Shoah Foundation's Visual History Archive online. Had she been referenced in the archive or given further testimony? When I entered "Hela" and "Goldstein" into the search fields, the match that was returned was that of an interviewee who had that birth name, interviewed under the name of "Helen Colin." On opening the viewing page of Helen Colin, the "Biographical Profile" in the Visual History Archive confirmed she had been an inmate at Bergen-Belsen. The segment-level keyword search made it possible to further confirm that she was liberated at Bergen-Belsen. The information I had gleaned from her first ten seconds of testimony given led me to two full testimonies (there are two versions of her testimony in the Visual History Archive) that accounted for six additional hours of audio-visual testimony provided by Helen Colin. Another piece of metadata let me know that she had been interviewed in Houston, Texas, by the Holocaust Museum Houston in 1991 and by USC Shoah Foundation in 1996. As a result of ten words spoken in 1945, on June 8, 2016—71 years after she had first stated the date and her name—this metadata helped me to locate her in Houston, Texas. I could meet her and ask her about the historic day she bravely stood in front of the British Movietone camera at Bergen-Belsen.

I played the clip to Helen, who nodded knowingly and was surprised that I had the footage. She confirmed that she remembered the incident well. Until speaking with her I didn't realize that the young woman heard in the reel screaming in Polish at the SS several minutes before she appeared at the microphone was in fact Hela Goldstein. Remembering her own anger at the time, she explained that she was incensed at how disrespectfully the former camp guards were treating the corpses. Upon hearing her protests, one of the film crew invited her to address the assembled SS to camera. It was her anger that got her noticed. During the 2016 conversation with Helen Colin, she explained that when she stepped up to the microphone to speak, she had feared for her life. Just a few days prior, the SS guards who were lined up in front of her had held power of life and death over her. To confront them with her personal story was an act of significant courage, for which she told me she was prepared to die.[6]

In these rare few minutes of footage, German perpetrators and surviving victims of the Holocaust are seen together in the same physical space. While this was a largely contrived event orchestrated for the purposes of an ongoing propaganda battle (Shephard 2005), several things remain striking about the scene. Hela Goldstein and several other surviving victims are clearly observable spontaneously berating the Nazis. Their indignation at their former captors is palpable. Hela accepts the invitation of the British to address the former guards and local dignitaries, choosing to address the perpetrators in their own language, German—the language of her enemy. In speaking to the camera, she made a conscious choice to be in the public eye. Defiant in the face of her enemy, she used her own words to establish the veracity of her own experience.

Hela Goldstein was one of hundreds of thousands of surviving victims of the Holocaust who had no choice but to live with traumatic memory, but nevertheless chose to be witness to it, and gave form to her witness through testimony, allowing society to encounter her as an individual. Throughout this book we will examine the testimony of many surviving victims who provided testimony about their own experiences using different media and genres at different points in time across their lives in what I refer to as the "Trajectory of Memory." Helen Colin, the first of those known to have documented her testimony on camera, laid the foundation of what was to follow. She provides a natural starting point for a closer look at the theory and practice of how testimony evolves over time.

The Trajectory of Holocaust Memory

There is an observable trajectory to memory, witness, and testimony. The trajectory is dynamic, constantly evolving, and influenced by external forces. While the past remains fixed, how it is experienced in the present is ever changing (Smith 2001) Sometimes it is silent, sometimes it is vocal, at times it is literal, and at other times exegetical, public, or private. Regardless, the past always remains present in the memory of the surviving victim at each phase of their unfolding life and influences their identity and the choices they make. Paul Ricoeur (2007) observes a simple three-step trajectory in the epistemology of the historical sciences that follows a pattern of 1) testimony and record of testimonies; 2) questioning of the records; 3) and written historical representation of the past. This broad pattern may not always follow the same chronological or temporal sequence, but its historiographical elements—which roughly translate as record, analyze, and represent—endure. It is well established that objects from the past "endure through time and encapsulate a 'silent' trajectory of human—object relations, sustaining the past in the present" (Kidron 2012, 3). People also have an ongoing, silent relationship with their past, which from time to time finds form through testimony.

In this book we will attempt to understand more about how surviving victims of the Holocaust have lived with memory, bore witness to atrocity, and gave it form through testimony at different points through their lives. Roy Schwartzman describes "suturing" the past through testimony as an "ongoing often provisional process of creatively recrafting personal and collective identity after extreme disruption" (2015, 279). Stitching a patchwork of memories, the metaphor of an open wound still to be healed, is what he identifies as "disruptive trauma" (280).

Such trajectories of memory enable us to trace the relationship between memory, witness, testimony, and interpersonal conversation as experienced through the life of the individual and expressed through their public persona. These trajectories are constrained or facilitated by life cycle, geography, language, community, society, and media over time. Trajectories of memory are personal to the individual. What we see represented by testimony is merely the tip of the iceberg of the totality of memory—the moments in the life of the surviving victim when he or she has chosen to share an aspect of their memory through a testimonial act—like a speech, documentary film, or publication. The moment of witness, wherein memory is given form through testimony, is the gateway for society to enter a curated version of their lived experience.

When collected over time, these moments of revelation, representation, and conversation—which manifest along the timeline of their lives—build into a body of testimonial content. This body of testimony helps bridge their lived experience and our understanding of it. Some surviving victims choose silence, keeping their memories private until the day they die. Maybe their memories are too painful to reveal, or they are never made public for other personal reasons. For others, moments of public witness are few and far between. Still more survivors produce a steady representation of their past in the present. While the collective and public trajectory of Holocaust memory adds up to a vast collection of testimonial representations over several generations, for each surviving victim, most of the memories they have are only ever experienced as deeply personal and private pain.

To help navigate the theoretical framework of this book, there are four key terms that require definition. Their application will become clearer as the book progresses.

> *Memory* is an involuntary state of being by which our sensory experiences, perceptions, and actions change us continuously and what we later become (Thomson and Madigan 2005, 1). Memory has many forms that comprise the retained sum of the experiences of an individual. "To be useful a memory has to be recalled" (Kandel 2007, 215), which for those who experienced violence is at times involuntarily as "memory of the traumatic experience remains powerful for decades and is readily reactivated by a variety of stressful circumstances" (343).
>
> *Witness* is a voluntary state of being in which the individual volunteers to be publicly associated with the events they experienced and remembered. To be a witness does *not* require the individual to give specific form to their memory; the witness simply *is*. Being witness to the past is profoundly internal and private and helps shape personal identity. It also has a public face whereby, "a witness carries memory and calls on others to hear him, and through him, the past he bears" (Booth 2006, 72). A witness does not need to testify. The very public presence of the witness links the experience of

the past to the present. "To bear witness then is to remember, to be a living memory, to guard the past, to ask others to do likewise and to illuminate the traces of the past and their meaning" (73). Anyone can fulfil the role of a witness, but only the eyewitness can give testimony.

Testimony gives form to the experience of an eyewitness. It is how an eyewitness makes a conscious choice to communicate a part of *who they are* through physical representations of their past. Testimony is *any form* of first-person representation of a personal memory to which the testifier is a living witness. It may include film, creative and performative arts (theatre, dance, music, art, photography), social media, and immersive media. Testimony is not narrative but can be and often is expressed as such.

Encounter is a dialogue with an eyewitness in search of subject-focused meaning. An encounter could be as literal as a conversation, a verbal engagement between two people. In its applied form, encounter is also form of testimonial literacy, whereby testimonial sources are encountered using a dialogic method. Encounter with the testimony provides the individual to engage it *as if* in conversation with the subject.

Each surviving victim is a living person, an individual who was once dehumanized and targeted for death. Their voice gives them a name, history, and place in society. That said, they are not testimonial marionettes; they make their own choices about what they will and will not say about their lives at any given point and in any given context. Becoming a witness evolves over time (Cohen 2014) and is enabled through world events and cultural moments that facilitate the representation and confrontation of the Holocaust in broader society, as well as the life cycle of the individual. These moments include publishing key documents, erecting Holocaust museums, conducting significant war crimes trials, releasing major films, enacting of national policies and legislation, creating educational curricula, and recognizing Holocaust memorial days. There has been an explosive growth of institutions, representations in popular culture, the ongoing politics of memory, and testimony-based publications. These have all contributed to a growing culture of Holocaust memory (Wollaston 1996), in which the faces, voices, words, and presence of each surviving victim has become increasingly prominent.

Such trajectories are not specific to the Holocaust and have universal applicability. "Memory—the ability to acquire and store information as simple as the routine details of daily life and as complex as abstract knowledge of geography and algebra—is one of the most remarkable aspects of human behavior" (Kandel 2007, 10). These skills begin young and mature over time, whereby, "memory performance develops throughout childhood, probably as a result of the more effective use of memory capacity through increasingly more sophisticated memory strategies" (Baddeley 2013, 223). Every human being therefore has a set of formative memories physically encoded in their brain and may be retrieved across the lifespan of the individual. While "physical and cognitive function change as we get older . . . semantic memory continues to grow" (244). Such identity-forming memories remain valid over a lifetime.

Daniel Kahneman's concept of the "experiencing self" and "remembering self" helps navigate between what surviving victims went through during the events of the Holocaust, and how they came to recount them:

> The experiencing self is the one that answers the question: "Does it hurt now?" The remembering self is the one that answers the question, "How was it on the whole?"
>
> *(Kahneman 2011, 381)*

Kahneman's point is that when painful memories are eventually socialized, each traumatic life event has an associated meaning to its memory, in which the way we reflect upon the past is different from how we experienced it. Deeply traumatic memories influence identity, life decisions, personal relationships, individual psychology, and religious views long after the experience is over. Trauma aside, experiencing such events is a life-shaping force that cannot be undone and evolves in the surviving victim's present in relation to their current time, place, and persona. The temporal distance to events influences what the surviving victim feels able to say about them. The geographic and cultural milieu contextualizes what they may or may not say—some places do not feel safe, while others are empowering. As understood through the Jungian concept of the *individual* (internal identity) and *persona* (external identity) (Jung 2017), both the *individual* and their *persona* change over time too. Their emotions, psychological state of mind, period of life cycle, and people that surround them either constrain or facilitate their willingness to speak. While the trajectory of memory is not unique to surviving victims of the Holocaust, tracing the arc of memory, witness, and testimony among surviving victims of the Holocaust who experienced genocidal violence throws into sharp relief how those who survive traumatic events go on to live their lives.

The symbiosis between personal lived memory and its representations in broader society is at the heart of this book's inquiry into testimony. What surviving victims feel able to say at any given moment in their life is often determined by factors outside of their control. The surviving victim—who promised to bear witness on behalf of those who could not—is subjected to these personal and societal forces. Understanding who the surviving victims *are* as living people and what is reasonable for them to convey at any given point in time helps define the trajectory of memory from a position of empathy and trust. Skills of the listener include the need for empathetic listening, better understood in psychology as "perspective-taking," whereby "the perspective taker considers what that other person would think, feel, or do, and then, returning to her own perspective, ascribes these thoughts, feelings, or intentions to her" (Maibom 2020, 10).

This book will explore the object-subject dynamic of testimony and reframe testimony around a Buberian, "I-Thou" relationship (Buber 1970). Dori Laub identified that because of the coercively totalitarian and dehumanizing effect of the

Holocaust there was no longer an "other" to which one could say "Thou" (Felman and Laub 1992, 82). Testimony is a means to provide a "Thou"—a rehumanizing path through which the surviving victim can convey their inner memory of loss and pain to a trustworthy and humane listener. Testimony is not text, it is an extension of the life of the individual, an invitation to encounter who they are through what they share.

By rethinking testimony as a *relationship* it becomes possible to see beyond the *persona* (object) and experience the *individual* (subject) through *encounter*. We will explore how to remove the objectification of the surviving victim and their narrative—by creating an analytic discourse that avoids objectification. By removing (or reducing a dependency on) the subject-object relationship "I-It," both the surviving victim and the observer of testimony can enter a subject-subject *encounter* as a mode of unfolding co-existence and mutual learning. This book will evaluate whether I-Thou can provide a new testimonial modality based upon a subject-subject discourse. This modality includes how one comprehends testimony created in the immediate aftermath, as well as after the witness is no longer able to be in dialogue in the present, a time on the trajectory of memory described by Marianne Hirsch as "postmemory" (Hirsch 2012). If testimony is no longer read through its form but as an extension of being, a new literacy of testimony may be possible. This literacy would extend beyond literary criticism and narratology, to an ontological immersion in the life of the witness as expressed through their testimonial representations. Testimony may then be reconsidered as a *type of relationship*, rather than a *form of representation*. The person that testifies only does so because they have something to say about who they are, not because they are an artisan of historical production. Whatever he or she produces helps explain their lived experience, and therefore the modality of testimony can always be read as an extension of who they are.

This book introduces the idea that there are modalities of memory, witness, and testimony. Typologies of Holocaust memory and trauma have been explored (Langer 1991; Browning 2003; Amir 2018) with some success, demonstrating that not all memories are the same. I will not attempt a new typology of memory here, but rather observe that surviving victims live their memories through four distinct *modes of being*.

The first mode is that of *being alive* after the threat of death. The genocidal events experienced by surviving victims were designed to eliminate life. *To be* with no further obligation to anyone or anything is a fundamental right of those who survived. The soft accusation that survivors were "silent" after the Holocaust fails to recognize their fundamental right *to be*; they have the right to silence, privacy, recovery, and anonymity.

The second modality is that of *being witness*. To be an eyewitness to life-threatening terror was not avoidable to Jews trapped within the Nazi genocidal world. Jews were incarcerated and murdered because of who they were, not what they did. Outliving that assault and becoming a living witness to its lethality was not a choice. But it is a choice to self-identify publicly as that witness. To *be witness* to those events does not necessitate saying anything about them, but it does demonstrate a vulnerability to place one's identity into the public sphere.

A third mode is that of *being a testifier*. A testifier is a person willing to give form to memory. They are not the testament itself, although their existence is testament to the possibility of survival. Taking on the identity of spokesperson—whether to remember the dead, seek justice for those that were lost, assuage guilt, or try to make comprehensible to others that which the testifier may not fully comprehend themselves—places significant constraints on the testifier. The testifier lives with the *crisis of witness*: you won't understand, and even if you say you do, you don't (see as follows and Chapter 2: The Crisis of Witness). To *be a testifier* is to grapple with the limitations of representations, and nevertheless be willing to testify.

The fourth mode is the state of *being in conversation*. *Being in conversation* is a state that changes the understanding of the witness from being an object of history to a subject in the present. In conversation, the identity of the surviving victim is no longer constrained by form, because they *are* in the present. Being in the present allows those who have not suffered the same experience and may not fully understand the meaning of what is being said to still enter a subject-subject relationship. This process humanizes the surviving victim as a living person contributing to society in the present, rather than as relic of the past. It also creates new testimony borne from human encounter. Therein lies the possibility that two authentic forms of being—the witness and the witness of the witness—collide to create a reading of the past that is beyond its mere objectification.[7]

These modalities take us inward, to recognize that every surviving victim is best understood not by what they produce, but by who they are:

> Just as there is a relation to the outer object, an outer attitude, there is a relation to the inner object, an inner attitude. It is readily understandable that this inner attitude, by reason of its extremely intimate and inaccessible nature, is far more difficult to discern than the outer attitude, which is immediately perceived by everyone.
>
> (Jung 2017, 427)

The surviving victim speaks as someone who lives in their own present, which includes presents that are now in the past. The past thus continues to manifest itself in each of their lives in unique ways. What each person chooses to disclose at any given point is an extension of who they *are* at that moment in time. This theoretical framework for understanding testimony proposes that there is an ever-changing relationship between modalities of *being*, *types* of memory, and *forms* of witness.

Rehumanizing the source of testimony—as an extension and expression of *being* rather than as a mere representation of historical facts—provides a framework for the resuscitation of testimony. This approach does not mean that testimony does not contribute to history; testimony can and should be treated as a documentary source, but it is not limited to being documentary alone. Moving away from the objectification of the surviving victim as an artefact and their testimony as mere source moves us toward the subjectification of their role as an ongoing living witness in an unfolding struggle to live with the past in the present, thus helping to resolve the crisis that being witness creates.

This book approaches memory, witness, testimony through encounter, using a new theoretical framework. These are underpinned by concepts, which require some elucidation at the outset, so that their later use is clear.

There is a *crisis of witness*, explored in detail by Shoshana Felman and Dori Laub in *Testimony* (1991). The crisis of witness describes the difficulty the surviving victim experiences when confronting the possibility of speaking about things that are unspeakable. It is the dilemma faced by the surviving victim who wants to talk about their experience but also knows the audience will not fully understand. The crisis of witness also involves the limits that language imposes on the surviving victim (Langer 1991), because it is not designed to carry the meaning of such extreme experience. It runs aground on a society that is closed to listening or creates a cultural phenomenon out of atrocity memories; these are symptoms of Holocaust memory, witness, and testimony in crisis.

Identity is at the heart of memory, witness, and testimony, as it is an extension of who the individual is, as well as what they have seen and experienced. Dori Laub describes his own coming to terms with his past stating:

> There is, in each survivor, an imperative need to tell and thus to come to know one's story, unimpeded by ghosts from the past against which one has to protect oneself. One has to know one's buried truth in order to be able to live one's life.
>
> *(Felman and Laub 1992, 78)*

As just described, Carl Jung conceptualizes identity as a relationship between the *persona*—an external "mask" seen from the outside and experienced by others as an object—and *the individual*, who is the subject of inner feelings not experienced by others. This book broadly adopts this Jungian concept of the self to describe the difference between how the surviving victim understands themselves, and what they experience as an *individual*, versus how they represent themselves and are perceived as a *persona* from the outside. Taking this Jungian perspective provides a working framework for an encounter taken from a subjective perspective—as constructed from the inside looking out—thereby enhancing objective analysis of testimony when reviewed from the outside looking in.

This book conceptualizes *memory* as a dynamic extension of identity, which has an internal and external expression. The individual subjective forms of memory remain private, accessed through encounter. Memory expressed through the external persona is a representation of memory, but it is *not* memory itself. Kahneman's two forms of the self in relation to the past can be applied to surviving victims of the Holocaust. Each one lived through experiences and understood them in a particular way at the time (the experiencing self). Only later did they develop a perspective on the meaning of their experience "in sum" (the remembering self). The remembering self is expressed through testimony. The remembering self may reflect on what the experience in the past means "in sum" differently over time.

Individualizing how testimony is read is essential, especially when considering the vast corpus of testimonial literature that individual surviving victims have contributed to. Analytical forms, including source criticism, literary criticism, and narratology, reviewed through an interdisciplinary lens (Chapman and Vuohelainen 2016) have made testimony an object to study as a part of a genus of content. A notable exception is the work of Henry Greenspan (1998), who as a psychologist focused on listening to the subjects individually. Such analysis is important if we are not to consign testimony to commemoration alone, and not simply use it to fill in the gaps in history (Browning 2003, 85). That said, this book concerns itself with understanding the *individuality* of the testimonial author. As such, each subject is referred to as a "surviving victim," rather than the more typically used "survivor." Subjects throughout are referred to by their first names, because that is what people call them in their daily lives. In many cases, it was a name that was once denied them.

Testimony can be read from a text, listened to aurally, viewed on video, or experienced through talks, as well as performative and visual arts. All such modes of representation are experienced by what I describe as *the listener* (even when they are looking). A listener is typically defined as someone who hears a sound aurally. The listener to trauma however is also a participant and a co-owner of the traumatic event. Through listening, they come to partially experience the same trauma (Felman and Laub 1992, 57). This *deep listening* is also a part of testimonial literacy. In my own work I encourage my colleagues and students to "listen and listen again"—literally re-listening, re-watching, and re-reading the testimony a second time to deepen understanding beyond the text itself (see Chapter 7). When referring to "the listener" hereafter, I assume an individual who is willing to suspend critical judgement of the representational form, until such time as they have established a subject-subject understanding of the individual who is testifying and is willing to engage in deep listening as a part of their analysis and understanding.

Deep listening in turn leads to a dialogic encounter, in which the surviving victim and the listener are in "dialogue" with one another, even if they are not co-present. During the lifetime of the surviving victim, dialogic encounters may take the form of in-person conversations. Dialogic encounters can also be used as a critical analytic methodology whereby the listener takes a subject-subject position in relation to the original source. They question the source *as if* they were in conversation with its original author, asking "When did you write this? Why did you write this? To whom did you write it? What are you trying to say by this?" The listener asks these questions while respecting the struggles of the individual to give form to testimony. When the original source material is approached from the perspective of the individual (subject) rather than persona (object), it becomes possible to dialogue with the testimony in search of context and layers of meaning.

The concept of *testimony* used in this book is broad. Any historical or first-person-based narrative, document, photograph, artwork, or communication that is produced by a surviving victim about their experience, or derived directly from their experience, is considered testimony, and therefore fit for encounter. These conceptual lenses help us to better understand the trajectory of memory—how testimony develops over time in relationship to the forces that propel or resist it—and establishes a new mode of testimonial literacy through subject-subject encounter. We will now turn to explore this methodological framework for memory, witness, and testimony—and how it has developed over time—through theoretical analysis and testimonial case studies.

Notes

1 I use the term "surviving victim" throughout this book instead of the more typical term "survivor." The term "survivor" implies that individuals had greater agency than I believe most had. It has also come to represent a genus of people, and this book is about individuals. Those who did survive to witness do so on behalf of the dead and were themselves victims of the same threat of death. They are not witnesses to their survival. They are witnesses because of their victimization as Jews under threat of genocidal death.
2 Jane E. Wells, telephone conversation with the author, January 2021.
3 Transcription and translation courtesy of Maria Zalewska, with thanks.
4 The pronunciation of *Birkenwalde* or *Bergenwalde* is unclear, so it is difficult to know what Goldstein is referring to. *Birkenwalde* means Beechwood and there were beech trees there, but it is not a known name of the place. "Bergenwood" was not a name used for Bergen Belsen.
5 Translation courtesy of Karen Jungblut, with thanks.
6 Helen Colin, personal conversation with the author, June 8, 2016.
7 See https://medium.com/personal-growth/the-two-types-of-relationship-we-form-and-which-is-better-26339f572e7f.

References

Alexander, Jeffrey C. 2002. "On the Social Construction of Moral Universals: The 'Holocaust' from War Crime to Trauma Drama." *European Journal of Social Theory* 5, no. 1 (February): 5–85.
Amir, D. 2018. *Bearing Witness to the Witness: A Psychoanalytic Perspective on Four Modes of Traumatic Testimony*. 1st ed. London: Routledge. https://doi-org/10.4324/9781315146508.
Baddeley, Alan. 2013. *Essentials of Human Memory* (Classic Edition). 1st ed. London: Psychology Press. https://doi.org/10.4324/9780203587027.
Belsen, Bergen. n.d. "Bergen-Belsen Mass Graves." www.bergenbelsen.co.uk/pages/Database/DatabaseMassGraves.asp.
Berney, Leonard. 2015. *Liberating Belsen Concentration Camp: A Personal Account*. Self-published.
Blake, Brian, dir. 1985. *A Painful Reminder: Evidence for All Mankind*. London: Granada Television.
Booth, W. James. 2006. "Bearing Witness." In *Communities of Memory: On Witness, Identity, and Justice*, 72–111. Ithaca, NY: Cornell University Press.
Böser, Ursula. 2013. "A film Unfinished: Yael Hersonski's Re-representation of Archival Footage from the Warsaw Ghetto." *Film Criticism* 37, no. 2: 38–56.
British Movietone. (1945) 2016. "Belsen Concentration Camp—Reel 1 & 2–1945." Filmed April 24, 1945 in Germany. Vimeo video, 18:35. https://vimeo.com/157912217.
British Pathé. 1945. "British Troops Enter Belsen." Filmed April 1945 in Germany. Unreleased film, 5:03. www.britishpathe.com/video/british-troops-enter-belsen.

Browning, Christopher R. 2003. *Collected Memories: Holocaust History and Postwar Testimony*. Madison, WI: University of Wisconsin Press.
Buber, Martin. 1970. *I and Thou*. New York: Charles Scribner.
Chapman, Arthur, and Minna Vuohelainen. 2016. *Interpreting Primo Levi: Interdisciplinary Perspectives*. New York: Palgrave Macmillan.
Cohen, Sharon Kangisser. 2014. *Testimony and Time: Holocaust Survivors Remember*. Jerusalem: Yad Vashem.
Cook, Jeremy. 2018. "Holocaust Victim Hetty Verolme Returning to Bergen-Belsen." *Broadcast on BBC News*, April 16, 2018. YouTube video, 3:01. www.youtube.com/watch?v=h0bqf8K8RZQ.
Felman, Shoshana, and Dori Laub. 1992. *Testimony: Crises of Witnessing in Literature, Psychoanalysis and History*. London: Routledge.
Greenspan, Henry. 1998. *On Listening to Holocaust Survivors: Recounting and Life History*. Westport, CT: Praeger.
Hersonski, Yael, dir. 2010. *Shtikat Haarchion* [A Film Unfinished]. Film. www.pbs.org/independentlens/documentaries/film-unfinished/.
Hirsch, Marianne. 2012. *The Generation of Postmemory: Writing and Visual Culture after the Holocaust*. New York: Columbia University Press.
Jung, Carl. 2017. *Psychological Types*. Abingdon: Routledge.
Kahneman, Daniel. 2011 *Thinking, Fast and Slow*. 1st ed. New York: Farrar, Straus and Giroux.
Kandel, Eric R. 2007. *In Search of Memory: The Emergence of a New Science of Mind*. New York: W. W. Norton & Co.
Kidron, Carol A. 2012. "Breaching the Wall of Traumatic Silence: Holocaust Survivor and Descendant Person—Object Relations and the Material Transmission of the Genocidal Past." *Journal of Material Culture* 17, no. 1: 3–21.
Kushner, Tony. 1997. "The Memory of Belsen." In *Belsen in History and Memory*, edited by David Cesarani, Tony Kushner, Jo Reilly, and Colin Richmond, 181–205. London: Routledge.
Langer, Lawrence L. 1991. *Holocaust Testimonies: The Ruins of Memory*. New Haven, CT: Yale University Press.
Lipscomb, F. M. 1945. "Medical Aspects of Belsen Concentration Camp." *The Lancet* 246, no. 6367: 313–315.
Maibom, Heidi L. 2020. *Empathy*. 1st ed. London: Routledge.
Ricoeur, Paul. 2007. *A memória, a história o esquecimento*. Translated by Alan François. Brazil: Unicamp.
Schwartzman, Roy. 2015. "Sutured Identities in Jewish Holocaust Survivor Testimonies: Holocaust Survivor Identity Construction." *Journal of Social Issues* 71, no. 2: 279–293.
Shephard, Ben. 2005. *After Daybreak: The Liberation of Bergen-Belsen, 1945*. New York: Schocken Books.
Sington, Derrick. 1946. *Belsen Uncovered*. London: Duckworth.
Smith, Stephen D. 2001. "The Trajectory of Memory." In *Remembering for the Future*, edited by John K. Roth, Elisabeth Maxwell, Margot Levy, and Wendy Whitworth. London: Palgrave Macmillan.
Smith, Stephen D., and Rachael Cerrotti. "Episode 1: The First Testimony," September 11, 2021, in *The Memory Generation*, podcast, 38:06. www.memorygenerationpodcast.com/episode-1.
Thomson, Richard F., and Stephen A. Madigan. 2005. *Memory: The Key to Consciousness*. Princeton, NJ: Princeton University Press.

USHMM. 2019. "Tattoos and Numbers: The System of Identifying Prisoners at Auschwitz." https://encyclopedia.ushmm.org/content/en/article/tattoos-and-numbers-the-system-of-identifying-prisoners-at-auschwitz.

Waller, James. 2002. *Becoming Evil: How Ordinary People Commit Genocide and Mass Killing.* New York: Oxford University Press.

Wollaston, Isabel. 1996. *A War against Memory?: The Future of Holocaust Remembrance.* London: SPCK.

2
WHAT IT MEANS, AND WHAT IT DOESN'T

The Hanging Scene

It was January 1945, and *Appell* [roll call] had been called in Auschwitz I. Gallows had been erected on the *Appell Platz*. Victoria Ancona-Vincent was standing in a row of five women, as was typical of the *Appell* procedure. The gallows had been prepared for the execution of two women who had been part of the underground prisoner resistance movement. On October 7, 1944 the resistance movement had successfully destroyed the gas chamber and crematorium complex IV (then known as III) at Auschwitz-Birkenau. The girls, who had been working in the Union ammunitions factory, were accused of smuggling minute pieces of gunpowder (Kleiman 1996, seg. #54). It is estimated that as many as 30 women had smuggled enough gunpowder for an incendiary device large enough to burn down the complex (Harran 2017, 51). Not knowing all the names of women who were in the smuggling network, the Germans determined that four women—Roza Robota, Ala Gertner, Ester Wajcblum, and Regina Safirsztayn—were conspirators. They planned to hang two of them in the evening of January 5, 1945, for the returning day shift to witness (Ancona-Vincent 1995, 48), and two the following morning.

I had heard Victoria tell the story of that day many times. Victoria survived Auschwitz and the subsequent death march and was liberated by the Russians on April 24, 1945 (Ancona-Vincent 1995). On her return to Milan, she met British soldier Albert Vincent and ultimately made her home in Nottingham, England. She explained to me that she went to great lengths to disguise her Jewish identity; she assumed the identity of an Italian émigré by concealing her Auschwitz number under her shirt sleeve and teaching Italian, never mentioning that she was a Jew. Upon the opening of the UK National Holocaust Centre in September 1995, Victoria spoke in public about her experiences for the first time, 50 years after her liberation. She also published the testimony book *Beyond Imagination* (1995), which

FIGURE 2.1 Watercolor of the hanging scene from the morning of January 6, 1945 by surviving victim Zofia Rosenstrauch (later Naomi Yudkowsky), painted shortly after her liberation in 1945 and seen in the original album of paintings which serves as a visual testimony of her experiences

Source: Zofia Rozenstrauch (Naomi Judkovski) (1920–1996) The Last Execution January 1945, from the album Auschwitz Death Camp, 1945 Watercolor and ink on paper 26.5 x 36 cm. Collection of the Yad Vashem Art Museum, Jerusalem. Permanent loan of the Israel State Archive Photo © Yad Vashem Art Museum, Jerusalem.

she had penned for her son in the event of her passing. The manuscript had laid dormant in her personal archive along with several documents. These documents included a diary of events that she had inscribed and hidden in her shoe in the Fossoli concentration camp in Italy and in Auschwitz. Together, they demonstrated that she was acutely aware of the significance of her memory and the importance of documenting the details of history, even though she chose not to be a public witness for 50 years.

For the 11 months that followed our first meeting, Victoria spoke about her experiences several times a week at the newly opened UK National Holocaust Centre and schools in the East Midlands region of the UK. Victoria required a wheelchair, and so I would often accompany her to school visits to introduce her and listen to her testimony. I noticed that she always trembled before breaking down in tears when recounting the hanging scene. After a while, it occurred to me that there must be a reason that scene was more emotional for her than the packed and deadly six-day train ride in cattle wagons, selections, hunger, exhaustion, and

22 The Crisis of Witness

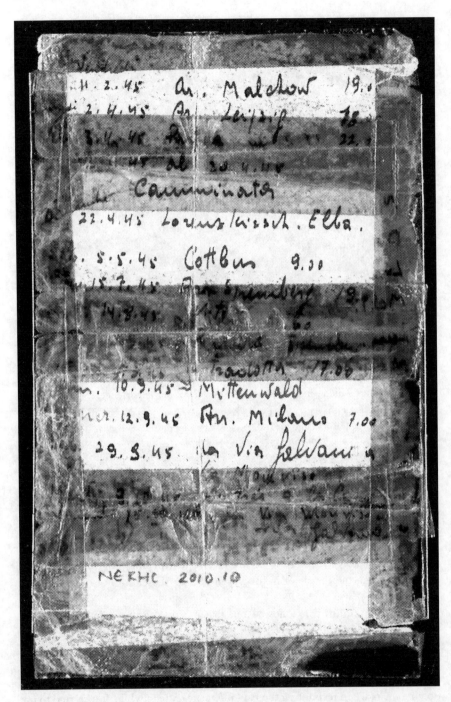

What It Means, and What It Doesn't 23

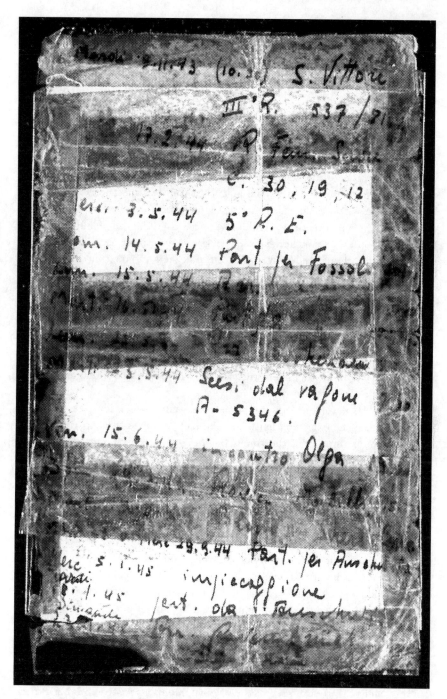

FIGURE 2.2A AND 2.2B Front and rear of paper diary hidden in the shoe of Victoria Vincent née Ancona, from November 9, 1943 the day she was captured in Milan until her return in September 1945

Source: Photos © from the collection of the National Holocaust Centre and Museum.

fear she also experienced watching the daily selections on the *rampe* (platform) (Ancona-Vincent 1995). I wondered why, so I asked her.

Victoria explained that her sister Olga was standing next to her at the *Apell*. The two young women had not seen each other for the seven months following Victoria's arrest in Milan on November 9, 1943. They only accidentally found each other again in Auschwitz-Birkenau. A few months later, they stood together watching the hanging scene. She also explained that in the same row of five girls was the sister of one of the girls being hanged. Whatever the range of actions and emotions of her experienced self—the self that feels the pain (Kahneman 2011)— it was the presence of the grieving sister that had a lasting and traumatic impact on Victoria's remembering self. She and Olga still had one another, unlike the bereaved sister who was now alone in that deadly place.

She also explained that since childhood she was "technically blind," and wore thick coke-bottle lenses in her glasses. Her glasses were hanging on by a piece of string, and that should they have fallen off and been trampled in the mud, she would be "dead by nightfall." She explained that she considered herself in immediate danger of death. While she was no use to the resistance movement in the camps, the two girls about to hang were her heroes. "I just wanted to put one foot in front of the other and say, 'Take me!', but I just could not do it. I just wanted to live another day."[1] Third, she told me that the camp hierarchy had erected a Christmas tree at the *Appell Platz*. As it was the evening of January 5, 1945, the Christmas tree was still standing in the vicinity of the gallows. Victoria described her anger when recounting this episode: "How dare you!"

Victoria had never once in her public presentations mentioned any of these details, nor had she explained her tears. She had described her experiencing self (what she went through at the time), but not her remembering self (how she reflected on that experience in sum). The audience had witnessed the persona but not the individual. I asked her to go back to the beginning of the testimony that she would typically present in public events and explain why she chose each episode. What at first appeared to be a chronological recounting of Holocaust history, was in fact a series of interconnected short stories, each with an implicit exegetical meaning—family values, resistance, trust, love, fear, anger, and hope. What she recounted as a single historical narrative could be broken down into a series of short parables, each with its own implicit meaning. As she talked with me, I realized that the narratological consequences for understanding the *source* and *purpose* of testimony as she described it were significant. It was not one thing (a recounting of history), it was two intricately woven strands of what happened and what that meant to her. The testimony only existed because what happened in front of the gallows had meaning to her.

As Victoria explained the reason for telling the hanging scene story, it was clear that the *source* of the testimony was the original trauma associated with her experiencing self as an individual, which she re-experienced during the talk. When she retold the story, she relived the experience. She was not crying about the women who were hanging on the gallows. The tears were related to the trauma she had experienced *herself* that day as an observer of the atrocity. The *purpose* of the testimony was to overcome that traumatic moment in her life, not to retraumatize herself. She told the story of that day as an educator, but the trauma could not be contained. It was central to her identity and the very reason for giving the testimony in the first instance. When she cried, what was being witnessed on stage in the school gym was the trauma of her re-experiencing her own past, which was completely distinct from her talking about the women being hanged. Each time she spoke, the trauma broke through her otherwise precisely structured narrative. I had inadvertently encountered trauma-informed testimony.

Every time she told her story, she relived the same events and the associated trauma and was subsequently re-traumatized by it. But if "trauma is redeemed only when it becomes the sources of a survivor mission" (Lifton 1980, 113–126), Victoria had placed herself in a good position to redeem it by making it her mission to repeatedly tell her story in public. It had taken many years to break through the silence, but Victoria seemed to understand that "re-living the feelings, memories, or sensations of traumatic experiences is a normal, healthy reaction as the mind attempts to digest and understand trauma" (Weingarten 2003, 115). In the absence of any form of counseling 50 years prior and without any form of closure, she took on a mission to educate young people. It offered a form of narrative closure and her own means to achieve transitional justice, all rolled into a one-hour high school class.

In contemporary justice processes that have followed genocide and mass violence in the last 25 years—such as the recent international tribunals (ICTR, ICTY), truth commissions (e.g., the Truth and Reconciliation Commission in South Africa), and the International Criminal Court—it has been determined that the role of the surviving victim includes: the right to truth, the survivor's right to vengeance and remedy, and the right to participate (Soueid et al. 2017, n.p.). Victoria did not have access to such judicial processes (notwithstanding the International Military Tribunal at Nuremberg) or any support as a surviving victim in the immediate post-Holocaust period. Nevertheless, 50 years later she accomplished all these objectives—the right to truth, vengeance, remedy, and participation—through public presentation of her testimony that enabled her own her own story and therefore her own identity:

> The point at which survivors are ready to share their story, the survivor has ownership of the story and must be clear about who she wishes to reveal the information to and what information she wishes to reveal.
>
> *(Herman 1992, 201)*

I witnessed how Victoria made a personal choice to speak in public, despite the pain it re-inflicted, to define the truth of her own experience and to deliver it her own way. She was also ready to attain justice by using her testimonial narrative as her personal form of narrative vengeance. By controlling her own story, she was ensured that she was no longer defined by her persecutors, but by herself. Victoria had no interest in seeking physical or monetary remedy. What she sought was to reclaim her own voice and use it to influence the next generation. Even though she experienced re-traumatization every time she spoke, the overriding benefit of rehumanization and her ability to prosecute narrative revenge was worth the pain. As she exerted her right to participate, her remedy was the reclamation of her own identity.

There was an additional dimension to her trauma-informed narrative. The purpose behind her willingness to witness in public was to share the meaning of her experience through her remembering self, which she distilled to a single sentence:

> It does not matter whether you are a Christian, a Muslim, or a Jew, always remember, this could happen to you.[2]

Her statement implies a call to action, because her goal is to persuade listeners to act (Nance 2006, 19). Victoria's universal message to her listeners was that everyone is implicated in memories of the past, because the only way to avoid your own group becoming the next victim is to protect all groups. Having discovered that Victoria's public testimony was imbued with exegetical commentary, I began to wonder whether all Holocaust testimonies—written, audio, or video—had similar hidden exegetical meaning, rather than only the obdurate historical fact.

When I visited Victoria Vincent in her hospital right before she died in August 1996—just one year after she first found courage to speak—she told me with confidence that she had told the woman in the bed opposite her that she was a Jew and that she had showed her the Auschwitz number (A5346) on her arm. Victoria had moved along her own trajectory of memory from *being silent* with her memories, to *becoming witness* to her memories when she publicly attended the opening of the UK National Holocaust Centre, to then *being a testifier* in the form of educational talks, a book publication, and media appearances, to *encounter* with the woman in the hospital. She went through that entire trajectory in less than a single year, having waited 50 years to reveal her identity. Her willingness to contribute to historical knowledge through recounting her past began a process that changed her identity. Testimony had become a mode of being for her.

Witness and the Many Forms of the Present

Testimony is, at its heart, an historiographical form. Whatever the layers of metaphor and exegesis that are woven into it, first and foremost it is a recounting of personal experience related to historical events. But unlike historical documents that are fixed in time and place and therefore evidential, "individual memory does not function like an archive of lived experiences deposited somewhere in the brain but is rather constructed anew at each moment of recall" (Smith and Watson 2001, 16). As well as being a source, testimony is also a subject (Tumblety 2013). If the role of historiography is to create a "certain kind of relationship to the past mediated by a distinctive kind of written discourse" (White 2020, 1), testimony can be considered one such discourse. But "there remain many contested and unresolved questions about how memory can be meaningfully interrogated by historians" (Tumblety 2013, 7). Going further, Pierre Nora describes an intractable tension between history and memory, whereby memory "accommodates" and "nourishes," while history is "suspicious of memory, and its true mission is to suppress and destroy it" (Nora 1989, 8–9). Memory and its derivative representation, testimony, can indeed "accommodate" the present because memories are related to historical experience, but are not fixed in time and place by it in the way that documents are:

> Put another way, we do not have memory as much as remembrances, or even performances of remembering, where what is remembered is shaped fundamentally both by the meaning of the initial experience to the individual in question, and by the psychological—and inextricably social—circumstances of recall.
>
> *(Tumblety 2013, 7)*

Narrative testimony can never be pure documentation because it is a form of storytelling, and therefore deploys literary devices and metaphor. The hanging scene described by Victoria at Auschwitz was a metaphor for the execution of Victoria's own identity. Even if she conceived it subconsciously, it was her way to inform her audience that the German authorities not only robbed the two women of their lives, but everyone watching too. As Lawrence Langer suggests, life and death merge in metaphor:

> One unintended effect of this festival of destruction is that anyone studying the subject [of the Holocaust] is not spared the impact of watching metaphor merge with reality until it permanently disfigures our traditional ideas of living and dying.
>
> *(Langer 2020, 287)*

Victoria Vincent made a concerted effort to be fact-based in her reporting. She documented the historical dates of events on a single piece of paper hidden in her shoe for two years. That document is fixed in time and place, making it a form of evidence (see Figure 2.2). When she wrote her memoir *Beyond Imagination* (1995), she chose to publish a short, fact-based account of her experiences. She even said it was "beyond imagination" in the title, dispelling any misconceptions that it was fiction. But when she put her narrative into the public domain, she started to speak in public and thereby place her testimony in the context of her current-day life as a public persona. Holocaust memory in British society was also newly entering public discourse in 1995. "Few could have predicted the amount of public interest and media coverage shown in the lead up to and marking of the liberation of Auschwitz in January 1995" (Pearce 2014, 67). The fiftieth anniversary of the Liberation of the camps, the announcement of the Imperial War Museum's Holocaust galleries, and the launch of the Survivors of the Shoah Visual History Foundation (now USC Shoah Foundation) gave Victoria impetus to participate.[3]

Even in the short period that Victoria was speaking about her life, there were several forms of the present in the giving of her testimony. There was the present she described *within* the testimony itself, the unfolding chronological scenario in which she would go back in time to describe that present, now in the past (the relived present). Then there was the present she had lived with every day since, infused with the trauma of the past. Her present was still overshadowed by the complications of the past, including being wheelchair-bound and subject to nightmares (the hidden present). In personal conversation, she described her nightmares and other symptoms of post-traumatic stress to me, as well as the constant charade of hiding her identity. There was also the successful, well-adjusted smiling teacher that all the students loved to learn from (the successful present). She had always been a highly intelligent young woman prior to the Second World War and had grown into a wonderful and beloved teacher. Then there was her relationship with present-day society, which conditioned how she would identify herself in public and what she felt comfortable to say about her past (the conditioned present). This included concealing her Holocaust identity to her Italian language students who never knew she was a Jew in the Italian resistance or incarcerated in Fossoli or Auschwitz.

Prior to August 1995, when Victoria called the UK Holocaust Centre and we met for the first time, the conditioned present was the principal barrier to her finding her voice. The conditions associated with it felt threatening and intimidating. Ultimately, they were too psychologically insurmountable for her to risk identifying with her relived present in the current present. For 50 years she re-ran the spool of her relived present and coped with her hidden present. There was no place to surface the reality of her true self. Anything that could potentially disrupt her hidden present was not worth the risk. She could not reject the only safety she had, which was her successful present; there was more for her to lose than gain. The risk-reward of going public was not in her favor.

Then society began to change. Popular culture began recognizing the Holocaust through films like *Sophie's Choice*, *The Holocaust* mini-series and *Schindler's List*. There was widespread commemoration of the fiftieth anniversary of the liberation of the camps; the opening of the UK National Holocaust Centre; and her making friends she could trust (including myself). All these events created a more welcoming present for her, a context in which the psychological and social barriers to being publicly identified as a surviving victim of Auschwitz were lowered or removed. As she developed confidence in her ability to communicate her past, her conditioned present was in a constant state of change. What had started as external social and cultural changes facilitated her ability to engage with her past in the present, becoming an internal, psychological set of changes. She no longer needed to be afraid of her hidden present, no longer needed the façade of her successful present (she could be successful and open) and was less conditioned by society. Victoria had been living in many forms of the present for decades, which is true of many surviving victims to this day.

FIGURE 2.3 Victoria Vincent at the UK National Holocaust Centre 1995
Source: Photo © National Holocaust Centre and Museum.

In the case of Victoria Vincent, she became less vulnerable the more accepted she felt through her acts of remembering. Andrew Pearce observes that Britain was then "more aware and receptive to the Holocaust than any time previously" (2014, 193). Its

> communicative memory—once the sole property of survivors—was finding form and dissemination through initiatives such as the Library of Holocaust Testimonies series launched in January 1993 and the British Library's *Voices of the Holocaust* oral history project of the same year.
>
> (193)

In addition to the change in societal context, the presence of the UK National Holocaust Centre gave Victoria a physical and institutional place with which to associate, and the people at the Centre offered her community. The alignment of these unique circumstances afforded her an opportunity to contribute to history, public conscience, and collective memory.

But not all agree that memory should be source and subject in this way. The fraught relationship between memory and historiography is taken up by Paul Ricoeur:

> The problem of the relation between individual memory and collective memory will thereby be put to rest. Historiography will again take up this

problem. And it will arise once more when history, presenting itself in turn as its own subject, will attempt to abolish the status of the womb of history commonly accorded to memory, and to consider memory as one of the objects of historical knowledge.

(Ricoeur 2004, 95–96)

Ricoeur's approach to historiography places memory as a static object in service of historiography, rather than an extension of the lived experience of the individual or society in the present. Although Ricoeur's assertion direct opposes the hypothesis underlying this book, it does have clear merit as an unambiguous way for memory to be entwined in the writing of the past. It does not deny that memory exists, the veracity of its content, nor that it can greatly contribute to knowledge and understanding. In typifying memory this way, Ricoeur appears to accord documentary status to memory, much like evidence. Not all historians agree on this latter point, although Christopher Browning does conclude "the overall value of survivor testimony for writing Holocaust history" (Browning 2003, 84), to which Zoë Waxman adds, "what testimony can do is supply meaning" (Waxman 2012, 150).

Making memory an object of the past transforms it into an instrument of the historiographer alone, rather than existing as a subject in its own right. Oren Baruch Stier sees the writing of history and collective memory as being distinct forms of representing the past:

> Even though both history and memory select items from the past in their attempts to describe and appropriate it, history tends toward elucidation, clarification, and differentiation, while memory tends toward simplification, mythologization, and identification: that is, toward symbolization.
>
> *(Stier 2015, 4)*

Yosef Hayim Yerushalmi notes that "memory and modern historiography stand, by their very nature, at radically different relations to the past" (1982, 94), which reminds us to not confuse the two. He goes onto observe that "the Holocaust has engendered more historical research than any single event in Jewish history, but I have no doubt whatever that its image is being shaped, not at the historian's anvil, but in the novelist's crucible" (98). Historian Dan Stone observes that the meaning of history does not come ready-made, suggesting the creative process lies with the historian also: "the meanings we give to the past are forged by the creative act of writing history" (Stone 2012, 2). Somewhere in the mix of documentary fact and creative storytelling lies narrative testimony as part history and part story. Holocaust testimony describes the past while remaining a product of the present.

Testimony may be viewed by some as an historical source, by others as a quasi-spiritual text, although it may well be possible for testimony to "retain a 'special' status and be an important historical source" (Waxman 2012, 145). Testimony retaliates against the Nazi view of history as depicted in Himmler's October 1943 Poznan statement, that the mass murder of the Jews was to be "an unwritten and never to be written page of glory in our history" (Breitman 1991, 243). Elie Wiesel went so far as to counter Himmler by asking, "Why don't we claim [the Holocaust] as a glorious chapter in our eternal history?" (Wiesel 1967, 288). Despite difficulties in using survivor testimony as a historical source, the overall value of survivor testimony for writing Holocaust history has been affirmed by historians, "provided it is accompanied by critical analysis" (Browning 2003, 84). Testimonial sources are a unique type of source material that combines historical reporting, storytelling, memorial texts, and personal commentary. They provide rich resources for research as well as being their own form of writing history (historiography).

If the aforementioned "rights"—truth, vengeance, remedy, and participation—are to be fully accorded to surviving victims, the memory-as-object modality suggested by Ricoeur and their reductive enshrinement in society leaves the surviving victims far short of attaining full agency. When the subjects of memory are objectified and iconized, they lose the rights associated with asserting their own past in the present. Even though they remain living people, they are analyzed by their testimonial work product, not by who they are as people. That said, the individual surviving victim may still exercise their rights and claim their own agency after they have produced testimony as a fixed form. After Victoria had published her book and established the facts about her past, she exercised her rights to truth, vengeance, remedy, and participation, and continued to develop as a person in the present. As she took on a new mission, testimony helped her address her own trauma. Victoria developed a virtuous memory cycle in which the more she engaged society with her testimony, the more remedy and participation were found. Having the final word on her tormentors and engaging the next generation of learners was her revenge. The memory cycle in the current present would have stopped, had the publication of her book as an object of history been her only testimonial act. It would have been reviewed and analyzed as new object of history and the sum total of her memory, rather than a momentary window (the date of publication) into her continuously unfolding trajectory of memory in the present which unfolded all the more rapidly after her testimony was published.

When surviving victims speak about their past, they put words to memories that they experienced once, then had to live with, and re-live permanently. The words they share at any given point in time are not the entirety of those memories, only those that they feel comfortable sharing in that moment. They are a partial rendering of the past, a set of carefully curated insights into an otherwise vast ocean of emotions, feelings, and details. Such memories do not merely describe the speaker's relation to the past but place her quite specifically in reference to it (Antze and Lambek 1996, xxv). They also place her in reference to the present too. As time goes by she can create fixed memories in the past (such as a publication) as well as generate new memories in the present (such as a public talk or documentary) that appear to extend or even contradict prior published testimony. When audio-visual testimony is recorded, it happens in a particular moment in time and becomes a record of the past. The data contained within that one interview can thereafter be mined by the historiographer as an object of history, while the subject continues as a memory subject in the present. The new object of history—the interview—takes on its own life as a subject too, contributing to discourse in the ongoing present. When we record videotaped testimonies "we begin with separate narratives and end with collective memory" (Langer 1991, 21).

In the twenty-first century, "teachers, students, filmmakers, genealogists, storytellers, and *community* activists are putting their mark on a practice that has been relegated to historians until recently" (MacKay 2016, 18). There is a symbiosis between the collective conscience and subjects of historical memory who are asked to contribute to collective memory through the sharing of audio and videotaped memories. In addition to institutional projects, "people all over the world are talking about oral history, learning about oral history, and conducting oral history *interviews*" (MacKay 2016, 17). The digital present is creating a new opportunity for more testimonies and easier access to them, whether they were written in 1945 and only now made accessible on a digital platform, or recorded on a digital device today.

Oral history is made up of "speech and counter speech" composed of a "conversation with a person whose life experience is regarded as memorable" (McMahan 1987, 187). As such, the many forms of the present experienced through testimony manifest themselves during that conversation through time, place, language, context, and technology. As the temporal trajectory of testimony unfolds, the history of the world changes around it, as does the life cycle of the individual. Testimony that was written in 1935 (we will later explore Nazi era testimony given before the Holocaust itself occurred) has a different tone to that which was written in a ghetto in 1943 or a displaced person camp in 1946. Place has a significant bearing on what is sayable, because the context in which the testimony is given changes the nature of testimony itself.

Janine Oberrotman (née Binder) was interviewed by David Boder on August 4, 1946 at the Jewish Committee Home for Adult Jewish Refugees in Paris. The interview was conducted in German, for approximately 30 minutes, using audio only (Binder 1946). Janine was later recorded in 1995 for two hours in English in the comfort of her home in Lincolnwood, Illinois by the USC Shoah Foundation using video (Oberrotman 1995), and again in 2004 for over five hours by the United States Holocaust Memorial Museum (Oberrotman 2004) also using video. In 2016 she was recorded for the USC Shoah Foundation's "Dimensions in Testimony" program for two-and-a-half days in a large green-screen volumetric video studio at the USC Institute of Creative Technologies in Playa Vista, California. All four testimonies were taken across a 70-year timespan in vastly different contexts with vastly different results. Had she declined to speak to David Boder, we would not have the immediacy of her memory from 1946. If she had not been willing to give several days to answer questions in 2016, we would not have the detailed memories in her "Dimensions in Testimony" interview, which benefit from 70 years of further reflection. The question might be, which is the authentic testimony of Janine Oberrotman? The correct answer is: all of them.

Janine's first interview with David Boder was in German, which meant that both interviewee and interviewer were speaking second (or third or even fourth) languages. At one point in her interview Janine asks Boder if she can switch to

Yiddish, as some German vocabulary was proving difficult for her (Binder 1946). At the point an interviewee is struggling to find a word, it is unlikely they are tapping their deepest emotions. Language changes not only the nature of what is said, but also what is sayable. Speaking in a mother tongue plays a fundamental role in emotion (Lindquist et al. 2015). Yet in the USC Shoah Foundation Visual History Archive of 51,562 accessible testimonies of Jewish surviving victims (at the time of writing), approximately 40,570 (79%)[4] appear to have given their testimony in a language *other* than their mother tongue, either because it was the language of their adoptive home or the language of the audience they anticipate will listen to them. Even when the witness remains fluent in their adopted language, it is rarely the language they used during the years of Nazi persecution, providing another form of disconnect from the experienced self (the language in which they experienced the events) and the remembering self (the language in which they report the events).

Their adopted language is also a part of their new present, which differentiates them linguistically from their prior present, which at some level they are trying to put behind them. The inverse is also true. There are times when recounting memories creates a safe and comfortable space for a return to a surviving victim's mother tongue. Jeremiah Kirschenbaum began his testimony in English and reverted to Yiddish, which provoked a particularly emotional moment, in which he recalled his uncle Izik Kirschenbaum and paused to gather himself for a full 24 seconds (Kirschenbaum 1996, seg. #10). It appeared that the change of language brought about a change of emotion. In a recent interview, I asked interviewee Ichak Kalderon Adizes to speak in his mother tongue, Ladino, even though as the interviewer, I was not able to ask him questions in Ladino. For the first 45 minutes of the interview, I asked questions in English and followed along with my (basic) Spanish comprehension as he talked about home and family and traditions in the language he had spoken at home as a child. This allowed Ichak the freedom to recount his childhood more precisely using words, songs, and emotions about his pre-war life. He included several Ladino songs and lullabies that he would unlikely have shared had he been answering in English. It was evident during the interview that speaking in the Ladino language enabled him to speak more directly from his emotions than during the English portion of the interview, which we switched to at the point the Bulgarians began deporting the Jews of Skopje, Macedonia (Adizes 2021). Jeffrey Shandler makes the point that

> most Jewish Holocaust survivors have spoken more than one language over the course of their lives. Many grew up in richly polyglot environments, shaped by contact among multiple ethnic communities, shifting political powers, and expanding educational and cultural possibilities in the decades before World War II.
>
> *(Shandler 2020, 87)*

The result is that many surviving victims were not speaking their mother tongue when giving their audio-visual testimony.

Surviving victims of the Holocaust testify because they are witness to an experience, not necessarily because they *understand* that experience. It is important to make a distinction between recounting events in the past and comprehending them in the present. The speech and counter-speech that underpin testimony work out of an understanding between historian and informant (McMahan 1987). The "information" most valued by the observer-listener is not that of historical data—which can be obtained from documentary or historiographical sources—but that of human experience wherein "the subjective dimensions and dynamics of memory become a virtue" (Pearce 2018, 13). This has specific application in the educational environment, where learners confront memory in the form of testimony. I observed while I was director of the UK National Holocaust Centre that after the survivor speakers at the museum delivered their short-form public testimony (typically 45–60 minutes in length), that the audience virtually never asked them to clarify an historical point, such as: "Did boys stay with their fathers and girls stay with their mothers during the selection irrespective of their age?" Questions virtually always would focus on emotions and consequences, such as: "How did you feel when you realized your mother was dead?" or "Do you hate the perpetrators for what they did to your sister?" The questions relate more to the present than to the past. The audience was curious to know what the Holocaust had come to mean in the present more than they wanted clarification about what happened in the past.

The need to understand the past in the present is a natural fit with the role of the surviving victim's remembering self, because the surviving victim can respond by explaining what it had come to mean to them in sum, at that point in their life. It is also the reason that I did not witness a single school group that heard Victoria talk about her past explain *why* she told the story of the hanging scene. The audience took it on face value that she was describing a hanging scene, not that it was a metaphor for something deeper in her own life in the present. Once I asked her the question about why she cried at that moment, she was more than willing to share it with me, but it was necessary to know what to ask. Her audiences came away knowing that watching the hanging had been distressing for her to watch. It was always an intensely emotional moment in her testimony which she relived with the same intensity every time. The audience just never knew *why*.

Victoria's reflection, "whether you are a Muslim, a Christian, or a Jew, beware it can happen to you," is similar in tone to the landmark 1996 speech given by Yehuda Bauer to the Bundestag. He is reported to have stated, "Next time the question is, who will be the Germans and who the Jews?" Clearly, genocidal persecution is not unique to Germans, neither is suffering unique to the Jews. After her 50-year silence Victoria hoped to influence actions in the current world predicated on an understanding of the Holocaust, as passed down through victims' and survivors' literary testimony (Young 1990, 11). Her mission when recounting her past was to move her audience to action in the future should they see the suffering of a new group of victims. She hoped that memories of the death of two young women in Auschwitz, and the tears they saw her shed, would impart a moral imperative to act, thereby extending the trajectory of memory beyond her own lifetime.

Victoria's trajectory underpins Noah Shenker's observation that we all receive testimonies "not as enclosed capsules of memory but as constantly mediated, contested and fragile acts of remembering" (Shenker 2015, 1). How we encounter testimony must therefore exceed mere rhetorical obeisance to the text. We should seek an understanding of the consequences of testimony for society, if only because the surviving victims were themselves willing to navigate its complex conditions. For that to be possible, it is necessary to understand how a dehumanizing past can be rehumanized in the present.

Rehumanizing the Past

The mass murder of the Jews during the Second World War was a profoundly dehumanizing event that completely denied the victims' subjectivity. Ordinary men and women (Lower 2014) simply could not kill *en masse* until their victims had been conceptually and psychologically transformed into less-than-human creatures (Lang 2010, 225–227) and conditioned to respect and defer to authority (Browning 1992). Jews were described as vermin by Nazi propagandists. They were stripped of citizenship rights, economic independence, education, employment, travel, sports, arts, and entertainment. These dehumanizing restrictions, which included the so-called Law for the Restoration of the Civil Service, were the beginning of an economic assault on the Jews (Reicher 2004). Later they were rounded up and made to live in ghettos in squalor with no personal agency (Cohen 2006). They were separated from families, forced to work as slaves, and forced to hide and flee. Under-nourished, their names were replaced with numbers, and they were stripped naked, physically assaulted, tortured, and raped. Eventually, they were shot, gassed, and burned (Kogon et al. 1993; Venezia 2009).

Everything they suffered was a dehumanizing assault on their humanity, as Jews and as people. Ghettos were established to collect inhabitants into a nameless mass that could be easily controlled (Berenbaum 1997, 71; Tory 1990; Markowska 2008). The Einsatzgruppen killing squads pulled men, women, and children out of their homes, and lined them up naked on the edge of pits of corpses (Klee et al. 1991). The cattle wagons that transported Jews from ghettos to death camps (Cole 2011) treated them like animals. The entire concentration camps system—the daily *appell*, the work *kommandos*, food rations, sleeping quarters, sanitary conditions, camp hierarchy, selections, and the penal code—was designed to be inhumane. Women underwent a continual assault upon their bodies (Ephgrave 2016).

Upon death, there are typically sacred rites of passage in which the life of a human being is respected and dignified within the Jewish tradition (Colls 2021). But there are no names, dates of birth, dates of death, or final resting places for most of the Jews who were murdered during the Holocaust. Nazi policy toward the Jews was designed to be de-humanizing because for the Nazis these "were not, after all, fully human beings; they were a subhuman species" (Sabini and Silver 1993). Hitler's ideological fanaticism enabled a redemptive and potentially genocidal antisemitism. His calculated pragmatism and murderous fury would explode into unlimited destruction and death. Everything flowed from that urge, its toxicity seeping into memory, witness, and testimony to this day.

There is a crisis of witness which emanates from the dehumanizing, debilitating events of the Holocaust themselves. Never had any group of people been subjected to such widespread, determined, genocidal brutality, in which camps built for work and death were revolutionary institutions (Goldhagen 1996, 457). The Jews of Europe had experienced persecution for centuries (Evans 2011) and the crescendo of genocidal hatred channeled this long history of hate towards innocent civilians of Jewish heritage. The Holocaust's devastating consequences of erasure and the brutal trauma carried by its surviving victims still confounds the expected norms of human behavior. This remains true even 75 years after the end of hostility and genocidal killing, and the tens of thousands of volumes that have been published about these events. No one individual can adequately convey the complexity of the events or their meaning. For those who did not live through it—which is almost everyone alive today—the ability to understand the layers of meaning within a single surviving victim's narrative is severely limited, creating disconnection at the very point readers should become most connected to it.

The Holocaust is particular to Jews and yet has had increasing relevance for those who do not identify as Jewish. This cultural transformation has been achieved "because the originating historical event, traumatic in the extreme for a delimited particular group, has come over the last fifty years to be redefined as a traumatic event for all of humankind" (Alexander 2002, 6). Those who survived were not only silent emblems of the radical evil (Kant 1960) that was associated with the broadly dehumanizing destruction of Nazi ideology. Over time they developed their own narrative of the anti-Jewish hatred they experienced. The tension between the unique and universal is another dimension of the crisis of witness. What makes the genocide of the Jews so challenging is its specificity—the pursuit of a racially pure national community in Germany through legislation (Burleigh 1997, 159). Such was their dependency on the law, an instrument by which life itself could be legally extinguished (Bazyler 2017), to the extent that as Richard Rubenstein points out "the Nazis committed no crime at Auschwitz" (Rubenstein 1975, 87).

All Jews everywhere were to be murdered because of their racial heritage was "put into state policy" on January 20, 1942 at the Wannsee conference (Bazyler 2017, 29). Witness to the genocide of the Jews is a uniquely Jewish experience, because only Jews were targeted by that policy, even if other groups were targeted for genocide under other policies. The Nazi regime committed genocide against the Roma and Sinti, governed by separate policies. They also committed war crimes against Soviet Prisoners of War under other policies. So too the mass murder of disabled and the mentally ill had their own policies. The Nazis committed multiple genocides and crimes against humanity, at the same time, sometimes in the same place, governed by different laws, policies, and practices. It is not correct to say that there were many victim types during "the Holocaust," if by "the Holocaust" we mean the genocide of the Jews. It is however correct to observe "a strong causal link between racial thinking, on the one hand, and murderous population policy and genocide, on the other" (Roseman 2017, 31), which resulted in the persecution of many groups. The genocide of the Jews would only retrospectively fall under the definition of genocide as defined in the Convention for the Prevention and Punishment of the Crime of Genocide. The intent to murder all Jews without exception was at the time a crime without a name.

The list of atrocities committed by the Nazis can be overwhelming, which speaks to the nature of the violence. Just reading off the many types of victims takes work on the part of the listener, particularly where there is a complete lack of first-person testimony. It is likely that readers of this volume have never heard a first-hand account from many of the groups listed next.

The plan to kill Soviet intellectuals upon the invasion of the Soviet Union in 1941 was a forerunner to the genocide of the Jews (Streit 1986), as the Nazis equated communist intellectuals with "Bolshevist Jews." The rounding up, deportation, and murder of Roma and Sinti who were subjected to a "bewildering number" of laws and decrees (Weiss-Wendt 2015, 2) also constituted genocide. Racial-hygienic legislation commenced with the July 14, 1933 Law for the Prevention of Hereditarily Diseased Progeny (Burleigh 1997, 160). This law led to the creation of the T4 program that targeted 70,000 adults for state murder, including chronic schizophrenics, epileptics, and long-stay patients (123). Homosexuals were governed by Paragraph 175 of the Reich Criminal Code, which was extended under Nazi rule, resulting in increased prosecution in the 1930s. After serving jail sentences for "homosexual acts," the accused were transferred to concentration camps where many subsequently died (162). The use of 13.5 million civilians and prisoners of war for forced labor (Plato et al. 2011, 3) constituted a part of the National Socialist "wartime employment of foreign workers' policy wherein workers from across the continent were forced to work in factories, and 'most were killed'" (Plato et al. 2011, 443).

Of the 5.7 million Soviet Prisoners of War taken by the German armed forces, 3.7 million died in captivity. This mass lethal incarceration for work constituted acts of human slavery and was outlawed long before the Second World War by the Slavery Convention of 1926. These experiences resulted in the dehumanization of its victims and several parallel genocides, crimes against humanity, and war crimes. Everyone had their own trauma and their own memories. Very few gave testimony. They have the same rights to truth, vengeance, remedy, and participation as surviving victims of the Nazi era in Germany. USC Shoah Foundation *did* include many of these groups in relatively small numbers within its Visual History Archive, although most are not translated from their original languages, making them difficult to access for a mainly English-speaking audience.

When each testimony is listened to individually, there is no tension between competing narratives. Each is heard one at a time and has its own efficacy. Human suffering and trauma cannot be compared, because we experience pain on an individual basis, even when an entire group is targeted. The unique set of events that unfolded happened in the life of the individual and it remains their personal and private pain. Human suffering can only ever be experienced (by the experiencing self) and recounted (by the remembering self) and listened to as having its own unique character. That said, what Jews say about their suffering as individuals and as a group has profound impact on group identity as well as universal application. Understanding the causes behind what happened to Jews specifically, and to a number of targeted groups during the period of the Third Reich, have value because they help us understand how to prevent it. If witness about the Third Reich was solely about Jews for Jews, then there would not be the proliferation of testimony that we have today. Holocaust testimony is not only about rehumanization of Jews as Jews; it also has application to the rehumanization of traumatic experience as humans that has meaning for many groups that suffer, which is why it resonates within the collective conscience the place where most of us encounter testimony day-to-day.

Limits of Collective Conscience

The trajectory of memory within the life of an individual surviving victim is guided by invisible forces at play in their own life, as well as in the broader society that constrains or allows what is revealed at any point in time. There are just two options available to the surviving victim: either they keep their memories private, or they make them public. Once memories are public, they form a part of a high-stakes history within the collective conscience in which "simply stated it is who wants whom to remember what and why" (Burke 2013, 108). The Holocaust was the outcome of an ordinary sequence of political and societal events, which had extraordinarily devastating outcomes. These outcomes and the processes that led to them are still subject to inquiry and understanding within the societies that "remember" in the present. Peter Burke in his formulation of cultural history suggests "an approach to the past which asks present minded questions but refuses to give present-minded answers" (Burke 2013, 2).

There are two aspects to inquiry about the Holocaust as historical past: what happened (establishment of the facts) and why (establishment of the reasons). This history has high stakes because what happened is still contested (Seymour and Camino 2017) not only by outright deniers, but also by communities and countries that have a reason to protest the facts as presented, or to frame them in a more politically expedient or convenient manner, because "the crucial issue in the history of memory is not how a past is represented but why it was received or rejected" (Confino 1997, 1390). In other words, there can be "unintended consequences in the history of historical writing as well as the as in the history of political events" (Burke 2013, 2). This is especially true of societies that grapple with violent pasts.

Debates in Germany about the role of the Wehrmacht (Beorn 2014), inquiry into the role of the Vatican during the Holocaust (Zuccotti 2000), or the reshaping of historical perspective in Poland (Gross 2012) are high stakes because their implications are profound for those who inherit those histories. For example, if testimonies demonstrate that citizens of a country were more complicit in the Holocaust than previously thought, local politics can call into question the veracity of the surviving victims' memories. For example, in the Ukraine, Rossoliński-Liebe observes that "non-Jewish communities ignored the voices of the survivors, marginalizing their stories, and some communities even presented them as a political campaign against the Ukrainian people" (2020b, 222). These confrontations with the past often occur at a political or cultural level wherein "Holocaust remembrance remains a contested space where history is simplified in order to serve political ends" (Seymour and Camino 2017, 6). When surviving victims speak about their experiences, their narratives become a constituent part of a collective conscience, which is far from resolved in many countries. In the context of the individual trajectory of memory, how a society views the past is one of the many constraints placed on the surviving victim. What they wish to say about their own memories may contradict the prevailing historical-political view, thereby making it more difficult for the surviving victim to speak.

Notwithstanding the contested nature of the history and meaning of the Holocaust, commitment to remember it has become nearly universal. Societies far removed from the epicenter of the theater of violence, such as the UK and the USA, now hold national commemorations, establish memorials, and support public programs (Pearce 2014). The International Holocaust Remembrance Alliance (IHRA) currently has 36 member states whose delegations are appointed to unite "governments and experts to strengthen, advance, and promote Holocaust education, remembrance, and research worldwide" (IHRA n.d., para. 1). Even with its growing universality, it is necessary to be aware that the motivations for remembering the Holocaust vary (Wollaston 1996, 2). Testimony will therefore be viewed within the collective conscience:

> What is most misleading about confusing mnemonics with memory is that it obfuscates agency. Mnemonics (museums, memorials, artistic representations, and commemorative practices) are initiated, or carried to fruition, by particular individuals and groups, acting out of various particular motives. When we treat the aggregate of these mnemonics as an index to how, and how much, a society "remembers," the result is pure mystification.
>
> *(Novick 2015, 48)*

French Sociologist Maurice Halbwachs is credited with being one of the first to recognize that memory was not limited to personal and subjective experience. He described personal recollections as existing within "social frames" woven into history.[5] In *La Mémoire Collective* he notes that "individual memory could not function without words and ideas, instruments the individual has not himself invented but appropriated from his milieu" (Halbwachs 1980, 50). The milieu to which he refers creates the setting in which a community of memory forms and functions. Alon Confino further helps us frame how to think about the relationship between memory and society, suggesting there is "great advantage in thinking about the history of memory as the history of collective mentality" (Confino 1997, 1389). Paul Ricoeur is not so convinced that the relationship between the individual and society is so clear cut. He states that the overriding question, "is memory primordially personal or collective?" is a paralyzing dilemma (2004, 93). But if a community of Holocaust memory does exist beyond that of the personal memory of the surviving victim, it is a synthesis of societal structures such as memory, history, tradition, language, ethnicity, culture, and nationality. Together, these shape the environment in which self-understanding of the past evolves. In other words, collective memory is not a national or community archival repository. Instead, society shapes collective memory, making the past part of their own memory, then people use these memories to render their lives in more meaningful terms (Antze and Lambek 1996, xviii). Ricoeur poses a rhetorical question:

> Does there not exist an intermediate level of reference between the poles of individual memory and collective memory, where concrete exchanges operate between the living memory of individual persons and the public memory of the communities to which we belong?
>
> *(2004, 131)*

It is a simple question, to which there is not a simple answer. The memory of living persons who survived the Holocaust and the public memory of the Holocaust within the community to which we belong is set in an ever-changing social context and dispersed across many countries, which were either occupied by Germany or were a part of its history. Perceptions of historicity, national identity, and narrative vary by place and evolve over time, as illustrated by Rossoliński-Liebe in his study of Germany, Poland, Lithuania, Belarus, and Ukraine (2020a). Each country has its own distinct mnemonic and historiographic trajectories that parallel or contradict the individual trajectories of memory of the surviving victims in those countries. The "concrete exchanges" to which Ricoeur refers are markedly different in the US, Israel, and the UK, none of which were occupied or lost their Jewish community to the Final Solution. "Concrete exchanges" are different than those of the Ukraine, Lithuania, or Slovakia, where the Jewish communities were decimated and there were varying levels of complicity. Nazi proxy states such as Hungary, Croatia, or Italy are different still.

As a result of these differing concrete exchanges, all aforementioned countries have surviving victims and active commemoration programs, but they confront vastly different interpretations of the Holocaust. They have created different "Holocausts." IHRA exists to find a common political and historical understanding to at least agree upon what the Holocaust was in history, and to create principles on how to talk and teach about the Holocaust in the present. To add further complexity, because of the decimation of many pre-war Jewish communities, there is not an established culture of witness-led commemoration, and therefore is difficult to establish a "concrete exchange" which involves the surviving victims or their descendants, with the exception of outspoken voices such as Marian Turski (Poland), Irena Veisaite (Lithuania), and Charlotte Knobloch (Germany).

The events of the Holocaust are also very difficult to convey within the collective conscience that they become simplified tropes. Geoffrey Hartman observes the difficulty of extracting a guiding image from what he calls the "black sun" of the destruction of the Jews, which produced "a melancholy as disabling as anything ever known" (Hartman 1994, 2). The "black sun" casts a shadow over the endeavors of public witness, serving as both its main motivation and major hindrance. The surviving witness seeks to explain the meaning of the melancholy of the Holocaust which defies interpretation within normally accepted constructs in the collective conscience, and result in summarizing the "complex narratives of the Shoah, simplifying, condensing, and distilling these narratives and producing meanings for cultural consumption" (Stier 2015, 2). The "black sun" thus presents a metaphorical concept that may also be a "metaphor for the darker side of modernity" (Landau 1998, 5) demonstrating that commonly accepted modes of historical comprehension within the collective conscience may not suffice.

Saul Friedlander describes the historiographical process as needing time to confront the reality of the material and describes the need for "working through" (Hartman 1994, 260). He describes the need to balance the numbing distancing of intellectual endeavors with the powerful emotional impact of the subject matter. However, he states that the overriding problem is that "neither the protective numbing nor the disruptive emotion is entirely accessible to consciousness" (Hartman 1994, 261). Friedlander admits that the need to balance the text of the Holocaust (the facts) with the context (their meaning) is problematic, even for professional historians who are close to the topic. Yehuda Bauer also struggles to balance knowledge with interpretation, fearing that "symbolic descriptions that occupy, quite legitimately, the centre of the literary stage in Holocaust literature, become just another escape route for the superficial" (Bauer 1978, 46). Holocaust witnessing is therefore a constant challenge—an ongoing compromise between the difficulties of language, the presentation of fact, and the limitation of paradigms into which the Holocaust can fit in the collective conscience. James Young finds a way to live with the constraints of the collective conscience:

> So long as we are dependent on the vocabulary of our culture and its sustaining archetypes, it may not be possible to generate entirely new responses to catastrophe. It may now be possible however, to respond from within our traditional critical paradigms with self-critical awareness of where traditionally conditioned responses lead us in the world.
>
> *(Young 1990, 192)*

Maurice Blanchot's comment "learn to think with pain" (1986, 145) provides a means by which the "black sun" metaphor may find practical meaning in the collective conscience. Such pain in its most fundamental form is found in the emotions embedded in the witness of the surviving victim. While the traditional documents that historians have relied upon to tell the story of the past are necessary for the reconstruction of the past, the Holocaust has emerged as one of the first significant world-changing histories to be written by the very people the perpetrators sought to destroy. For those individuals to be rehumanized and contribute fully to the society wherein they have made their home, their role as witness to the past needs to be understood beyond them being an object of the past. They need to be heard and understood as subjects in the present.

The Crisis of Witness

We now turn in more detail to the crisis of witnessing the Holocaust, and the inherent dilemma Laurence Langer identifies as a double bind (1991)—the very thing you must understand is impossible to understand. This dilemma is at the heart of every representation, narrative, and interpretation of the Holocaust, in which communication is constrained by language and comprehension. This crisis is true for the witnesses themselves. If they do not speak, their experience remains unheard. If they do speak, it is mediated and therefore no longer the original experience, in which case silence may be the only authentic way to communicate such a past. Jean François Lyotard (1988) describes such retelling as a form of non-verbal communication; survival is not about what is said, it is about being alive. But if Terence de Pres is correct that "the denial of death comes finally to be the denial of life" (Des Pres 1976, 206), acknowledging the all-consuming death of the past demands speech over total silence. Can reimagining the past by empowering survivors with the rights of truth, vengeance, remedy, and participation, free it from the double bind of the "dilemma of witness?"

The dilemma of witness pervades what was intended to be the ultimate silencing event—all Jews were to be silenced permanently. The specifics of what occurred can be described in simple ordinary words and numbers. We can enumerate how many barracks there were in the camp, describe what the soup tasted like, and calculate how many people were gassed at a time. However, that which needs to be explained—how that experience felt and what it means metaphysically to survive it—resists narrativization. To help explain the crisis, Lawrence Langer quotes surviving victim Magda F., who said,

> to understand us, somebody has to go through with it. Because nobody, but nobody understands us. You can't. No [matter] how much sympathy you give me . . . you're trying to understand me, I know, but I don't think you [can]. I don't think so.
>
> *(Langer 1991, xiv)*

To rephrase Magda: To understand an event, one must live through it. Since only the surviving victims have lived through those events, nobody outside of their personal experience can understand them. It does not matter how much sympathy the listener feels toward them or how hard they might try to comprehend their experience; it is just not possible to do so.

Magda's evaluation of the challenges to understanding testimony return us to the hermeneutics of memory. It is possible to describe what happened because every event was associated with a particular time, place, people, and action. Nevertheless, we struggle to interpret what the Holocaust means, which is at the heart of the dilemma of witness. There is only one type of historical memory unique to each surviving victim—the one which is borne out of experience. It is deeply personal and unique to the individual. Among the thousands of testimonies that I have reviewed, I have yet to come across two that are identical, even where some features are shared.

Finding shared meaning relies on an acquired "memory" in which the listener adopts an understanding of the past through watching, reading, or confronting the retelling of another's experience. One memory *is*, the other memory *acquires*. The former speaks, putting personal pictures and feelings into words. The latter listens, reconstructing the past. The hermeneutic failure is precipitated when the narrator and listener confront the same set of events, but do not draw the same meaning from them. The narrator fails to find the words to describe what she experienced, how she feels, and what the memory means. The listener fails to understand what the words mean outside of the normal everyday definition or the gravity of the metaphysical meaning, because there is no existing reference point for that type of experience.

This tensile relationship pervades all forms of narrative retelling and is not unique the extreme circumstances of the Holocaust. However, the tension creates a particular crisis in respect to the Holocaust, as both narrator and listener struggle to convey and comprehend the memory of human suffering in the same way. In this confusion, a breach of shared understanding is created that needs to be bridged. The crisis is thus not only a narrative one; it is also a crisis of identity. As the surviving victim fails to find words that adequately convey the complexity of her experience and being, she asserts that words alone cannot meaningfully convey the experience. Her identity is formed by more than words, but is nevertheless forced to use words as the most readily accessible communication tool available. The surviving witness knows that the listener cannot experience what she experienced through the words at her disposal but insists he must listen to them anyway in order to try to comprehend.

A surviving victim is a witness because of what they saw and experienced (their personal and individual memory), but also because of who they have become in the present. Once they choose to identify publicly (beyond immediate family), they move from passive memory of the past to active memory in the public domain in the present (even if the public space is a relatively safe one, such as at a Jewish community event or memorial). To *become* a witness transmutes passive private memory into active public memory through a change in the surviving victim's status as a self-identifying witness. A witness is no less a witness if they remain silent. There are three modes of witness: 1) A surviving victim who lives with memories and keeps their identity and the memories private; 2) A surviving victim who identifies openly as a living witness to the atrocities of the past and chooses not to give testimonial form to their experience (such a witness may attend a ceremony, or list their name somewhere, or attend a social club for other surviving victims); and 3)

A surviving victim who gives testimony in public via an archive, education program, or museum.

In a 1983 address to the American Gathering of Holocaust Survivors, Elie Wiesel encouraged surviving victims of the Holocaust to recount their memories:

> I know how difficult it is to speak. You have children, you have friends and don't want open wounds—why should you? But you must. When you choose not to speak, your story will not be told, not even in silence. You are more than a witness, you are a hundred witnesses.... You must share. You must!
>
> (Shenker 2015, 35)

Wiesel's strong request for the surviving victims to "speak" and "share" came at a time when relatively few had done so. The Yale Fortunoff Archive had been established just four years prior in 1979. It would be a decade before the USC Shoah Foundation would begin filming in 1994. He directly confronted the dilemma of witness when he insisted that silence will not be sufficient to convey the meaning of the deeply held and painful memories that his audience had. All of those at the gathering were already identifying as witnesses just by being present at the public event. But without words, memory and witness are not given form. Wiesel understood that there was power in giving form to witness in numbers. Today Yad Vashem counts more than 125,000 testimonies in its collection, 60% in video formats.

If "to bear witness to the Holocaust is to *bear the solitude* of a responsibility, and to *bear the responsibility* of that solitude" (Felman and Laub 1992, 3, emphasis in original), the very essence of the witness is to be alone with memory. Testimony is the reverse—it is the vehicle by which the witness gives public form to the events through narrative, photography, audio, video, or multimedia formats. Testimony may also take the form of visual art, music, dance, poetry, works of fiction, documentary film, narrative film, and even social media short-form testimonial representations, such as those of Tik Tok star Lily Ebert (@lilyebert). To testify is therefore to make public the loneliness of witness for the benefit of those who are not able to be a witness (the dead) and for those for whom the act of witness may be beneficial (the living).

Through all of its many representations, the paradox of witness is illustrated by two counter-imperatives that accompany acts of testimony: "You won't understand!" and "You must understand!" Notwithstanding the difficulty of comprehension, Lawrence Langer posits that the doubt surviving victims have that their experience can be understood "underestimates the sympathetic power of the imagination" (1991, xvx). An empathetic imagination creates the possibility that the crisis of the double bind can be overcome. Applying the subject-subject framework of I-Thou enables a closer and more empathetic comprehension of the past. The tension between testifier and listener means the testifier grants the imagination of the listener the power it deserves, and according to Langer the surviving witness also retains the right to doubt the listener's imaginative ability. That doubt will always exist, because as Magda F. stated, "to understand [it] you have to go through . . . it," and nobody but the victims went through it. When the surviving victim states, "even if you think you understand you do not," they help the listener to think more empathetically. The imagination need not be powerful enough to understand the complexity of the experience, so long as it is courageous enough to enter the debilitating world of the witness dilemma. Far from being about narrative, witness is about being willing to enter a state of shared being together.

The Mandate

Olga Lengyel states in her testimony published in 1947:

> In setting down this personal record, I have tried to carry out the mandate given to me by the many fellow internees at Auschwitz that perished so horribly. This is my memorial to them. God rest their souls! Frankly, I want my work to mean more than that. I want the world to read and resolve that this must never, never be permitted to happen again.
>
> (Lengyel 1947a, 208)

By stating that it "should not be permitted," she accuses those who actively or passively permitted her own suffering, and simultaneously suggests that to permit genocide is to participate in its outcome. As previously discussed, the narrative of survival is never documentary evidence alone, rather it is a form of historical exegesis (Young 1990, 11). This does not mean that historical facts do not matter or are not correct, only that there is a higher goal beyond documentation, which includes the role of the dead. Czeslaw Miłosz recognized the duty to respect the dead and places demands upon historians to use their skills to construct the past with precision:

> Those who are still alive, receive a mandate from those who are silent forever. They can fulfil their duties only by trying to reconstruct precisely things as they were, by wresting the past from fictions and legends.[6]

Such a *mandate* enforces the preservation of "fact" from those who cannot provide their own witness (the dead), making it incumbent upon "those who are still alive" to fulfil their demands, including the surviving victims. The *mandate* does not insist on memory being the vehicle to represent the past, but rather a precise and scientific reconstruction of events "as they were." It is important to be clear that paying attention to factual accuracy is not the same as objectifying data. The memorial, literary, and fictive processes have their place, but Miłosz underscores the ongoing need for historical integrity and rigor. The tension between the facts and their interpretation is addressed by Alvin Rosenfeld when he states, "if facts always supersede fiction, it is questionable whether literary works have any role" (Rosenfeld 1988, 65). He goes on to clarify that "genre is not itself an indicator of fidelity to history, so much as a reflection on the writer's ability to absorb history into myth and legend" (80). The mandate does not contradict the position that testimony is exegetical, it just demands that exegesis—including mythologizing the Holocaust—be true to the underlying facts. As Jonathan Webber stated about the site at Auschwitz, there are many

> peoples who see their own Auschwitz in Auschwitz . . . which clearly represent an historical view by their proponents, but none the less distort and manipulate the complexities so as to . . . make them more digestible within the systems of their own cultural and political preoccupations.
> (Webber 1992, 17)

The intention of the *mandate* is to preserve the integrity of the historical past in the present and to always respect the source. Terence Des Pres, in his foundational work *The Survivor*, observes that "the denial of death comes finally to be a denial of life" (Des Pres 1976, 206). By extension, denying the past also denies the present. The *mandate* demands that the surviving victim tell their story, and for humanity to respect the weight of its meaning, not only for the sake of the past, but also the present.

There is another dimension to the mandate. Surviving victim, Gisella Perl, reflects upon the "message" of the dead:

> The dead are speaking to you here. The dead who do not ask you to avenge them but only to remember them and to be watchful that no more innocent victims of German inhumanity ever swell their ranks.
> (Perl 1948, 12)

This demand from the dead was first published by Perl in 1948, invoking the ultimate witnesses of mass murder. As the dead call out in silence, they universalize the purpose of witness on their behalf. Perl underscores that there is first the possibility of being victims, and second being victimizers (Davidson and Charney 1992, 18). Witnessing therefore carries an implicit and universal warning that anyone could find themselves on either side. Jürgen Habermas reflects that such a similar *mandate* exists for Germans as an obligation and warning from their own history, writing that, "these dead have above all a claim to the weak amnesiac power of a solidarity which those born later can now only practice through the medium of memory" (Habermas 1988, 44).

In his memoir *Witness*, Samuel Drix refers to the "sacred duty I owe to the martyrs of Janowska camp and Ghetto Lwów so that they should not be forgotten" (Drix 1995, xv). Like Perl, he is a surviving victim, and states that he bears witness out of "duty to the souls that cry out 'remember us, don't kill us for the second time'" (xiv). Drix's self-imposed *mandate* is commemorative in nature. He makes no attempt to reconstruct "precisely things as they were." He only personally commits to remembering those who became its victims, some of whom he knew personally.

The dead are the only ones who can make the ultimate demand to remember the meaning of their loss, as even the surviving victims have "the inexperience of dying" (Blanchot 1986, 37).[7]

In Arnost Lustig's *A Prayer for Katerina Horowitzova*, the "ashes," like the *mandate* of the dead, are inescapable and all-pervasive:

> No one living would ever be able to escape them. . . . These ashes will be contained in the breath and expression of every one of us . . . they will be contained in books which haven't yet been written . . . no one will be able to get rid of them, for they will be the fond, nagging ashes of the dead who died in innocence.
>
> (Lustig 1973, 50–51)

The dead make their own demand on humanity. Those who were threatened by the same death—its surviving victims—understand it best. It is not only the fact that these dead died, but the manner of their death that makes their demand upon the living greater. Blanchot's observation that "if in death there is something stronger than death, it is dying itself" (1986, 47) clarifies that *how* these people died, and who they were as Jews, contains the power of the *mandate*. The surviving victim is their interlocutor. She can describe the cold-blooded genocidal murder of the Jews, and at the same time help make sense of their deaths for the living. Without the word of the surviving victim, memory of the Holocaust—and with it the memory of the dead—takes no form at all. This is why Elie Wiesel so empathically implored the witnesses in his audience to put their private memories into public words.

Motivations to transition from being an anonymous surviving victim, to then becoming a self-identifying witness, to then becoming a testifier about the experience, differ from one person to the next. For surviving victims, testifying could be about revenge, historical duty, or a commemorative act. Regardless, there is a particularly difficult motivating factor that troubles the conscience of many surviving victims: guilt. Guilt that they survived when their family did not, guilt about how they survived, what they did to survive, guilt that they get to live a full life free of oppression (Nutkiewicz 2003; Leys 2007).

Whatever its motivation, fulfillment of the mandate to speak on behalf of the dead for some happened within days of liberation. For others, it took over 50 years. For some it is yet to happen. For others it never will. The *mandate* may motivate the surviving victim to witness on behalf of the dead, but the surviving victim must themselves choose when and how to carry out that *mandate* within the constraints of their personal courage and the limits of language itself. Witness cannot be forced, even by the dead.

Resolving the Dilemma

The dilemma of witness and the fulfilment of the mandate may be resolved through *encounter*. The double bind of witness is broken when the listener knows that it will not be possible to understand the entire meaning of what is being said, but nevertheless is still willing to encounter the witness. That is, they acknowledge the humanity of the surviving victim no matter what they say, or what they understand. Using the Buberian I-Thou construct, the listener no longer objectifies the experience of the witness or the form of their words. Instead, they "stand in relation" to the one who is witness to the events and respects the essence of their being (Buber 1970, 60). In Buberian ontological philosophy, *I-It* objectifies the experience of the other, turning them into a thing. In Kantian philosophy, the world of experience is the world of phenomena (Wood 1969, 35) in which the thing-in-itself exists as such. The Buberian *I-Thou*, on the other hand, recognizes those things that make up the experience of the individual are included within the encounter. They are superseded by acknowledging the entirety of their being, wherein "real meeting involves the transcendence of all such subjective mediation to arrive at an authentic immediacy" (Wood 1969, 54).

At this point, the thing-in-itself meets us (Buber 1960, 157) when the object becomes a new subject. The witness changes from being an artefact of history to a state of unmediated being, because "the basic word *I-Thou*, can be spoken only with one's whole being" (Buber 1970, 62). At the heart of Buber's assertion is his determination that "all actual life is encounter," wherein "nothing conceptual intervenes, between I and You, no prior knowledge and no imagination" (Buber 1970, 62). The encounter is one in which the listener temporarily suspends objectivizing the individual in favor of engagement, adopting an empathetic position from the perspective of the subject. If the surviving victim is accepted for who they are, irrespective of what can be determined about what they saw and how they explain it, their being is experienced through the encounter, whether through language or silence. Just because the surviving victim cannot find words does not mean they do not have something to say.

In the I-Thou encounter, no conditions need be set by either party. The witness need not make demands of the listener to try to understand, because they are assured of their full attention. The listener does not objectify the surviving victim or her narrative as being limited to being a thing-in-itself, because in addition to the object encountered, they fully recognize the being who envelopes it. They commit to being witness to things they may never fully comprehend, such as her humiliation, dehumanization, the murder of her children. The fear of being misunderstood, an insufficient witness, misconstrued, or misrepresented are removed when both parties recognize the humanity in each other.

Throughout the rest of book, as we examine how language, evidence, and experiences of the Holocaust constrain its narrative, we will apply the I-Thou testimony framework to more closely observe how the crisis of witness may be alleviated through encountering being over form.

Notes

1 Victoria Vincent, personal conversation with the author, 1995.
2 As broadcast by the BBC and remembered by the author, September 17, 1995.

3 Victoria Vincent unfortunately did not get to give her USC Shoah Foundation testimony prior to her unexpected death in 1996.
4 This is a rough estimate because almost all interviewees speaking English, Hebrew, Russian, Spanish, and Swedish are unlikely to have started life speaking those languages. There may be some exceptions, such as Jews living in the former Soviet Union who spoke Russian as a first language or who spoke Hebrew at home. There is at least one British Jew, Leon Greenman, who was deported to Auschwitz. I have made a 1% adjustment (410 testimonies, which I believe is on the high side) to account for these exceptions.
5 Maurice Halbwachs (1877–1945) was the first scholar who pioneered work on collective memory. For further reading see: Halbwachs (1980).
6 Czeslaw Miłosz's Nobel Prize speech, December 8, 1980.
7 Blanchot does not refer specifically to Holocaust survivors in this instance. However, he suggests that death is only learned once, and hence nobody except those that have learned its lesson (he uses the school classroom as an example) understands it.

References

Adizes, Ichak. 2021. *Interview by USC Shoah Foundation*. Los Angeles, CA: Visual History Archive.
Alexander, Jeffrey C. 2002. "On the Social Construction of Moral Universals: The 'Holocaust' from War Crime to Trauma Drama." *European Journal of Social Theory* 5, no. 1 (February): 5–85.
Ancona-Vincent, Victoria. 1995. *Beyond Imagination*. Newark, NJ: Beth Shalom.
Antze, Paul, and Michael Lambek, eds. 1996. *Tense Past: Cultural Essays in Trauma and Memory*. New York: Routledge.
Bauer, Yehuda. 1978. *The Holocaust in Historical Perspective*. Seattle, WA: University of Washington Press.
Bazyler, Michael. 2017. *Holocaust, Genocide, and the Law: A Quest for Justice in a Post-Holocaust World*. New York: Oxford University Press.
Beorn, Waitman Wade. 2014. *Marching into Darkness: The Wehrmacht and the Holocaust in Belarus*. Cambridge, MA: Harvard University Press.
Berenbaum, Michael. 1997. *Witness to the Holocaust: An Illustrated Documentary History of the Holocaust in the Words of Its Victims, Perpetrators and Bystanders*. New York: HarperCollins.
Binder, Janine. 1946. "Interview by David Boder." https://voices.library.iit.edu/interview/binderJ.
Blanchot, Maurice. 1986. *The Writing of the Disaster*. Lincoln, NE: University of Nebraska Press.
Breitman, Richard. 1991. *The Architect of Genocide: Himmler and the Final Solution*. 1st ed. New York: Knopf.
Browning, Christopher R. 1992. *Ordinary Men: Reserve Police Battalion 101 and the Final Solution in Poland*. 1st ed. New York: Harper Collins.
Browning, Christopher R. 2003. *Collected Memories: Holocaust History and Postwar Testimony*. Madison, WI: University of Wisconsin Press.
Buber, Martin. 1960. *The Knowledge of Man*, edited and translated by Maurice Friedman. New York: Harper Torchbooks.
Buber, Martin. 1970. *I and Thou*. New York: Charles Scribner.
Burke, Peter. 2013. *Varieties of Cultural History*. Oxford: Polity Press.
Burleigh, Michael. 1997. *Ethics and Extermination: Reflections on Nazi Genocide*. Cambridge: Cambridge University Press.
Cohen, Sharon Kangisser. 2006. "The Experience of the Jewish Family in the Nazi Ghetto: Kovno—A Case Study." *Journal of Family History* 31, no. 3 (July): 267–288. https://doi.org/10.1177/0363199006287786.

Cole, Tim. 2011. *Traces of the Holocaust: Journeying in and Out of the Ghettos*. London: Bloomsbury Publishing.
Colls, Caroline Sturdy. 2021. "'For Dust Thou Art, and Unto Dust Shalt Thou Return': Jewish Law, Forensic Investigation, and Archaeology in the Aftermath of the Holocaust." In *Routledge Handbook of Religion Mass Atrocity and Genocide*, edited by Sara E. Brown and Stephen D. Smith. London: Routledge.
Confino, Alon. 1997. "Collective Memory and Cultural History: Problems of Method." *American Historical Review* 102, no. 5: 1386–1403.
Davidson, Shamai, and Israel Charney, eds. 1992. *Holding on to Humanity*. New York: New York University Press.
Des Pres, Terrence. 1976. *The Survivor: An Anatomy of Life in the Death Camps*. Oxford: Oxford University Press.
Drix, Samuel. 1995. *Witness: A Holocaust Memoir*. London: Fount Paperbacks.
Ephgrave, Nicole. 2016. "On Women's Bodies: Experiences of Dehumanization during the Holocaust." *Journal of Women's History* 28, no. 2 (Summer): 12–32. www.proquest.com/scholarly-journals/on-womens-bodies-experiences-dehumanization/docview/1807847564/se-2.
Evans, Harold. 2011. *A Convenient Hatred: The History of Antisemitism*. New York: Facing History and Ourselves.
Felman, Shoshana, and Dori Laub. 1992. *Testimony: Crises of Witnessing in Literature, Psychoanalysis and History*. London: Routledge.
Goldhagen, Daniel. 1996. *Hitler's Willing Executioners: Ordinary Germans and the Holocaust*. London: Little-Brown.
Gross, Jan Tomasz. 2012. *Neighbors: The Destruction of the Jewish Community in Jedwabne, Poland*. Princeton, NJ: Princeton University Press.
Habermas, Jürgen. 1988. "Concerning the Public Use of History." *New German Critique* 44 (Spring–Summer): 40–50.
Halbwachs, Maurice. 1980. *The Collective Memory*. New York: Harper and Row.
Harran, Ronnen. 2017. "The Jewish Women at the Union Factory, Auschwitz 1944: Resistance, Courage and Tragedy." *Dapim (Haifa)* 31, no. 1 (2017): 45–67.
Hartman, Geoffrey, ed. 1994. *Holocaust Remembrance: The Shapes of Memory*. Oxford: Blackwell.
Herman, Judith. 1992. *Trauma and Recovery: The Aftermath of Violence—From Domestic Abuse to Political Terror*. New York: Basic Books.
International Holocaust Remembrance Alliance (IHRA). N.d. "A World That Remembers the Holocaust." www.holocaustremembrance.com/world-remembers-holocaust.
Kahneman, Daniel. 2011 *Thinking, Fast and Slow*. 1st ed. New York: Farrar, Straus and Giroux.
Kant, Immanuel. 1960. *Religion within the Limits of Reason Alone*, translated by Theodore M. Greene and Hoyt H. Hudson. New York: Harper.
Kirschenbaum, Jeremiah. 1996. *Interview by USC Shoah Foundation* (Interview 23,513). Los Angeles, CA: Visual History Archive.
Klee, Ernst, Willi Dressen, and Volker Riess. 1991. *Those Were the Days: The Holocaust as Seen by the Perpetrators and Bystanders*. London: Hamish Hamilton.
Kleiman, Kay. 1996. *Interview by USC Shoah Foundation* (Interview 11,028). Los Angeles, CA: Visual History Archive.
Kogon, Eugen, Herman Langbein, and Adalbert Rückerl. 1993. *Nazi Mass Murder: A Documentary History of the Use of Poison Gas*. New Haven, CT: Yale University Press.
Landau, Ronnie. 1998. *Studying the Holocaust: Issues, Readings and Documents*. London: Routledge.

Lang, Johannes. 2010. "Questioning Dehumanization: Intersubjective Dimensions of Violence in the Nazi Concentration and Death Camps." *Holocaust and Genocide Studies* 24, no. 2 (Fall): 225–246. https://doi.org/10.1093/hgs/dcq026.

Langer, Lawrence L. 1991. *Holocaust Testimonies: The Ruins of Memory.* New Haven, CT: Yale University Press.

Langer, Lawrence L. 2020. "My Life with Holocaust Death." *The Journal of Holocaust Research* 34, no. 4: 271–287.

Lengyel, Olga. 1947a. *Five Chimneys: The True Chronicle of a Woman Who Survived Auschwitz.* New York: Ziff Davis.

Leys, Ruth. 2007. *From Guilt to Shame: Auschwitz and After.* Princeton, NJ: Princeton University Press. www.jstor.org/stable/j.ctt7t727.

Lifton, R. J. 1980. "The Concept of the Survivor." In *Survivors, Victims, and Perpetrators: Essays on the Nazi Holocaust*, edited by Joel Dimsdale, 113–126. New York: Hemisphere.

Lindquist, Kristen A., Jennifer K. MacCormack, and Holly Shablack. 2015. "The Role of Language in Emotion: Predictions from Psychological Constructionism." *Frontiers in Psychology* 6: 1–17.

Lower, Wendy. 2014. *Hitler's Furies: German Women in the Nazi Killing Fields.* New York: Mariner.

Lustig, Arnost. 1973. *A Prayer for Katerina Horowitzova.* New York: Harper and Row.

Lyotard, Jean-François. 1988. *The Differend: Phrases in Dispute.* Manchester: Manchester University Press.

MacKay, Nancy. 2016. *Creating Oral Histories Second Edition: From Interview to Archive.* London and New York: Routledge.

Markowska, Marta. 2008. *The Ringelblum Archive: Annihilation—Day by Day.* Poland: KARTA Centre.

McMahan, Eva M. 1987. "Speech and Counterspeech: Language-in-Use in Oral History Fieldwork." *The Oral History Review* 15, no. 1: 185–207. www.jstor.org/stable/3674965.

Nance, Kimberly A. 2006. "Can Literature Promote Justice? Trauma Narrative and Social Action." In *Latin American Testimonio*, 1st ed. Nashville: Vanderbilt University Press.

Nora, Pierre. 1989. "Between Memory and History: Les lieux de mémoire." *Representations* 26 (Spring).

Novick, Peter. 2015. "The Holocaust Is Not—and Is Not Likely to Become—a Global Memory." In *Marking Evil: Holocaust Memory in the Global Age*, edited by Amos Goldberg and Haim Hazan, 47–55. New York: Berghahn Books.

Nutkiewicz, Michael. 2003. "Shame, Guilt, and Anguish in Holocaust Survivor Testimony." *The Oral History Review* 30, no. 1 (2003): 1–22.

Oberrotman, Janine. 1995. *Interview by USC Shoah Foundation* (Interview 1190). Los Angeles, CA: Visual History Archive.

Oberrotman, Janine. 2004. Interview by USHMM Oral History. Accession number 2004.11. https://collections.ushmm.org/search/catalog/irn514926

Pearce, Andy. 2014. *Holocaust Consciousness in Contemporary Britain.* 1st ed. New York: Routledge. https://doi.org/10.4324/9780203484210.

Pearce, Andy, ed. 2018. *Remembering the Holocaust in Educational Settings.* 1st ed. New York: Routledge. https://doi.org/10.4324/9781351008648.

Perl, Giesella. 1948. *I Was a Doctor in Auschwitz.* New York: International Universities Press.

Plato, Alexander von, Almut Leh, and Christoph Thonfeld. 2011. *Hitler's Slaves: Life Stories of Forced Labourers in Nazi-Occupied Europe.* 1st ed. New York: Berghahn Books.

Reicher, Harry. 2004. "Nazi Laws: An Infamous Date." *The National Law Journal* 26, no. 31.

Ricoeur, Paul. 2004. *Memory, History, Forgetting*, translated by Kathleen Blamey and David Pellauer. Chicago, IL: University of Chicago Press.

Roseman, Mark. 2017. "Racial Discourse, Nazi Violence, and the Limits of the Racial State Model." In *Beyond the Racial State: Rethinking Nazi Germany*, edited by Devin O. Pendas, Mark Roseman, and Richard F. Wetzell, 31–57. Cambridge: Cambridge University Press.

Rosenfeld, Alvin Hirsch. 1988. *A Double Dying: Reflections on Holocaust Literature*. Bloomington, IN: Indiana University Press.

Rossoliński-Liebe, Grzegorz. 2020a. "Introduction: Conceptualizations of the Holocaust in Germany, Poland, Lithuania, Belarus, and Ukraine: Historical Research, Public Debates, and Methodological Disputes." *East European Politics and Societies* 34, no. 1: 129–142.

Rossoliński-Liebe, Grzegorz. 2020b. "Survivor Testimonies and the Coming to Terms with the Holocaust in Volhynia and Eastern Galicia: The Case of the Ukrainian Nationalists." *East European Politics and Societies* 34, no. 1: 221–240.

Rubenstein, Richard L. 1975. *The Cunning of History: The Holocaust and the American Future*. New York: Harper & Row.

Sabini, John P., and Maury Silver. 1993. "Destroying the Innocent with a Clear Conscience: A Sociopsychology of the Holocaust." In *Political Psychology: Classic and Contemporary Readings*, edited by Neil J. Kressel, 206. New York: Paragon House.

Seymour, David M., and Mercedes Camino, eds. 2017. *The Holocaust in the Twenty-First Century: Contesting/Contested Memories*. 1st ed. London: Routledge.

Shandler, Jeffrey. 2020. *Holocaust Memory in the Digital Age: Survivors' Stories and New Media Practices*. Stanford, CA: Stanford University Press.

Shenker, Noah. 2015. Reframing Holocaust Testimony. Bloomington, IN: Indiana University Press.

Smith, Sidonie, and Julia Watson. 2001. *Reading Autobiography: A Guide for Interpreting Life Narratives*. Minneapolis, MN: University of Minnesota Press.

Soueid, Marie, Ann Marie Willhoite, and Annie E. Sovcik. 2017. "The Survivor Centered Approach to Transitional Justice: Why a Trauma-Informed Handling of Witness Testimony Is a Necessary Component." *George Washington International Law Review* 50, no. 1: 125–179.

Stier, Oren Baruch. 2015. *Holocaust Icons: Symbolizing the Shoah in History and Memory*. New Brunswick, NJ: Rutgers University Press.

Stone, Dan. 2012. *The Holocaust and Historical Methodology*. New York: Berghahn Books.

Streit, Christian. 1986. "The German Army and the Policies of Genocide." In *The Policies of Genocide (RLE Nazi Germany & Holocaust): Jews and Soviet Prisoners of War in Nazi Germany*, edited by Gerhard Hirschfeld. London: Routledge.

Tory, Avraham. 1990. *Surviving The Holocaust: The Kovno Ghetto Diary*. Cambridge, MA: Harvard University Press.

Tumblety, Joan, ed. 2013. *Memory and History: Understanding Memory as Source and Subject*. London: Routledge.

Venezia, Shlomo. 2009. *Inside the Gas Chambers: Eight Months in the Sonderkommando of Auschwitz*. Cambridge: Polity.

Waxman, Zoë. 2012. "Transcending History?: Methodological Problems in Holocaust Testimony." In *The Holocaust and Historical Methodology*, edited by Dan Stone, 143–157. New York: Berghahn Books.

Webber, Jonathan. 1992. *The Future of Auschwitz: Some Personal Reflections*. Oxford: Oxford Centre for Post-Graduate Hebrew Studies.

Weingarten, Kathy. 2003. *Common Shock: Witnessing Violence Every Day: How We Are Harmed, How We Can Heal*. New York: Dutton.

Weiss-Wendt, Anton. 2015. *The Nazi Genocide of the Roma: Reassessment and Commemoration*. 1st ed. New York: Berghahn Books.

White, Hayden. 2020. *Figural Realism: Studies in the Mimesis Effect*. Baltimore, MD: Johns Hopkins University Press.

Wiesel, Elie. 1967. "Jewish Values in a Post-Holocaust Future: A Symposium." *Judaism* 16, no. 3.

Wollaston, Isabel. 1996. *A War against Memory?: The Future of Holocaust Remembrance*. London: SPCK.

Wood, Robert E. 1969. *Martin Buber's Ontology: An Analysis of I and Thou*. Evanston, IL: Northwestern University Press.

Yerushalmi, Yosef Hayim. 1982. *Zachor: Jewish History and Jewish Memory*. Seattle, WA: University of Washington Press.

Young, James Edward. 1990. *Writing and Rewriting the Holocaust: Narrative and the Consequences of Interpretation*. Bloomington, IN: Indiana University Press.

Zuccotti, Susan. 2000. *Under His Very Windows: The Vatican and the Holocaust in Italy*. New Haven, CT: Yale University Press.

3
THE CONSTRAINED WITNESS

There is a beautiful and touching scene in Claude Lanzmann's *Shoah* (1985). A small boat is shown drifting along slowly on the River Narew through the verdant Polish countryside. A man's voice singing in Polish can be heard. It is lonely, haunting, and plaintive:

> A little white house lingers in my memory.
> Of that little white house, I dream each night.
>
> *(Lanzmann 1985, 4)*

The subtitles do not continue, but the singing does. When the stanza finally comes to an end, Szymon Srebrnik is shown in the boat, silent with his thoughts. Then, other local people comment in voiceovers:

> When I heard him again my heart beat faster. Because what happened here was a murder. I really re-lived what happened.
>
> *(Lanzmann 1985, 5)*

Szymon is then shown walking through a forested landscape, silent, apparently lost in his thoughts. Finally, three minutes after we first see Szymon Srebrnik, he comes to a standstill and states in German:

> It's hard to recognize but it was here. They burned people here. A lot of people were burned here.
>
> *(Lanzmann 1985, 5)*

Over the next two minutes of film, Szymon confirms that this was the place the gas vans came and bodies were burned. Surveying the scene, he continues,

DOI: 10.4324/9781003147220-5

Bodies were thrown into these ovens, and the flames reached the sky. It was terrible. . . . And no one can understand it. Even I, here, now.

(Lanzmann 1985, 6)

Szymon is physically alive, but he is represented as being dead inside. As he walks through the former death camp in silence, we are led to believe that he has no narrative that can describe his experience there. His testimonial witness at Chełmno in *Shoah* is limited to reprising songs from his childhood and confirming the physical location of the crematoria. The camera creates a "narrative" with few words. It is Szymon's *presence* at Chełmno that is the retelling. Szymon then observes the tranquillity of the location:

It was always peaceful here. Always. When they burned two thousand people—Jews—every day, it was just as peaceful. . . . Just as it is now.

(Lanzmann 1985, 6)

Szymon creates an eerie image of mass murder. It was not likely to have either been as quiet or as dignified as the memorial site at Chełmno was when the filming took place. In selecting those words from Szymon's reflections, Lanzmann wants the viewer to understand the work of killing Jews at Chełmno as being carried out quietly and methodically in the forest. There would have had to have been significant activity to accomplish the task; murdering 1,000 people a day takes organization and manual labor. But it was not like the highly industrialized complexes at Auschwitz-Birkenau and Majdanek, where the killing centers were combined with manual labor. There was not a large infrastructure at Chełmno; it was a rural death camp where killing took place in the forest, as surviving victim Michael Podlchlebnik confirms. "When [the] inmates returned from the woods in the evening, they said that they had been burying Jews from Klodawa in a common grave in the woods" (Podlchlebnik 1945, n.p.). Since the Jews had already been murdered in the gas vans, the victims had already been silenced. An occasional gas van would arrive and leave. There were only the sounds associated with the disposal of corpses. Otherwise, the forest would indeed have been peaceful.

The film moves later to a meeting between Szymon and local villagers outside of the church at Chełmno. Szymon is shown silently looking on as Lanzmann encourages them to give their side of the story. Szymon is in the picture, but entirely out of the dialogue, as the narrative has shifted from Szymon's own memory to the memory *of* Szymon, as the villagers describe the little boy who was once in chains (Lanzmann 1985, 95). As the procession of the "Immaculate Conception" passes by—consisting of young girls dressed in white to symbolize unspoiled purity—Szymon passively looks on. The villagers discuss with Lanzmann that Jews had been brought to the church in advance of being placed in gas vans (97). They also discuss the reasons behind the murder of the Jews, one churchgoer concluding, "It was God's will. That's all!" (Lanzmann 1985, 100) Without contributing to the discussion, Szymon is a silent artefact juxtaposed with the vocal and excitable

Polish locals. There is little doubt that Szymon understands what the Polish locals are saying, but at no point does he answer for himself or challenge what they say.

Szymon Srebrnik has a particularly unusual story, as one of few surviving victims of the Holocaust who experienced being murdered. Szymon was shot at Chełmno during the final Nazi retreat from the camp and left for dead. As occasionally happened, the bullet missed his vital organs:

> I went outside in the first group of five. Lenz ordered us to lie down on the ground. He shot everybody in the back of the head. I lost consciousness and regained it when there was no one around. . . . The wound was not deadly. The bullet went through the neck and mouth and pierced the nose and then went out.
>
> *(Holocaust Education & Archive Research Team n.d.)*

Szymon is witness to Blanchot's concept of something stronger than death itself—dying (Blanchot 1986). Szymon was both killed *and* survived. The silent and confused Szymon on film, who states his disbelief at being back at the site of mass murder—including his own—becomes the living embodiment of the dead. His perpetrators had assumed he *was* dead and therefore unable to witness their cruelty. He, like those in the areas marked as mass graves around him at Chełmno, was supposed to have taken his secret with him. Unlike most surviving victims, who cannot claim to have witnessed death itself, Szymon crossed a metaphysical boundary line. In the eyes of the viewer, the formerly "dead" child sailing down the river Narew singing childhood songs is powerful cinematic imagery. We get the impression he was doing nothing different on camera at Chełmno than he had done in the previous 34 years—remaining silent. What had changed was his willingness to re-live the past, at a place where words had no meaning. But Szymon Srebrnik was *far* from a silent witness.

His depiction in *Shoah* as largely confused, disoriented, and mute is a cinematic construct that does not represent either the individual or persona that is publicly available to encounter. Szymon first gave testimony June 29, 1945 to Acting Judge Władysław Bednarz, in Koło for the Łodz District Court (Holocaust Education & Archive Research Team n.d.). In his testimony, he gives detailed descriptions of the gas vans at Chełmno and the killing process. He names and identifies many perpetrators and victims:

> The van doors were locked with a bolt and a padlock. Then the engine was started. The exhaust fumes entered the interior of the van and suffocated those inside. The exhaust pipe went from the engine along the chassis and into the van, through a hole in the car's floor, which was covered with a perforated sheet of metal. The hole was located more or less in the middle of the chassis. The van's floor was also covered with a wooden grate, just like the one in the bathhouse. This was to prevent the prisoners from clogging the exhaust pipe.
>
> *(Holocaust Education & Archive Research Team n.d.)*

He was also able to name 14 of the 15 *Sonderkommando* stationed at Kulmhof (Chełmno), at least four of whom were later convicted of their crimes. In a remarkable feat of memory recall he names them as,

> Bothmann, Piller, Lenz, Runge, Kretschmer, Hafele, Sommer, Gorlich, Laabs, Burstinger, Gielow, Richter, Burmeister, Schmidt and one more whose name I cannot recall.
> (Holocaust Education & Archive Research Team n.d.)

Szymon Srebrnik also testified at the Eichmann Trial in Jerusalem on June 6, 1961. In his testimony (USHMM 1999a) he offers details about the shooting incident, including his own "execution." During his statement he also presents the scar of the bullet wound to the judge as physical evidence of the verbal testimony he gave about the shooting. Srebrnik also provided audio-visual testimony to the United States Holocaust Memorial Museum (Srebnik 1991); USC Shoah Foundation for five and half hours (Srebnik 1997); and contributed testimony now available through the Video Testimony Resource Centre at Yad Vashem.[1]

In his testimony for USC Shoah Foundation Szymon provides detailed descriptions of cruelties he saw and endured:

> I told them about the shooting spree that Hafelle and Bothman did, they placed bottles on each head of the Jews and shot them, if they hit the bottle the Jew was saved and if they hit the head the Jew fell, and his brain spilled all over. The judge asked me how many survived? I said almost everyone died.
> (Srebrnik 1997, seg. #241)[2]

In addition to the oral histories, the film reels of footage taken by Claude Lanzmann show that Szymon was filmed for a total of five hours and eight minutes during the filming of *Shoah*. A review of the footage reveals that Szymon is a lively, talkative family man who can be seen playing and singing with his grandchildren. He is also seen discussing details of his experience with Polish locals at length during the filming trip, which did not make the final cut. He speaks fluently in Polish, Hebrew, German, and Yiddish throughout the filming process. The image of him standing awkward and silent amid the overbearing Catholic churchgoers disappears, revealing a relaxed, easy-going Szymon Srebrnik who smokes while the villagers chatter around him.

Lanzmann did not use the extensive footage of Srebrnik in long, interpersonal conversations with other local Poles. Nor did he use footage taken during the boat trip filmed along the Narew River, in which Lanzmann interviewed Srebrnik, who responded in un-faltering German (Srebnik 1991). The misrepresentation of Szymon Srebrnik in *Shoah* by Lanzmann is within his artistic license to create a constructed persona. There is no attempt to represent either the persona that Szymon had developed for himself—one that is a confident, engaging, and eloquent public witness—nor do we encounter the individual as revealed in his other testimonies.

FIGURE 3.1 Szymon Srebrnik testifies at the Eichmann Trial June 1961

Source: Accessed at United States Holocaust Memorial Museum, courtesy of The Steven Spielberg Jewish Film Archives of the Hebrew University of Jerusalem.

Footage of his testimony (Figure 3.2) shows that he spoke for five hours and 21 minutes in 1997. His testimony is more than twice as long as most testimonies, which average two hours and 15 minutes, demonstrating that he is neither a reticent nor silent witness as depicted in *Shoah*. It was likely to have been an extremely poignant and thought-provoking moment for Szymon to return to Chełmno in 1979. His lack of words may be a natural outcome of that experience. However, the image that Lanzmann portrays of a man who is silent and alone with his memories runs counter to the fact that Lanzmann likely cast him because he was already an established public witness in Israel. He was one of just two survivors to provide testimonial evidence for the Chełmno trial of 1945. Szymon Srebrnik was not muted, and greatly contributed to the understanding of a death camp from which only four Jews are known to have survived the war (USHMM n.d.). He is also not alone in his struggle to find words.

Limits of Language

In the same film, *Shoah*, the aforementioned other surviving witness of the Chełmno death camp, Michael Podchlebnik, says through his translator that "he is only human and he wants to live. So he must forget. And let's not talk about that." In so saying, he invites viewers to encounter him as a human being, along with his need to forget, rather than as a rote narrator of past events. At that moment

The Constrained Witness   59

FIGURE 3.2   Szymon Srebrnik smoking during filming outside of the Catholic church at Chełmno

Source: Created by Claude Lanzmann during the filming of Shoah. Used by permission of the United States Holocaust Memorial Museum and Yad Vashem, the Holocaust Martyrs and Heroes' Remembrance Authority, Jerusalem.

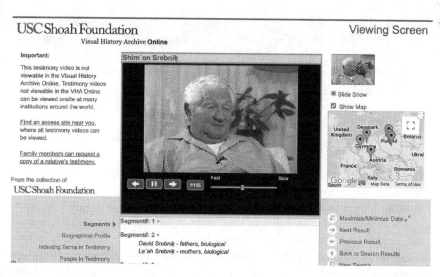

FIGURE 3.3   Szymon Srebrnik (Shim'on Srebnik) viewing screen in USC Shoah Foundation's Visual History Archive

Source: Used with permission of USC Shoah Foundation.

he drops the persona that he has prepared to present to the camera and reveals the individual. Not talking about "that" allows for a deeper comprehension of what "that" represents in his life in the present.

As with Szymon Srebrnik, *Shoah* portrayed Michael Podchlebnik as a relatively silent witness. Yet, the original interview with him for the film was 117 minutes in length, during which he spoke fluently and coherently about his experiences. Like Srebrnik, he had likely been cast because he had provided testimony in June 1945 to the Chełmno trials, which showed him providing specific historical details:

> At about 8 AM the first car from Chełmno arrived. When the van's door was opened, dark smoke with a white tint belched out from the inside. . . . After three or four minutes had passed three Jews went into the van. The corpses were haphazardly piled one on another as high as half-way up the side of the van. Some of those murdered died holding their loved ones in their arms. The corpses generally did not look bad. I did not notice anyone with their tongue sticking out of their mouths or with any unnatural bruises. . . . The van in which the victims were gassed could take 80–90 people at a time. During my stay in Chełmno, two cars were used simultaneously. . . . Twelve to thirteen vans a day arrived in the woods. On this basis I figured that about 1,000 people were gassed every day.
>
> *(Podlchlebnik 1945, n.p.)*

His testimony also included a description of how he unloaded the bodies of his own wife and children:

> The third van which came to Chlemonski's Square on that day (Tuesday) brought the bodies of my wife and two children—a 7-year-old boy and a 4-year-old girl. They were thrown out of the vehicle. I laid myself down near my wife's body and wanted to be shot. An SS-man approached me and said, "this burly man can still work very well."
>
> *(Podlchlebnik 1945, n.p.)*

Michael had clearly put his experiences on record years before, and it is reasonable that he avoids returning to the part of his past during which he witnessed the gassing of his own children because it was unspeakable in every sense of the word.

Aharon Appelfeld asserts that "The unspeakable is a secret. You can only surround it. You cannot speak about it" (Lewis 1984, 16). This provokes several questions. What counts as being unspeakable? In what ways might that which is unspeakable be surrounded? And what is the purpose of surrounding the unspoken? Unlike the double bind that inhibits speech, Appelfeld's assertion is not about the inability to narrate. Rather, he asserts the inappropriateness of narration that exposes something that demands protection, such as discovering the gassing of one's own children. The intensity of this type of experience, the depth of its personal, social, historical, philosophical, spiritual meaning, and consequences are all strands of pain that do not sit comfortably with a narrative retelling. The purpose of exposing the pain for no apparent reason may result in unnecessary re-trauma and humiliation, hence Appelfeld's suggestion to contain it rather than reveal it.

Surviving victims narrate "in order not simply to destroy, in order not simply to conserve, in order not to transmit, but write in the thrall of the impossible real wherein every reality safe and sound, sinks" (Blanchot 1986 38). Then clearly, they narrate outside the boundaries of the accepted norms of reporting. If "fact is stranger than fiction" (Oppenheimer 1996a, 24), the gruesome detail in texts of surviving victims often exceed the most excessive fictions. During the writing process, surviving victims relate the intense struggle that they endure to write down their experiences, which results in seemingly ordinary reporting.[3] It is therefore necessary to understand the difference between the events of the Holocaust as experienced by the surviving victim, the consequence of those events in the lives of the human beings who live with them, and how they choose to represent their experiences in text. These are *modes of memory*. First, Szymon Srebnik experienced being shot and remembers that moment vividly. Second, the consequence of being shot and surviving has traumatic consequences for Szymon. Nevertheless, third, he chose to go on record testimony in 1945, 1961, 1979, 1991, and 1997. These three modes of memory are not the same, even though they happened within the life of the same person. There are many more layers to the process of witness and its narratives than the text itself contains (Langer 1982). Through the I-Thou encounter, all three can be experienced in one place because all belong to the life of the individual. The things that remain unsaid are understood to be there nevertheless and encountered through being, not its representational form.

Hayden White's statement that "historical discourse could never come into existence at all [without] language" (White 2020, 5) is countered by Theodore Adorno's struggle with language and what might possibly be conveyed of an event through it. He is often quoted for his now famous dictum that "to write poetry after Auschwitz is barbaric" (Adorno 1967, 4), which emphasizes the difficulty of representing traumatic events in literary form. Commentators of the Holocaust often cite Adorno to describe their own reluctance to create an "aesthetics" of Auschwitz.[4] However, as Alvin Rosenfeld observes, the real issue is the deep anguish and immense frustration of the writer, stating that "all memoirists have known this radical sense of self-estrangement which handicaps any thinking and writing about the Holocaust, but which their books are written to break" (1988, 55). Adorno went on to qualify his original statement stating,

> the abundance of real suffering tolerates no forgetting . . . this suffering demands the continued existence of art [even as] it prohibits it. It is now virtually in art alone that suffering can find its own voice.[5]
>
> (Adorno and McDonagh 1979)

The apparent contradiction in Adorno's position shows how the Holocaust encourages a dichotomy of interpretation though language. Words and their meanings are divided. Jean François Lyotard refers to the difficulty of language as "the differend," which he describes as the "unstable state and instant of language wherein something which must be able to be put into phrases cannot yet be" (Lyotard 1988, 13). As an event on the extreme of human experience, language—whether reporting or metaphor—may not be sufficiently developed to carry the meaning conveyed by the Holocaust. Language is also limited through the perceptions of consequence and the meaning it may or may not have for a given audience. If the event is of little or no consequence to an audience outside the victim group, the necessity of finding the words is reduced, as there will be no desire on the part of others to understand them. Israel Charney, discussing perceptions of genocide (Totten et al. 1997, xiv), points out that "it is the simple nature of humans that we care more about ourselves first of all." If another person's tragedy is inconsequential to our own identity, there is little motivation for them to understand its meaning.

If on the other hand the Holocaust is believed to have collective meaning for society and its values, understanding it becomes highly consequential, in which case, a complete description belongs in the public domain, as do its interpretations. For such interpretations to be possible, a common language must be found to convey the facts and consequences of genocidal mass murder in a way the society it affects can understand it. In what Lyotard describes as "new rules for forming and linking phrases" he suggests that that which cannot yet be phrased should be phrased in "idioms which do not yet exist" (Lyotard 1988, 13). Creating a new vocabulary of the Holocaust may not be entirely possible or even desirable, but to create new meaning is necessary if the events are to be understood beyond anything other than their descriptions. The limits are therefore not the words, but what the words are understood to mean. Such were the extremes of experience during the Holocaust that mere reporting transmutes to metaphor, a problem Terrence Des Pres grapples with:

> It is as if amid the smoke of burning bodies the great metaphors of world literature were being acted out . . . death and resurrection, damnation and salvation, the whole of spiritual pain and exultation in passage through the soul's dark night.
>
> *(Des Pres 1976, 70)*

The difficulty of using of simile and metaphor to describe events is demonstrated through those who have attempted it. Alvin Rosenfeld implores readers to avoid metaphor wherever possible, while using metaphor in his denunciation of it. He states, in part quoting Elie Wiesel,

> there are no metaphors of Auschwitz, just as Auschwitz is not a metaphor for anything else. Why is that the case? Because the flames were real flames, the ashes only ashes, the smoke always and only smoke. If one wants 'meaning' out of that, it can only be this: at Auschwitz humanity incinerated its own heart.
>
> *(Rosenfeld 1988, 8)*

Metaphor cannot be avoided altogether, but even descriptive reporting reveals that commonly used words have layers of alternative meaning for the surviving victims. For example, they may use words with no metaphoric overtones, but which carry a different physical and metaphysical meaning when they describe everyday activities *in extremis*. Adjectives such as "cold," "thirsty," or "hungry" have an additional meaning translated through having felt *that* "cold," *that* "thirsty," or *that* "hungry." Some everyday nouns such as "oven," "bread," "corpse," "fence," or "food" have their equivalents embedded into a in concentrationary language. An "oven" is no longer a domestic appliance in which to bake bread, it is where corpses are burned, but an implement of mass murder. When Sonderkommando Dario Gabbai describes the "eight ovens" in the gas chamber and crematorium complex in Auschwitz Birekanu (Gabbai 1996, 2014), the word "ovens" doubles as a physical tool and a metaphor for the Holocaust itself. As such, ordinary words that may appear in the reports of surviving victims may well have secondary meanings that may not be understood by the reader. If "language alone cannot give meaning to Auschwitz" (Langer 1991, 27), the Holocaust is not best understood using definitions we presently ascribe to words that describe ordinary everyday activities.

At the time of writing, neither the Oxford or other dictionaries provide a definition of the term "selection" beyond its normative usage of "the act or process of selecting."[6] This definition describes, say, selecting a vegetable in a supermarket, although some definitions do include "the act of selecting one or more people or things from a group."[7] In respect to the Holocaust, "selection" is a euphemism for mass murder, as those not selected (to live) are condemned to death (and vice versa)—the meaning of which is contained within the new definition itself. Hence, "selection" is no longer the positive selection of personal preference, but it is reversed as a disruptive notion of having no choice in the face of death. There is also a transcendental meaning to the word "selection" that remains silent; the term contains the weight of the meaning of all the deaths that the "selection" represented "as a sign that something remains to be phrased which is not" (Lyotard 1988, 57).

The public may never hear the transcendental silence of the dead. Nevertheless, the empirical description of the "selection" needs to state its meaning in commonly understood language and not the euphemism of the perpetrators. Such a definition would state that individuals were chosen to live or to die, and that those who were chosen to live were reduced to dehumanized numbers. They tolerated abhorrent living and working conditions, and that those who were chosen to die by *not* being selected to live were murdered within hours of the "selection" process concluding. A fuller definition of "selection" needs to formally enter our vocabulary. Wiesel suggest this is best accomplished by "trying to tell the tale and as purely, as soberly [as possible]" (Lewis 1984, 158). He says that it is better to remain ignorant than to use language that trivializes the events. He continues, "if people know nothing, then one day they [can eventually] know [accurately], but if they know this trivialized, cheapened, distorted view, then ultimately they falsify memory."

The memory of atrocity always results in the loss of some of its original nature. The I-Thou encounter reduces the deficit in comprehension, because in encountering the surviving victim, atrocity is accompanied by an emotional and sensual reliving of the event. In personal conversation and on video, emotions are conveyed through intonation, physiognomy, and other biometric markers (Rao and Koolagudi 2015). The victim does not need to explain certain things that are implicit within his or her version of the atrocity. The surviving victim explains one thing, the recipient perceives another.

When Kitty Hart-Moxon describes the "sickly fatty, cloying smell" that she and her mother associated with "roasting meat" (Hart-Moxon 1997, 62) on their arrival at Birkenau, she does not invite her audience to imagine smells from their own kitchen. Rather, she is attempting to relate a universal smell sensation. Victoria Vincent describes the same smell sensation as "the very strong odor of burning flesh" (Ancona-Vincent 1995, 32). Vincent is more direct with her audience, invoking a more nauseating sensation of mass murder, but in both cases the surviving victims bridge unrelatable experience in relatable terms. Charlotte Delbo, on the other hand, takes pains to describe the absolute otherness of language and its meaning both during and after the Holocaust. She makes clear throughout her testimonial work that her Auschwitz experience was a different form of normality. By way of example, she attempts to explain the concept of thirst:

> Someone who has been tormented by thirst for weeks would never again be able to say: "I'm thirsty let's make a cup of tea." . . . 'Thirst' has once more become a currently used term. On the other hand, if I dream of the thirst I felt in Birkenau, I see myself as I was then, haggard, bereft of reason, tottering. I feel again physically that real thirst, and it's an agonising nightmare.
>
> *(Langer 1991, 8)*

In a further attempt to emphasize the gap between the Auschwitz experience and everyday living, Delbo switches between a scene at Auschwitz-Birkenau—where corpses are being stacked in the frozen yard—and an incident on the Boulevard de Courtais in Montluçon prior to the Second World War. Delbo relates waiting at the Nouvelles Galeries for her father and watching a delivery of mannequins for a display window:

> I had never thought of them as naked, without hair. I had never imagined them outside the display window. . . . To discover them thus made me as uneasy as seeing a dead person for the first time. Now the dummies are lying in the snow.
>
> *(Delbo 1995, 18)*

The sudden switch between her experience before and then during Auschwitz linguistically jolts the reader between realities. In her former life, she is an innocent young girl afraid of naked manikins. In the next scene she is a young woman apparently afraid of nothing, as she sees the "dummies"—corpses in Auschwitz—lying dead in the snow. She comments that she and fellow internees are consuming their daily soup ration when one of them notices one of the corpses in the pile moving. Ignoring the sign of life, Delbo relates their reaction:

"Eat your soup," says Cecile. These women no longer need anything.
I look too. I look at this corpse that moves but does not move me. I'm a big girl now. I can look at naked dummies without being afraid.

(Delbo 1995, 19)

Henry Greenspan acknowledges the impossible juxtaposition of "any single life living with such destruction" (Greenspan 1998, 19). There is a core of abnormality that remains. Among the many scenes that were filmed by Claude Lanzmann and not included in *Shoah*, there is a 20-minute reel of Szymon Srebrnik playing with his grandchildren in a garden, showing a man living a "normal" life. And yet we know that Szymon's own life had been far from normal. The differend applies itself to life experience as well as words. It is difficult to describe precisely why the picture of family normality is far from normal. The picture of the happy family and their unseeable past cannot be explained. Here we find the differend: there is something to say about this image, but if I say it, I will either fail to sufficiently convey what I mean, or normalize their abnormal experience.

If language normalizes abnormal experience, is there any merit in creating narratives knowing they will fall short of explaining the meaning of what happened? Elie Wiesel resolves this by suggesting that rather replacing silence with words, it would be better to "add silence to the words, to surround words with silence" (Lewis 1984, 167). This silence is experienced as vocal silence (time-based silence such as pauses where nothing is said) and narrative silence (words and concepts that are not voiced that could be). The silence of Srebrnik as he walked the site of

FIGURE 3.4   Szymon Srebrnik smiles as he sings "Happy Birthday" to his grandchild at a family gathering in Israel during the filming of *Shoah* (left) and standing at the former site of mass killing at Chełmno death camp (right)

Source: Created by Claude Lanzmann during the filming of Shoah. Used by permission of the United States Holocaust Memorial Museum and Yad Vashem, the Holocaust Martyrs and Heroes' Remembrance Authority, Jerusalem.

Chełmno in *Shoah* exemplifies how layers of silence surround the few words he uses to make more comprehensible his pain at that site, and at the same time "coalesce with the rest of their lives" (Langer 1991, 3), which includes struggling with all of those things that remain unsaid.

What we experience when we observe Szymon Srebrnik singing "Happy Birthday" to his grandchild in the garden with his family is a form of mnemonic dissonance. It is a dissonance experienced by both the surviving victim and the listener, neither of whom can fully inhabit each other's identity. To an attentive listener, dissonance is instructive, highlighting the inconsistency of the events described with current-day realities. In an I-Thou encounter, there is no need to resolve the dissonance, because it is recognized that the harmonization of the two realities—surviving victim and listener—is not possible. "If one theme links their narrative more than any other, it is the unintended . . . but invariably unavoidable failure of such efforts" (Langer 1991, 3). The dissonance does not indicate no reality, only a different form of reality that requires a different form of literacy. Hence, Lyotard describes Auschwitz as "the most real of realities" (1988, 58) because it impugns the realities that we consider normative. The lived experience of the Holocaust, including its many dissonant realities, is a normative experience for those who went through it.

The differend, then, is not only the differential between language and understanding, it also extends to the differential between lived experiences past and present. Such differends "must have something in common" with everyday reality to provide a link, and "must take place within one universe" (Lyotard 1988, 28). That single universe is found in the I-Thou encounter in which it is recognized that what is presented is not what the Holocaust was; "the basic point here is that one should not hypostatize the text, the context or the reader but attempt to understand the relations among them in tensely interactive terms" (LaCapra 1994, 5). The encounter between the remembering self and the listener takes place in the interaction between the surviving victim, listener, and the collective conscience. Here, language takes on new meaning because "after Auschwitz there is no word tinged from on high, not even a theological one, that has any right, unless it underwent transformation" (Lyotard 1988, 87). The Holocaust may not make sense when described through words that limit its meaning, but neither should it be nonsense to the society in which it is spoken. For it to make sense, it must be supported by evidence.

Who Is a Holocaust Witness?

The narrative crisis also produces a crisis of evidence, as by virtue of its nature it "produced no witnesses" (Felman and Laub 1992, 80) in the way that the term "witness" is ordinarily understood. To be a witness and to testify in a court of law is to commit one's narrative truthfully and independently and "*take responsibility*—in speech—for the truth of an occurrence" (204). Finding witnesses prepared to provide an account of the events of the Holocaust is not difficult, as even today there are more than 100,000 surviving victims persecuted as Jews during the Nazi era. Finding witnesses who can do so independently of a role within the events themselves is all but impossible. The witnesses are all implicated (involuntarily) in its happening and therefore understand its meaning from different perspectives to the general population who did not experience it first-hand.

Surviving victims were subjected to persecution and might therefore be deemed insufficiently independent to objectively bear witness. All Nazis and most Germans were arguably involved, if only through their passivity. Therefore, their witness may also be deemed unreliable.[8] Non-German Aryans could be classed as possible independent witnesses, but should they have seen something and chosen not to intervene, they may be tainted by either the guilt of their passivity, or viewed as tacit supporters of the Nazi genocidal efforts. If they chose to intervene, they were similarly involved through their acts of resistance and courage. Very few potential witnesses can claim such independence from the events themselves. Surviving victims have also participated in the war crimes trials since the admission of testimony to the Lüneberg trials in 1946 (Stewart 2019). However, there have been occasions when such testimony has been called into question (Wagner 2010) because there was a fundamental difference between the "experiential truth of Auschwitz as a site of pain and loss" and the legal concept "of Auschwitz as a site of minutely specifiable criminal acts" (Pendas 2006, 141–142).

Whether or not testimony is permissible as evidence, the role, function, and act of witness may be called into question through the traumatic and debilitating nature of the Holocaust experience. Dori Laub contends that the Holocaust requires reinstating the witness process through "repossessing one's life story through giving testimony" (Felman and Laub 1992, 84). Laub reflects that the Holocaust created an anti-I-Thou relationship, wherein the victim who was caught up on the inside of the Holocaust lost all sense of the other. "There was no longer anyone to which one could say 'thou' in the hope of being heard or answered" (82). In other words, the Nazis created the conditions of dehumanized solitude and the absence of relationships. When the surviving victim loses his or her own self-identity, they lose the ability to witness oneself.

> This loss of the capacity to be a witness to oneself and thus to witness from the inside is perhaps the true meaning of annihilation, for when one's history is abolished, one's identity ceases to exist as well.
>
> *(Felman and Laub 1992, 84)*

Laub goes on to state that the chroniclers of the time were ineffective as "the event could thus unimpededly proceed *as though* there were no witnessing whatsoever, *no witnessing that could decisively impact on it*" (84). His point is that if witness had been effective, the outcome would have been different. This may well be true, but that was not the aim of the chroniclers. They accomplished their goal in two respects. If one of the roles of witness is to provide accurate and timely testimony, the chroniclers were the closest first-hand reporters whose writing rises to the level of evidentiary documentation. Second, in creating their own documents, the victims who otherwise would have been silenced permanently have retained their identities, names, and narrative voices, which overcomes the obfuscating intent of the perpetrators. Not many of the victims had the capacity to create such witness in real time because the nature of the events restricted it. Testimony gives opportunity for those who did survive to overcome the debilitating legacy of silence and to become witness to their own experience after the fact. This restores their sense of self, which may have been lost in the anti-I-Thou experience of genocidal violence.

As previously described, there were many national religious and ethnic backgrounds persecuted by the Third Reich. Their persecution was further compounded by the fact that most concentration and work camps were not extermination centers by design. Not all Jews were murdered at extermination centers, and a considerable number of non-Jews were. Are non-Jewish surviving victims classified as witnesses of the Holocaust? Are such surviving victims able to speak on behalf of all the dead, or just some of the dead? Can they speak for all, or are they limited to describing their own particular kind of survival?

When defining who is a witness to what, it is important to recognize the type of experience of each surviving witness, and how it differs from person to person and group to group. "Survival" is a relative and unclear term at times. There is no question that a Jew incarcerated in Auschwitz-Birkenau was a victim of genocide there. But is a Polish political prisoner who survived in the same place, under the same circumstances, a survivor of genocide? If not, is there more than one Auschwitz, more than one memory of it, or more than one type of suffering that took place there? A "multiplicity of memories at Auschwitz" (Webber 1992, 8), suggests that Auschwitz is itself multiplicitous. There were many victim categories within the concentration camp system, and so outcomes differed based on the intent of the perpetrators. "What distinctions, if any, can be made between the Final Solution to the Jewish question and Nazi policies towards other ethnic and religious groups?" (Berenbaum 1990, 1) The complete destruction of European Jewry was the motivating objective of the anti-Jewish genocidal ideology. The surviving victims of that genocidal goal survived something different *in intent* to those who were not Jewish, even if they were incarcerated in the same place for another intent.

Searching for a qualitative difference in suffering has no merit from a moral perspective. However, from a witness perspective, it is important to know what the witness was witness *to*, and the perspective from which they witnessed it, in order comprehend that which is being witnessed. Does witness of the Holocaust, as defined by the Nazis as *der Endölsung der Jüdishe Frage* ("the Final Solution of the Jewish Question"), require a Jewish identity to fully experience what it meant to be threatened with genocidal violence? Can the Polish political prisoner who saw it with his or her own eyes in the same place be a witness to it too? There are a wide variety of victim voices affected by the Final Solution who were not Jewish, including rescuers, adjacent political prisoners, and perpetrators. Jewish surviving victim of Auschwitz Primo Levi initially deals with the Nazi concentration camp system, and he is certain of its unique nature, saying,

> up to the moment at which I am writing, and notwithstanding the horror of Hiroshima and Nagasaki, the shame of the Gulags, the useless and bloody Vietnam war, the Cambodian self-genocide, the *desaparecidos* of Argentina, and the many atrocious and stupid wars we have seen since, the Nazi concentration camp system remains a unicum, both in its extent and quality.
> (Levi 1988, 10)

However, just because *l'univers concentrationnaire* (Rousset 1951) is a unique infrastructure does not mean that any one group caught up within that *univers* had consistent experiences of victimhood. Primo Levi entitles chapter 2 of *The Drowned and the Saved* as "The Grey Zone," in which the perpetrators "shift onto others—specifically the victims—the burden of guilt, so that they were deprived of even the solace of innocence" (Levi 1988, 53). In the Grey Zone, internees could be victims through their own moral choices and actions. Adjudicating such moral dilemmas is a complex matter (Des Pres 1976; Bettelheim 1979, 1986, 1991; Pawelczynska 1979; Todorov 1996), particularly through the medium of testimony in which the individual might use their testimony to hide their decisions to enter the Grey Zone and compromise their innocence. The 2021 documentary film *Love It Was Not* details the relationship between Jewish internee Elena Citron and SS officer Wünsch in the Kanada section of Auschwitz-Birkenau. The 2022 film *The Survivor* is a feature narrative based on the true story of Harry Haft who was "made" to box to the death in Janowska, a sub-camp of Auschwitz. Haft clearly states that he had better privileges through his relationship with the SS guard (Haft 1995, seg. #14). Both internees compromised with the will of the German guards to survive. Are such surviving victims any less reliable as witnesses? Can they legitimately speak on behalf of the dead?

In addition to those within the *l'univers concentrationnaire*, the panoply of witnesses include hidden Jews, those on false papers, and those who escaped German occupied or controlled territory. Writer and scholar Yaffe Eliach, who was hidden as a child in occupied Lithuania during the Second World War, says of herself, "I did not view myself as a survivor, and I don't even now. While I was in hiding . . . I learned to listen, being among adults" (Lewis 1984, 31). If Hitler's intention was to murder the Jews from the outset (Dawidowicz 1987, xix), then at the point he assumed power in the Weimar Republic in 1933, all Jews within his jurisdiction were potential victims of the genocidal intent and conditions that were being created. Thereafter, any Jew leaving Germany could be identified as a "survivor" of that intent, without having ever experienced direct personal assault, deportation, ghetto internment, or camp life. If a refugee leaving Germany in 1935 considered themselves a surviving victim by virtue of birth, nationality, and place of domicile prior to the onset of genocide, how does this impact the status of a Catholic priest or Jehovah's Witness incarcerated in a concentration camp who placed themselves in harm's way through outspoken belief or conviction? It may be argued that they sacrificed more by following their convictions than the Jew who was able to flee unharmed. Might not such a "survivor" legitimately claim to be a witness by choice? It is equally valid to argue to the contrary that because they *did* have a choice, they could not bear witness to the "choiceless choice" that characterizes the quintessential essence of the Holocaust experience (Langer 1982, 72).

If Jewish and non-Jewish victims of Nazi persecution shared similar experiences in the same camps, differentiation can only be claimed on empirical grounds. While many differences of policy existed among inmate types and levels of privilege, an inmate in the same work *Kommando* nevertheless experienced the same physical persecution as the next inmate. They experienced the same back-breaking labor with an equal chance of dying from that work, and can therefore give equal insight into that experience. Any claim to uniqueness lies not in the description of survival, as it was neither the conditions in the camps nor the experience of the surviving victims that defined the uniqueness of the experience, but the nature of the intent. Defining the singularity of experience cannot be found in the physical experience alone. Jews in that same work detail experienced that same work because of a genocidal policy, which is qualitatively different in intent to the actual physical work being carried out by both.

Whatever the specific lethal intent of the Final Solution, the nature of survival changed based on place, policy, and time. There are theories that survival depended upon the active engagement of the individual, including physical and psychological strategies:

> To survive one had to want to survive for a purpose. One of the simplest ideas that prisoners hung on to . . . was revenge. . . . An idea that sustained many . . . was that of bearing witness . . . Some wanted to stay alive for those whom they loved . . . some were sustained by thoughts of the better world they would create. . . . Only active thought could prevent a prisoner from becoming one of the walking dead *(Muselmänner)* whom he saw all around him.
>
> (Bettelheim 1979, 293)

This position is not acceptable to many commentators, who see this thesis as "blame-the-victim syndrome" (Des Pres 1991, 69). Terence Des Pres criticizes Bettelheim's comment that "walking to the gas chamber was committing suicide," because it shows a blatant lack of understanding of the meaning of the Final Solution, and therefore how the death camps worked. Bettelheim was at one time incarcerated in Buchenwald Concentration Camp. He left for America in 1939 on his release, thus avoiding further detention. Although Bettelheim is an eyewitness, Des Pres describes his analysis as spokesman for the surviving victims as being "limited and misleading" (Des Pres 1991). Des Pres' distance as a non-Jewish academic based solely in the United States is significantly more removed than Bettelheim. Des Pres could not claim Bettelheim's personal experience on the inside of a concentration camp, nor a direct understanding of the nature of Nazi persecution. Bettelheim does present a plausible point: all surviving victims, virtually without exception, did try to survive the ordeal.

Observing the non-Jewish witnesses within the camp system helps us understand the similarities and differences among its surviving victims. Ella Lingens-Reiner was an Austrian doctor who was incarcerated, first in Ravensbrück and subsequently in Auschwitz-Birkenau, for attempting to assist a Jewish man's escape to Austria. She was considered "Aryan" in the camp system, but her hatred for Nazism did not endear her to her fellow Aryan captors. Simultaneously, she was under suspicion by the non-Aryan internees at Auschwitz-Birkenau, who naturally saw her as being too close to the Germans to trust. Writing in the immediate postwar period she reflects:

> My personal position was peculiar, because I was an 'Aryan', a 'German', and a doctor who could work professionally all the time. This made my survival possible. It gave me an opportunity to see the various facets of camp life, which others may not have known at all; it also saved me from the deepest sufferings and made it comparatively easy for me to achieve an analytical frame of mind, such as would have been impossible for those whose experiences were more horrible than mine. Last but not least, it created specific problems for me and thus forced me to think about the moral implications of my situation with particular care.
>
> *(Lingens-Reiner 1948, x)*

This insight makes clear that inmates had markedly different experiences in the same physical place. Tadeusz Borowski describes how he used the little privilege he had as a "political" prisoner to sum up his own struggle to come to terms with his survival, saying,

> with a tremendous intellectual effort, I attempt to grasp the true significance of the events, things and people I have seen. For I intend to write a great immortal epic, worthy of this unchanging, difficult world chiselled out of stone.
>
> *(Borowski 1976, 180)*

Lingens-Reiner and Borowski, among other non-Jewish surviving victims, indicate that witnesses of the Holocaust need not be Jewish to be a witness. However, each in their own way makes clear that they do not consider themselves to be the victims of the genocide of the Jews happening in the same place at the same time. The narrative of Holocaust survival, while speaking to the uniquely horrific trauma brought about by the Final Solution on all Jews, encompasses the witness narrative of non-Jews, whose perspective underscores what is known about Jewish suffering. It also illuminates what can and needs to be known about those who were not Jewish and suffered greatly as a part of the Nazi regime's ideological persecution.

There are other groups who were eyewitnesses to the Holocaust, whose perspective is essential to understanding how it transpired and who it involved. At this point most of the perpetrators have taken their memories with them, but the few that survived have an important key to understanding—what motivated them, what they saw, how they felt, and why they did it. Many of these questions will remain unanswered and unanswerable. Like the victims, there were contemporaneous accounts (Klee et al. 1991) and trial statements, but they are largely restricted to archival sources. *The Final Account* archive collected by Luke Holland is a rare and courageous attempt to gain insight into the minds of ordinary perpetrators living in German society (Smith 2021). The 250 interviews are not classified as "testimonies" in the same way that surviving victims have shared their experiences, as there is no attempt to truthfully witness the atrocities to which they were associated. However, through the interview process Holland was able to elicit insights into their states of mind at the time and seven decades after the events.

The *Yahad in Unum* archive, established by Catholic priest Father Patrick Desbois, is also a compelling addition to the body of first-hand witness interviews. The 8,000 interviews were conducted in eight countries with the people who lived in the Ukraine, Belarus, and the Baltic countries. They were eyewitness to the mass killings of the Einsatzgruppen beginning in June 1941 after the German invasion of the Soviet Union. The Yahad in Unum archive helps us understand how the Holocaust unfolded through the eyes of those who observed at a safe distance as their Jewish neighbors were slaughtered before their eyes (Yahad in Unum n.d.), in what Desbois describes in the title of his first book as the *Holocaust by Bullets* (Desbois 2008). This largely unexplored archive reveals a perspective not heard in the thousands of testimonies of surviving victims—that of the bystander. Like the perpetrator interviews collected by Luke Holland, these interviews offer researchers valuable insights that will further complicate what we know about German genocidal atrocity.

Testimony is a form of rhetorical justice. Descendants of the victims acutely feel the lack of justice and the gaping holes in their family trees. They still feel the weight of the crimes committed for which justice was never served. The surviving victims were to be permanently silenced, yet have been able to speak. Only a small number were ever called upon to be witness in trial, yet they take the stand in the court of public opinion when they submit their testimony to public archives and speak their truths. Even if justice cannot be served, their testimony is rhetorical revenge. The surviving victims who took the stand in Jerusalem to face Adolf Eichmann did so under the auspices of the court. Taking the stand was their form of revenge. They were able to speak to their oppressor as citizens of Israel, rather than the *untermenschen* of the Third Reich. The perpetrators, who rarely spoke their own truths, believed that their crimes would not be revealed by those who survived. Of the millions of Germans who were involved in the genocidal state, the Nuremberg process tried approximately 200. The subsequent trials involved fewer than a thousand cases (USHMM 2020), meaning most implicated in the atrocities never saw trial, confessed, or were named. In the absence of a justice process the witnesses only had one course of action, which was to turn memory into public testimony as their own form of rhetoric justice.

The Impossibility of Forgetfulness

Forgetting is typically understood to be "passive, and intrinsic to memory" (Antze and Lambek 1996, xxv). But when a witness makes a conscious decision *not* to recount things too difficult to confront, the absent memory remains. Marcel Routier observes three members of the women's orchestra in Auschwitz-Birkenau, who reunited in the 1970s:

> Forgetfulness has helped in various ways; the dimming of memory has enabled them to survive, and, like night birds, they feel painfully nervous of the glare of day . . . it is impossible for each to guess which part of life in the camp the others might have decided to forget.
>
> *(in, Fénelon 1977, 7)*

Any surviving victim who actively "decides" to forget certain things commits the "forgotten" memory to an unspoken and non-represented form of memory. Such shielding of memory is not forgetfulness, but rather an act of self-protection. Routier observed that each of the women was afraid to open the wounds of the other. In the ensuing conversation, two of the women suggested they had forgotten too much of the experience to write it down. Fania Fénelon replied that not only had she not forgotten anything, but that she had, "never left the camp; I'm still there, I've spent every night of my life there for thirty years" (Antze and Lambek 1996, ix). The stark contrast between the surviving victims who say they have forgotten and those who admit to still "being there" is striking, not least because of the polarity of their claims. Wiesel's observation that "any survivor will tell you he could have stayed *there*, and in a way that is where he still is" (Wiesel 1979, 222, emphasis in original) imposes a permanent sentence of incarceration upon surviving victims. Many state that memory of the camps did not leave them despite their attempts to forget an "insomniac faculty, whose mental eyes have never slept" (Langer 1991, xv). Whether or not a surviving victim decides to be a public witness, all of them live with their own traumatic past and have their own way of coping, including preventing painful memories to surface.

Trauma is itself traumatic (Richman 2019). The recounting of traumatic memory is a mnemonic reversioning of the original act, of which the retelling is also a form of re-enactment. There are dangers to both repression and retelling for both victim and perpetrator. Fania Fénelon reflected this difference in her attempt to escape the memory of the camps. She commented that after 30 years of silence, she tried to forget that which was unforgettable, eventually finding a way to "exorcise" the memory by publishing her experiences (Fénelon 1977, ix).

The silence of the perpetrators has a more sinister motive. The "I do not remember" heard in war crimes trials court rooms was described by Primo Levi as "fossilised and formulated lying" (Levi 1988, 17). In a 2020 interview that I conducted with Benjamin Ferencz, he described conditions during the Subsequent Nuremberg Proceedings #9, the Einsatzgruppen Case of September 1946 that he had prosecuted at Nuremberg. He stated that the case was an easy one to prosecute because of the overwhelming self-incriminating evidence. He also observed that "all of them lied" (Ferencz 2020). Levi observes that both surviving victim and perpetrator are "in the same trap." However, when the perpetrator suffers from it, "it is right that he should suffer" (Levi 1986, 12).[9] He observes that perpetrators avoid burdensome memories by forming a *cordon sanitaire* around themselves, as "it is easier to deny entry to a memory than to free oneself from it after it has been recorded" (Levi 1988, 18). Klaus Kleinau appears in *Final Account*, a documentary featuring former members of the SS curated from an archive of eyewitnesses to the Holocaust from the vantage point of the perpetrators. During the film Kleinau struggles to say, "I wouldn't have been a perpetrator if I'd had the courage to say 'no' at any point." You can see in his eyes that it's the first time he's admitted this out loud. "How can you say you are not a perpetrator when you were a member of the Death's Head SS unit?" filmmaker Luke Holland asks Karl-Heinz Lipok. "A valid question," says Lipok, with sincere regret in his eyes. "That's when complicity turns to guilt."

In addition to those who cannot forget, there are those who cannot remember because the absence of memory is part of the memory itself. This forgetfulness particularly applies to those too young to remember everything, or anything at all. Most surviving victims now were young people and children at the time. Susi Bechhöfer was only three years old when she and her sister were sent to England on the *Kindertransports*. In the mid-1980s, knowing virtually nothing of her past and by then named Grace Stocken (née Mann), at the age of 49 she decided to rediscover her past. Her long and complex journey brought to light a non-Jewish family in Germany as well as an Orthodox Jewish family in New York. She discovered her identity was Susi Bechhöfer, and that she and her twin had been sent to England by their mother Rosa in 1939. A family photograph of Bechhöfer with her husband and son carries the inscription, "Susi has laid to rest the events of her tragic life. But the memory of Rosa, the mother she never knew, will always be with her" (Josephs 1996, 86). The "events of her tragic life" were not, however, the events that she had searched for. What was missing from her memory, and what she wanted to restore, were details of her family and their ultimate fates. The "memory of Rosa" she had retained of her mother was an entirely imagined memory. She had no personal recollection of her mother, and only a few details of her life and death at Auschwitz. In her diary she writes of her mother's fate:

> I have this strong image which I cannot get out of my head. It is of Rosa, walking towards her death. As she is confronted with the gas chambers, with all the people naked and crammed in together, all the time she is thinking to herself—I did what I could, I did what I could for my twins.
>
> *(Josephs 1996, 147)*

She constructed this imagined memory of her mother—who might have died en route to Auschwitz, in a work *Kommando*, in the *Revier*, or on a "death march"—because she needed a memory to connect them. For surviving victims who were children, constructing detailed episodes in the correct order may not be possible or desirable, given the trauma associated with it. This does not mean, however, that they have no memory or they that have "forgotten" simply because this form of memory is different. Aharon Appelfeld, a child survivor of the Holocaust, wrote about his experiences during the Second World War and clarified the genre of his recollections: "I have never written a memoir. I was a child. . . . I remember all the events, but it is not a chronological memory; rather it is an inner memory, a secret memory" (Lewis 1984, 13).

Surviving victims say that there is no way to subsume such experiences. Anton Gill concluded that, "there is no return to the person he or she formerly was, nor is there any final laying of the ghost, no matter how well adapted once again the survivor may appear to be" (Gill 1989, 9). In *At the Mind's Limits*, Jean Améry discusses the memory of torture, concluding that there is no possible repression of the memory of torture:

> It was over for a while. It is still not over. Twenty-two years later I am still dangling by my dislocated arms. . . . In such an incident there is no 'repression.'
> (Améry 1980, 40)

It is impossible to forget such physical and emotional torture. The memory lives without form, influencing what is and is not said in the narrative. Langer identifies a variety of memory strata working within the surviving victims' narratives, including deep memory, anguished memory, humiliated memory, tainted memory, and unheroic memory (Langer 1991). This typology illustrates that memory expresses itself in different ways, allowing the former victim's experience to be understood on different, complex levels. When she recounted the hanging scene (see: Chapter 2), Victoria Vincent provided a narrative account of what happened that day, but all of the aforementioned non-vocalized forms of memory—deep, anguished, humiliated, tainted, and unheroic memories—were all a part of the unvoiced memory that she lived through each time she tearfully told the episode. Arriving at a definitive typology of memory, while helpful in observing patterns and imagining memory as an often-unseen extension of identity, is not applicable to traumatic memory, because each individual's experience and memory pattern is unique. Individual memory is more like a person's mnemonic fingerprint—a unique extension of their being.

In establishing an I-Thou relationship with the surviving victim—having a willingness to encounter the complex nature of being—also means entering the complex nature of memory. The memory we encounter in the I-Thou encounter—that which is stated, that which is hidden, that which will never be recalled—all coexist in the life of the surviving witness. From all the forms of memory that *are* in the life of the witness, some of them eventually take form as testimony, to which we now turn.

Notes

1 See: www.yadvashem.org/holocaust/video-testimonies.html.
2 Translated by Hagit Arieli-Chai, with thanks.
3 Personal conversations with Arek Hersh, Rubin Katz, Roman Halter, and Victoria Vincent.
4 Irving Howe suggests that Adorno "would not have been so naive so as to prescribe a line of conduct that would threaten their very future as writers." He then discusses reasons why Adorno might have said what he said, from the aesthetics argument, discussion around possible voyeurism attached to the subject through to discussion around Adorno's possible thoughts on primitive ("things are too terrible to look at") and protective ("knowledge is not a good thing when the knowledge is bad") approaches. Irving Howe, "Writing and the Holocaust," in, Lang, Berel (ed.), *Writing and the Holocaust* (New York and London: Holmes and Meier, 1988), 178–180.
5 Quoted by Sidra DeKoven Ezrahi (1992). In addition to Adorno's own clarification, Sidra DeKoven Ezrahi, expressing concern that this dictum has been taken as Adorno's final word on the matter, further explores his actual work, pointing out that he made many "returns" to Auschwitz.
6 "Selection," *Merriam-Webster Dictionary*, www.merriam-webster.com/dictionary/selection.
7 "Selection," *Collins Dictionary*, www.collinsdictionary.com/us/dictionary/english/selection.
8 It is interesting to note that the "Truth and Reconciliation Commission" in South Africa took a different line on this issue. Victims and perpetrators were able to bear witness to their own perpetration or victimization. However, this was a public hearing rather than judicial court and any of the individuals later committed to trial will be examined under the usual constraints applied in a court of law. This precedent does raise the question, however, whether public witness to one's own crime or victimization is an acceptable version of events, as both a record of events and a meaningful narrative for public analysis.
9 The memory of the perpetrators is a complex issue, as they are important witnesses, but because of their involvement they have a perspective that is difficult to incorporate.

References

Adorno, Theodore. 1967. "Culture Criticism and Society." In *Prisms*, translated by Samuel and Shierry Weber. London: Neville Spearman.
Adorno, Theodore and Francis McDonagh. 1979. "On Commitment." *Performing Arts Journal* 3, no. 3 (Winter): 58–67. https://www.jstor.org/stable/3245104
Améry, Jean. 1980. *At the Mind's Limits: Contemplations by a Survivor on Auschwitz and Its Realities*, translated by Sidney Rosenfeld and Stella Rosenfeld. Bloomington, IN: Indiana University Press.
Ancona-Vincent, Victoria. 1995. *Beyond Imagination*. Newark, NJ: Beth Shalom.
Antze, Paul, and Michael Lambek, eds. 1996. *Tense Past: Cultural Essays in Trauma and Memory*. New York: Routledge.
Berenbaum, Michael. 1990. *A Mosaic of Victims: Non-Jews Persecuted and Murdered by the Nazis*. New York: New York University Press.
Bettelheim, Bruno. 1979. *Surviving and Other Essays*. London: Thames and Hudson.
Bettelheim, Bruno. 1986. *Surviving the Holocaust*. London: Fontana Paperbacks.
Bettelheim, Bruno. 1991. *The Informed Heart: A Study of the Psychological Consequences of Living Under Extreme Fear and Terror*. London: Penguin Books.
Blanchot, Maurice. 1986. *The Writing of the Disaster*. Lincoln, NE: University of Nebraska Press.
Borowski, Tadeusz. 1976. *This Way for the Gas, Ladies and Gentlemen*. London: Penguin Books.
Dawidowicz, Lucy S. 1987. *The War Against the Jews: 1933–45*. Middlesex: Penguin Books.

Delbo, Charlotte. 1995. *Auschwitz and After*. New Haven, CT: Yale University Press.
Desbois, Patrick. 2008. *The Holocaust by Bullets, a Priest's Journey to Uncover the Truth Behind the Murder of 1.5 Million Jews*. 1st ed. New York: Palgrave Macmillan.
Des Pres, Terrence. 1976. *The Survivor: An Anatomy of Life in the Death Camps*. Oxford: Oxford University Press.
Des Pres, Terrence. 1991. *Writing into the World: Essays, 1973–1987*. New York: Viking Penguin.
Felman, Shoshana, and Dori Laub. 1992. *Testimony: Crises of Witnessing in Literature, Psychoanalysis and History*. London: Routledge.
Fénelon, Fania. 1977. *Playing for Time*. New York: Atheneum.
Ferencz, Benjamin. 2020. "Dimensions in Testimony." https://sfi.usc.edu/dit.
Gabbai, Dario. 1996 and 2014. *Interview by USC Shoah Foundation* (Interview 142). Los Angeles, CA: Visual History Archive.
Gill, Anton. 1989. *The Journey Back from Hell: Conversations with Concentration Camp Survivors*. London: Harper Collins.
Greenspan, Henry. 1998. *On Listening to Holocaust Survivors: Recounting and Life History*. Westport, CT: Praeger.
Haft, Harry. 1995. *Interview by USC Shoah Foundation* (Interview 1776). Los Angeles, CA: Visual History Archive.
Hart-Moxon, Kitty. 1997. *Return to Auschwitz*. Revised ed. Newark, NJ: Beth Shalom Holocaust Centre.
Holocaust Education & Archive Research Team (HEART). N.d. "Szymon Srebrnik: Chełmno Survivor Testimony." www.holocaustresearchproject.org/survivor/srebrnik.html. Accessed March 3, 2022.
Josephs, Jeremy. 1996. *Rosa's Child; The True Story of One Woman's Quest for a Lost Mother and a Vanished Past*. London: I. B. Tauris.
Klee, Ernst, Willi Dressen, and Volker Riess. 1991. *Those Were the Days: The Holocaust as Seen by the Perpetrators and Bystanders*. London: Hamish Hamilton.
LaCapra, Dominick. 1994. *Representing the Holocaust: History, Theory, Trauma*. Ithaca, NY: Cornell University Press. www.jstor.org/stable/10.7591/j.ctvrf8b30.
Langer, Lawrence L. 1982. *Versions of Survival: The Holocaust and the Human Spirit*. New York: New York University Press.
Langer, Lawrence L. 1991. *Holocaust Testimonies: The Ruins of Memory*. New Haven, CT: Yale University Press.
Lanzmann, Claude. 1985. *Shoah*. New York: New Yorker Films.
Levi, Primo. 1986. *Moments of Reprieve*. New York: Summit Books.
Levi, Primo. 1988. *The Drowned and the Saved*. London: Abacus Books.
Lewis, Stephen. 1984. *Art Out of Agony: The Holocaust Theme in Literature, Sculpture and Film*. Montreal: CBC Enterprises.
Lingens-Reiner, Ella. 1948. *Prisoners of Fear*. London: Victor Gollancz.
Lyotard, Jean-François. 1988. *The Differend: Phrases in Dispute*. Manchester: Manchester University Press.
Pawelczynska, Anna. 1979. *Values and Violence in Auschwitz: A Sociological Analysis*. Berkeley, CA: University of California Press.
Pendas, Devin O. 2006. *The Frankfurt Auschwitz Trial, 1963–1965: Genocide, History, and the Limits of the Law*. Cambridge: Cambridge University Press.
Podlchlebnik, Michael. 1945. "Chełmno Survivor Testimony." www.holocaustresearchproject.org/survivor/podchlebnik.html.
Rao, K. Sreenivasa, and Shashidhar G. Koolagudi. 2015. "Recognition of Emotions from Video using Acoustic and Facial Features." *SIViP* 9: 1029–1045. https://doi.org/10.1007/s11760-013-0522-6.

Richman, Sophia. 2019. "Ageing: Coping with Re-traumatization." In *The Handbook of Psychoanalytic Holocaust Studies: International Perspectives*, 1st ed, 67–73. New York: Routledge.

Rosenfeld, Alvin Hirsch. 1988. *A Double Dying: Reflections on Holocaust Literature*. Bloomington, IN: Indiana University Press.

Rousset, David. 1951. *A World Apart (L'Univers Concentrationnaire)*. London: Secker and Warburg.

Smith, Stephen D. 2021. "Luke Holland's 'Final Account' Is Unsettling: That's Why You Need to Watch It." *Forward*, May 13. https://forward.com/scribe/469537/luke-hollands-final-account-is-unsettling-thats-why-you-need-to-watch-it/.

Srebnik, Simon. 1991. Oral History by USHMM. Accession Number 1995.A.1272.134 | RG Number: RG-50.120.0134. https://collections.ushmm.org/search/catalog/irn502871

Srebrnik, Shim'on. 1997. *Interview by USC Shoah Foundation* (Interview 28097). Los Angeles, CA: Visual History Archive.

Stewart, Victoria. 2019. "Crimes and War Crimes: William Hodge & Co. and the Public Understanding of the Holocaust in Post-World War II Britain." *Law and Literature* 31, no. 3: 113–127. http://dx.doi.org/10.1080/1535685X.2017.1351723.

Todorov, Tzvetan. 1996. *Facing the Extreme—Moral Life in the Concentration Camps*. New York: Metropolitan Books.

Totten, Samuel, William S. Parsons, and Israel W. Charny. 1997. *Century of Genocide: Eyewitness Accounts and Critical Views*. New York: Garland.

United States Holocaust Memorial Museum (USHMM). 1999a. "Eichmann Trial—Sessions 66, 67 and 68—Testimonies of S. Srebnik, A. Lindwasser, D. Wdowinski, A. Oppenheimer." Film, June 6, 1961, 34:36. https://collections.ushmm.org/search/catalog/irn1001695.

United States Holocaust Memorial Museum (USHMM). 2020. "Postwar Trials." https://encyclopedia.ushmm.org/content/en/article/war-crimes-trials.

United States Holocaust Memorial Museum (USHMM). N.d. "Chelmno." https://encyclopedia.ushmm.org/content/en/article/chelmno.

Wagner, Julia. 2010. "The Truth about Auschwitz: Prosecuting Auschwitz Crimes with the Help of Survivor Testimony." *German History* 28, no. 3 (September): 343–357.

Webber, Jonathan. 1992. *The Future of Auschwitz: Some Personal Reflections*. Oxford: Oxford Centre for Post-Graduate Hebrew Studies.

White, Hayden. 2020. *Figural Realism: Studies in the Mimesis Effect*. Baltimore, MD: Johns Hopkins University Press.

Wiesel, Elie. 1979. *A Jew Today*. New York: Vintage Books.

Yahad in Unum. N.d. "In Evidence: Map of Holocaust by Bullets." www.yahadinunum.org/in-evidence.

4
ALL THAT IS REAL (AND SOME THAT IS NOT)

Sabina's Missing Face

In July 1998, I arrived at a home in Cape Town South Africa where the testimony of Pinchas Gutter's interview would be filmed. I was an advisor to the soon-to-be-opened Cape Town Holocaust and Genocide Centre. The Centre wished to interview all local survivors for their archive and museum. As one of the few on the team who had interviewed Holocaust surviving victims, I volunteered to conduct interviews with three of them living in Cape Town.

Pinchas Gutter sat opposite me, preparing himself for the interview as the camera crew set up their equipment. Even before we started the interview, I could see from Pinchas' overall demeanor that he was uncomfortable. He had given his audio-visual testimony twice before, once with the Neuberger Holocaust Centre in Toronto Canada (Gutter 1993) and again with USC Shoah Foundation (Gutter 1995), so he was no stranger to the process. He portrayed a calm exterior that made everyone in the room feel at ease, and yet he projected a sense of anxiety about what was about to transpire. As we waited for the crew to complete their preparations, Pinchas and I looked at one another across the room. He had vibrant blue eyes and full round face, with large metal-rimmed spectacles. As we looked at one another, without saying a word, I became aware that *the encounter* between us as witness and listener had already begun.

Pinchas started by talking about his childhood in the 1930s growing up in the Polish city of Łodz. He spoke so affectionately about his past that I felt a sense of emotional connection to his community in a way that I had not encountered in a video interview before. I had heard surviving victims speak about the past by describing their school, sports, clubs, family, and holy days. When Pinchas described being in his family's wine cellars, he provided more detail than I anticipated a child of his age could remember:

> My father started taking me down to our cellars when I was three—not to taste, but just to smell the wines and I would have to identify them. He

DOI: 10.4324/9781003147220-6

would give them numbers . . . and he would then allow me to smell and then he would mix them up, and then he would say what number is this, and what number is that, and that's how he started teaching me the wine trade . . . we had electricity, but we didn't use it on Friday night, because the place was lit with candles—you know with silver candelabra and candles, and the candles lasted until about midnight. My mother did all the serving and we had songs before the table, [and] during the meal. . . . My father would expound to everybody who was there, whether it was family or friends or guests, would expound on the weekly portion or some specific saying that he heard from the Rabbi and it went on just about until the candles were getting low.

(Gutter 1998)

I realized that Pinchas was not just describing his past to me—he was re-living it. Pinchas Gutter still has a remarkable visual memory. He was no more than eight years old when the Germans invaded Poland in September 1939 and just 13 when he was liberated from Terezin, almost six years later after being incarcerated in concentration camps. At 90 years old today, he is still able to describe scenes in the Warsaw Ghetto in vivid detail. He can still remember people, places, and dates with remarkable accuracy. He describes himself as a "camera . . . absorbing and recording with my mind and my body" (Gutter 1998, 17). Roving the streets of the ghetto, he was a young child recording the scenes playing out before his eyes.

In May 1943, the Gutter family was deported from the burning ghetto of Warsaw, where they had witnessed the heroic last stand of the Warsaw Ghetto Uprising. Every member was placed in cattle cars and shipped to Majdanek, the concentration and death camp near Lublin. The Germans carried out a selection on arrival. Pinchas and his father Mendel were separated from his mother Helena and twin sister. Pinchas then observed his sister (who he did not name in his testimony) and Helena being separated from one another. It is not clear which one had been given a better chance to live, but his sister had been pushed toward the children's area. He recounted the scene:

And my mother was screaming. And then she went towards— and she wouldn't give up my sister. And so they pushed my mother towards where there were children. A lot of other women went there too. And that's the last time I saw my sister and my mother.

(Gutter 1995)

Momentarily, Pinchas was also separated from his father in the doorway to the shower and disinfection room. He would never see any of them again. Pinchas Gutter was orphaned and registered to enter the camp. He describes asking a man whom his father had befriended in the ghetto if he had seen him. He states in his 1993 testimony that he asked the man,

"Where is my father?" And he said, "I am afraid your father is not coming out." And I started crying, but, I don't really know what the crying was all about. I am not sure, to this day I cannot remember the feelings that were going through my mind at the time . . . all I can feel is that [PAUSES FOR 2 SECONDS] I just didn't accept the fact my father did not come out.

(Gutter 1993)

In his 1995 testimony Pinchas recalls that the man "didn't answer" when he asked about the whereabout of his father. By contrast, in his 1998 testimony he states that he "grabbed him and said 'where's my father, where's my father' and he said 'no, your father will come—he tried' to make me feel relaxed." Each time he approaches this moment in his testimony there is a sense of unease, as he grapples with his memory on camera. In his 1995 testimony Pinchas reveals the struggle he had with his emotions in that moment of realization:

And I started crying, but . . . I wasn't crying because I didn't see my father. I am going to be quite honest. I was crying because I was crying.

(Gutter 1995)

What the transcript does not capture are the conflicting emotions that were on display in his facial features and body language as he relayed this terrible moment, which he described as when his "whole world came to an end." Pinchas circles back to the topic later, as he has something to further say about why he thinks he was crying:

I'm not sure what I was crying for. I was crying for myself, for my father [PAUSES FOR 3 SECONDS] relief maybe, that I wasn't killed. I was just crying. [PAUSES FOR 3 SECONDS]

The admission that he was relieved to be alive is indicated in the transcript by several emotionally loaded pauses, as he struggles to say aloud what had been on his conscience for five decades—the faltering admission that he felt relief that he had survived, even though his family had not. In 1998 he talks about his guilt:

[O]n the one hand I was glad that I was alive, on the other hand I was terrified and concerned because my father wasn't there. . . . I don't want to create false feelings about what happened then. When I think about . . . those few hours . . . it's almost as if there is an absence of feeling whatsoever, because the emotions and feelings should be able to be recreated in your brain—I cannot do it. Whenever I try to recreate I say no that's false, so it's not there and if it is there it's so deeply buried, you know, that it would probably take 1000 years of psychoanalysis to get it out. . . . So that's another void that I have because I feel at the moment of my father's death of his passing away, of his spirit going from his body, I wasn't there, because I was like nothing. I was a person without feeling, without emotions—without anything.

(Gutter 1998, 28–29)

In his 1995 testimony given to USC Shoah Foundation, after describing being separated from his twin sister at the selection ground, he never mentions her again. But in later interviews Pinchas describes his guilt when asked about the loss of his sister:

> I have an enormous amount of guilt about my sister, because she didn't survive. . . . I can picture her talking and I can picture her dresses but can't see her face. I can see her tresses—she had long golden tresses which my mother used to plait it in these long plaits like you see the Swiss girls and she had these beautiful golden tresses . . . but I cannot see her face and that is something that has been troubling me all my life. I remember my mother and father's faces very clearly. I can't remember my sister's face.
>
> *(Gutter 1998, 17)*

I subsequently returned to the testimony to review the transcript and watch the video (Gutter 1998). What I found 22 years later was a well-told, but relatively predictable audio-visual testimony, much like his two early testimonies. As I reviewed the video, I noticed that there were three distinct modalities to his testimony, each of which provided different data, thereby changing the testimony itself:

1. *Transcript Only*: raw text, to be read.
2. *Audio Only*: an aural-only experience that sets the pace and cadence of the words, and relies heavily on the mind's imagination. It is the most passive form of recorded testimony that allows the listener to transform words into their own images. It provides tone and a sense of fluctuating emotions through sound.
3. *Audio-Visual Moving Image*: when viewed together, sound and the visual image of the testifier include hand gestures, body language, physiognomy as well as visual references that reveal more about the time and place it was films—fashion, hairstyle, home environment—as well as the video format—black and white or color; 5:4 or 16:9 aspect ratio.

I have reviewed all testimonies of Pinchas Gutter using each of these modalities as well as making a visit to Poland with Pinchas to make a documentary about his search for his twin Sister Sabina, *The Void* (Smith 2001). It was my intent to better understand how the listener encounters the same testimony differently with each. The testimony is experienced not only through the words as transcribed, but also how they are delivered and experienced. It became clear that I did not have the same reaction or feel the same emotion when reading, listening, or watching the video testimony as I did when being in the room with Pinchas in 1998. Testimony has a *fourth modality* that can only be experienced once. It is driven by the trust and human connection that exists between interviewee and interviewer when the interview takes place. The personal encounter between Pinchas and I enabled me to experience something beyond the data associated to the testimony that was only possible to experience together in the room that day. It was the *encounter*.

Being-for-Itself or Something-Others?

Giving form to memory entails much more than recalling historical events. In *From Belsen to Buckingham Palace*, Paul Oppenheimer discusses how he assembled his memoir through four distinct means of memory retrieval, ranging from memories carried from the experience itself to the reconstruction of episodes through external prompts. He distinguished between the fragmentation and retrieval of his memory as it became calcified in text. First he confirms that he remembered "the major milestones of my life story," as well as "basic facts about all the places we lived before and during the war" (Oppenheimer 1996a, 21). He then describes a second phase of retrieval when he and his brother Rudi were interviewed for a book about Holocaust survivors and refugees in Birmingham. In the ensuing conversations "we tended to stimulate each other towards remembering events which, until then, we had both forgotten" (Oppenheimer 1996b, n.p). He demonstrates how they use fragments of disjointed memory to recreate or retrieve a more coherent whole through their conversation. Paul admits that there "were many incidents that had totally slipped my memory, but when Ruzzi (nickname of Rudi) mentioned them, it all came back to me quite clearly" (Oppenheimer 1996b, n.p.). Finally, his third phase of retrieval took the form of a substantial collection of personal documents that were left with Dutch friends when the family was deported.

Through his documents, he observed, confirmed, and elaborated on his story. They helped him establish facts and dates, and to regain a sense of his pre-Holocaust identity. Finally, Paul describes his own "accumulated knowledge" gathered through visits to museums, books by surviving victims with similar experiences, and historians' lectures. His search for meaning leaves his narrative open to criticism that he "borrowed" the memories and research of others. The danger of an assisted memory is that it becomes a patchwork mosaic. Re-assembling gathered memories is theoretically problematic as it provides many points of reconstruction that may be unreliable, but Paul is careful in his written text to qualify his use of third-party material. He claims that his "accumulated knowledge does not necessarily alter what I have to say about my personal story, but it has assisted my understanding of the context of my experience" (Oppenheimer 1996a, 22). Paul's careful reconstruction is not a method explicitly used by many surviving victims, although their memories are likely also multi-sourced. Kitty Hart-Moxon reports that she made a point of "not reading a single book or researching a single item" to preserve her account as testimony. Later, she adds that she did discuss many things with her mother who survived with her, "because there were a lot of things that she had remembered that I had perhaps forgotten."[1]

Other surviving victims also consciously recalled their memories. Janina Bauman talks of diving "deep into the past, forgetting my present age and becoming a young girl again" (Bauman 1991, n.p.). She too qualifies her method, writing that, "I made an effort to be faithful not only to the facts but also to my own thoughts and feelings at the time. I tried hard not to let my present knowledge, my present mature reflection interfere with my memories" (Bauman 1991, n.p.). Her honesty in attempting to detach herself is admirable, although her recall is not likely divorced from the filters of her subsequent life experiences. That said, Bauman is careful to omit historical references to things that she was unaware at the time from her text. She assures her readers that her eyewitness account "does not pretend to be a historical document" (Bauman 1991, n.p.). In the foreword to Helen Lewis's *A Time to Speak*, Jennifer Johnston relates that Lewis, "tells her story with awesome integrity and in her hands it becomes more than just her story, it becomes history" (Lewis 1992, ix). The "integrity" she refers to is the frankness with which Lewis deals with episodes such as the suicide of her relatives when the Nazis invaded the Republic of Czechoslovakia on March 15, 1939 (Lewis 1992, 11), and her husband's death in the camps (125). Johnston asserts that her memory is "more than her story," meaning it is a story that is shared by many others.

The way in which testimonies are "more than her story" can be understood through Hegelian dialectics, wherein a "being-for-itself" (the One) contains within it "something-others" (the Many) (Hegel 2010, 152–154). In this context, if being-for-itself is the meta concept of testimony and the something-others are individual testimonies, then "each is a One as well as one of the Many" (Hegel 2010, 154). The *ideality* of testimony contains all testimonies and each testimony is a representative of the collected voices, which have similarities but are not identical. No single surviving victim's narrative can represent the experience of another's, let alone represent the history as a whole. Each of them do contain the essence of the Holocaust as the Being-in-itself, namely the story of the genocide of the Jews as told by those who survived it (the One), but which cannot be sublimated by any single testimony (the Many).

This structure helps place testimony in context as a source of history. Each testimony can be considered a type of document that can contribute to the knowledge history, provided it is understood as something-other like any other source would be—a partial and personal report that reveals a small part of a complex historical scenario. History (the One) is always made up of multiple such sources (something-others) that together provide the essence of the history but are not the complete picture. The victim who was highly restricted at the time and lacked access to information can only report what they saw. This report may only be a fraction of what could be known concerning the specific place they were in and were witness to, but it can still contain the essence of the whole. The nature of events requires many such reports and other sources to triangulate the complexity of the circumstances. Reading testimony in this manner does not undermine the value of each source, it merely underscores the need for multiple narratives and sources. That said, testimony does not exist as a utility in the service of history (although it does contribute to historical knowledge), but rather providing agency to the surviving witnesses to contribute from what they know and who they are. Their need to respond to what occurred to them, and explain it to others, is an extension of their being:

> Where men and women are forced to endure terrible things at the hands of others—whenever, that is, extremity involves moral issues—the need to

remember becomes a general response. Spontaneously they make it their business to record the evil forced upon them. . . . Here, and in similar situations, survival and bearing witness become reciprocal acts.

(Des Pres 1976, 31)

If survival and bearing witness *are* reciprocal acts, it follows that all surviving victims witness their survival by merely existing. Such witness thereby carries with it a moral message, even when the narrative may not itself be moralizing. However briefly encountered, the testimony carries the weight of the entire history for the listener. The meaning of the testimony lies not only in the suffering that the one individual testifying endured, but by implication the suffering of all Jews at that time and the abject immorality of the perpetrators. Testimony is witness to all the crimes that were committed as much as it is to the personal suffering it inflicted on the individual testifying. They are all a part of the One as well as being something-other.

Testimony has been widely accepted as a form of eyewitness *proof* that any given experience as narrated in the testimony took place as described. Surviving victims have given testimony in the relative safety of being unquestioned as witnesses and shielded from unwarranted criticism.[2] François Lyotard does *not* call into question the truthfulness of their statements, but he does suggest testimony be placed within a different dialogical context. He observes that proof can be cited as evidence, provided there is consensus over how it can be adduced (Lyotard 1988, 54). A dialogical framework might be usefully deployed to question such proof. However, surviving victims have largely preferred to avoid critical readings of their testimonies, in part out of the fear that it might question the veracity of the events themselves. The logic follows that if their testimony is representative of the Holocaust (the One) but the accuracy of their individual statement is called into question, then it may question the veracity of the Holocaust itself. Testimony has instead acted as a "proof" for the existence of the Holocaust rather than a source like any other. In an I-Thou reading of testimony, judgment is not suspended. On the contrary, because the listener comes from a place of deep respect and the witness trusts the listener's motivation, the need to question and verify is all the greater. The fear of questioning testimony is based on the original offense and the attempt of apologists to deny it. Through an I-Thou relationship trust is sufficiently established to be able to ask difficult questions without calling into question the veracity of the events or how they are being described in the testimony itself. I have regularly asked surviving victims to clarify inconsistencies or inaccuracies into their narrative without calling into question their survival or the truth of the Holocaust.

The crime of genocide includes the attempt to wipe out all evidence of the facts. The many testimonies that describe the burning of documents, the destruction of the sites of mass killing, and the exhumation and burning of corpses all show that the perpetrators intended to deny their atrocities before they were even completed. Any eyewitness to those crimes provides evidence the Nazis and their apologists would want to discredit and destroy.[3]

Where there is sensitivity around testimony is that calling eyewitnesses into question could appear to align with the perpetrators' objective to hide the truth and discredit its witnesses. Seeking clarification is not the same as denying that it is truthful. Human memory is not a form of documentation, it is a stored mnemonic impression of events as experienced by an individual who lived through them. Once shared as testimony, the impression that memory has made takes on a communicable form that allows those who did not go through an experience to understand it from the perspective of someone who did. Contained within that impression are *hard data* (places, people, dates), *descriptions* (sights, sounds, and events), *reactions* (emotions and feelings), and *reflections* (beliefs and worldview). These elements of testifying provide information, contribute to knowledge, inspire insight, convey emotion, and provide subjective opinion.

Reading and listening to testimony requires understanding these requisite parts and what constitutes data, feeling, opinion, or conjecture. If a date is wrong, it can be corrected—such errors don't invalidate the rest of the testimony. If the name of a camp is erroneous, the memory of the testifier may be called into question—it does not mean the camp did not exist or that the testifier was not in that camp. I may not agree with the opinion of the testifier that a subjective opinion such as "the Ukrainians were worse than the Germans" because empirical evidence makes clear that it was the Germans (not the Ukrainians) that were the architects of the genocide of the Jews. Nevertheless, the witness may have encountered Ukrainians more often and in more brutal circumstances, and therefore has the right to that opinion in the context of their own testimony. It is my role as the reader to know *why* they might have drawn that opinion, not to counter it on face value only. During an interview with Nimrod Ariav he explained to me,

NIMROD: One morning there [was an] action . . . it was one German and hundreds of Lithuanians and Ukrainians, SS . . . these sons of guns were more murderous than the Germans [Pauses for 3 seconds] And I will never forget . . .
STEPHEN: . . . how did you know they were Ukrainians and Lithuanians?
NIMROD: They speak Ukrainian and Lithuanian . . . the truth is that it was not the Germans that killed my father.

(Ariav 2016 seg. #47)

Nimrod's anger comes from the direct experience of his father being murdered by an auxiliary. He is not sure whether it was a Lithuanian or Ukrainian as it was his aunt that witnessed the killing directly and did not remember the specific nationality of the perpetrator but he remains angry, and blames the nations of the collaborators he saw in his town. Nathan Alterman turns his anger into rhetoric revenge.

> I wish Stalin would be alive today so he would take all the Ukrainians and slaughter them like cattle, . . . because they slaughtered most of the Jews in the Ukraine . . . of course the Germans gave them the permission to do so. But they done the job. They done the job.
>
> *(Alterman 1997 sg. #17)*

Not all surviving victims are so angry, searching instead for a rationale. "They hated the Jews and they hated the Poles and they figured the Germans were going to help them" (Finkel 2015, seg. #101). In these examples, the Ukrainians' actions were perceived as being more egregious than the actions of the German authorities. A sophisticated reader of testimony knows how to fact check the *hard data*, be interested in the complex *descriptions*, empathize with the human *reactions*, and be curious to understand the *perceptions*. Nathan Alterman clarifies, "I wasn't scared of the Germans, I was scared of the Ukrainians" (#17). His anger towards the Ukrainians is based on the fear he had lived with as a young person, knowing how to evade the Germans, but being afraid of his own neighbors.

An I-Thou ontological reading of testimony requires the testimony to be experienced with all its intricacies and nuances. It is a critical framework that comes from a place of curiosity, not judgement. The opinion that some surviving victims say that their Ukrainians neighbors were worse than Germans, cannot be countered on empirical grounds. Rather, it enquires *why* the surviving victim feels the way they do about Ukrainians. Testimony documents history as experience, not as historical fact. Testimonies (something-others) inform what the Holocaust (the One) is not, and vice versa.

Testimony and Its Many Forms

The term "testimonies" has come to commonly refer to audio-visual history archives that have grown since the late 1980s. The advent of personal audio recording devices in the 1970s, then widespread access to video capture in the 1980s, followed by crowdsourced, multimedia oral history projects have indeed focused testimony on audio-visual formats more recently. However, testimony belongs to no single medium; it is the result of the decision of the witness to give any form to their experience in whatever medium they choose. Initially, this was largely in written form, the David Boder audio collection of 1946 being a rare exception. Today testimony continues to amass through the visual arts, performing arts, memoirs, fiction, poetry, documentaries, narrative films, memorials, museums, commemorations, tours, education programs, social media channels, conferences, and speeches—all ways through which surviving witnesses have given form to witness. Each provides a different voice, or form of representation.

The choice of medium for surviving witnesses is not limited to only one. Kitty Hart-Moxon published her first memoir, *I am Alive*, in 1961. She then made her first documentary *Kitty: Return to Auschwitz* in 1979, followed by a second memoir and three further documentaries. As a trustee of the Holocaust Educational Trust, she was a frequent speaker in their Lessons from Auschwitz program (HET n.d.). She was a guide for several teacher's trips to Poland on behalf of the UK National Holocaust Centre, where she was also a frequent speaker to school groups and a contributor to the forever interactive biography project. Kitty also spoke at the Stockholm Forum in 2000, which was attended by over 46 country delegations (Fried 2006) and gave audio-visual testimony to the USC Shoah Foundation. Each of these public-facing witness activities are *modes* of testimony. Her speech at the

Stockholm Forum was not a biographical account of her experience, but her presence as a witness gave weight to her words and meaning to the gathering. Speeches are their own form of testimony, informed by, but not necessarily about her Holocaust history. Her presence and that of other surviving victims validated the reason for the gathered diplomats to endorse the Stockholm Declaration (IHRA 2000). Each witness spoke with intelligence and conviction, but it was their presence at the conference that brought the discussion into sharp focus, irrespective of the specific testimony or invocation they shared at the podium. How could they *not* endorse such a declaration while in the presence of Elie Wiesel, Ben Helfgott, Hedi Fried, and Kitty Hart-Moxon? Being present and being willing to speak on behalf of the dead is the essence of testimony.

On January 30, 2012, artist and surviving victim Roman Halter passed away at the age of 85. As a former friend and personal mentor, I took a moment to reflect on his life and experience. A search of the USC Shoah Foundation's Visual History Archive revealed that Halter had *not* given an audio-visual testimony. This was surprising because Halter was an active member of the Holocaust survivor community in the United Kingdom. He participated in Holocaust Memorial Day activities and had been the subject of "Generations," an intergenerational family history project displayed at the United Nations in 2010 (United Nations 2010). It became clear that Halter had specifically chosen not to give an audio-visual testimony in favor of other forms of testimonial representation. In addition to writing a memoir, *Roman's Journey* (Halter 2007), Halter had spent his life as an artist grappling with the meaning of his experience through drawing, painting, and stained glass.

Halter's stained-glass windows can be found at the National Holocaust Centre, and *Lohamei Ha Getaot* (The Ghetto Fighters Museum) in Israel. His windows feature themes from his Holocaust experience, such as a mother and child in a weeping Madonna-like pose. The mother may be his own mother, who was murdered in the Chełmno death camp, or it may represent all Jewish mothers who wept for their children during the Holocaust. I do not believe that Halter intended his testimonial art to specify a particular mother, rather, he wished to invoke the memory of all mothers who suffered. Through an I-Thou encounter with his visual testimony, Halter prompts the viewer to ponder the relationship between love and loss. On his passing I went to the small abstract painting that he had given to me, to discover it too was a mother and child. The mother has her eyes closed and is weeping. Unlike the Madonna pose, her child is turned away from her, back-to-back (Figure 4.1). There is no embrace, and no protection for her child.[4]

Halter's artwork also extended into the world of his nightmares. A series of watercolor paintings depicts the rolling green countryside of the Dorset Downs, an idyllic area of English countryside where Halter had a home. The Dorset Downs were his retreat from urban life, his safe place to be with his family far away from painful memories. He describes how, in his dreams at night, the Nazis would come to the Dorset Downs and carry out *Einsatzgruppen*-type mass shootings or Death Marches through the verdant English countryside (see Figure 4.2). Halter reports

All That Is Real (and Some That Is Not) 89

FIGURE 4.1 Mother and child painting by Roman Halter. 9 x 14 cm

Source: Acrylic on card. Courtesy of Stephen D. Smith.

90 The Crisis of Witness

> The 'Death March' from Dresden in March 1945 of our group of Jewish Slave Metal workers keeps recurring in my dreams again and again. Here I dreamt on Mond. 27th Nov. 2006 at 1:28 am. that I helped to carry Ing. Nussbaum. (But we never carried him, although he was marked category A, he was shot on the 2nd day of our 'Death March'. We walked in a landscape that resembled the landscape of Dorset. After weeks of being cooped-up, night and day in the factory on 68 Schandauer Str. in my dream I could smell the fresh air of this march and enjoy it. (I sleep with my window open tho' it's winter)

FIGURE 4.2 "Death March." Roman Halter. Watercolor and hand-written description of the dream associated to it

Source: (Courtesy of Ardyn Halter and the Roman Halter Estate).

that he would awaken from his nightmare and sketch his dream, which resulted in a series of watercolors.

When the surviving witness agrees to "give testimony" in an audio-visual format, they do so principally to document history. The life history methodology, as used by the USC Shoah Foundation, requests that the interviewee provide detailed hard data prior to the interview. This data includes up to 40 pages of information on specifics names, dates, places, family, ghettos, camps, and other experiences. The recording set-up, which includes a professional camera and interviewer from a formal archive, contributes to the interview's sense of being a documentation program. However, once the interview begins, the mode becomes that of storytelling. The interviewer is not fact-checking or seeking specific historical details. Rather, they allow the interviewee to tell their own story in their own words. Some require prompting, while others know precisely what they want to say and have little need for the interviewer to be there. Regardless of mode, the motivation, context, and medium of delivery shape what is said and can be said about the Holocaust in testimonial form.

Testimony is a "form of remembering" (Langer 1991, 2) that involves the shaping of memory and can take many forms. Etymologically, "testimony" derives from the Latin *testis*, which means "to witness." Therefore, to testify is literally "to make witness"—an etymological reminder that "as witness and testimony are made, so is knowledge" (Young 1990, 19). The emotional engagement that testimony engenders is such that can at times appear to represent the Holocaust itself. It is necessary to have the literacy skills to read it for what it is—one individual's partial insight into a fragment of their experience, among tens of thousands of others who shared likewise, and who represent millions more who could not.

Henry Greenspan challenges how testimony is perceived, indicating that it "suggests a formal finished quality that almost never characterizes survivors' remembrance" (Greenspan 1998, 3). He advises that testimony should be replaced with the concept of "recounting," as it "connotes the provisional and processual nature of retelling" (Greenspan 1998, xvii). Recounting envisages a witness narrative that is not complete either as text or internal discourse. To recount provides the surviving victims opportunity to reflect on the experience in an ongoing way. For recounting to be a viable alternative to testimony, it must coincide with how the surviving victims wish to speak about their past, many of whom provided testimony on only one occasion. Some surviving victims consider their role as providing a form of proof for the purpose of documentation, not an ongoing exploration of their past in the present. It is difficult for them to grasp that while the events they experienced in the past do not change, an ongoing recounting would give them a deeper appreciation of their own past over time. For Greenspan's valuable concept of recounting to affect the narrative process of witness, it must be incorporated into the methodology of audio-visual testimony itself. Recounting is a mode of testimony which methodologically is a subject-subject encounter, rather than a report about the past. All audio-visual testimony, irrespective of its other methodological considerations, should encourage the recounting of the past in the present.

Past in the Present

Returning to Kahneman's concepts of reliving the experience (the experiencing self) and reflecting on the past in the present (the remembering self), the surviving victim of the Holocaust lives with both modalities:

> Testimony cannot efface the Holocaust. It cannot deny it. It cannot bring back the dead, undo the horror or re-establish the safety. . . . But neither does it succumb to death, nostalgia, memorializing, [or] ongoing repetitious embattlements with the past. . . . It is a dialogical process of exploration and reconciliation of two worlds.
>
> *(Felman and Laub 1992, 91)*

The "two worlds" that Felman and Laub refer to could be applied to the world of the experiencing self, which relives specific moments from the past, and the world of the remembering self, which reflects on the past from the present. Because of the overwhelming pain it caused, Holocaust testimony succumbs to loss, guilt, nostalgia, memorializing, mythologization, and battles with the forgotten past. Testimony is the struggle to bring the world of the past into that of the present, for it to be better understood, if never completely so, by those who did not live through it.

The surviving victim ordinarily does not have sufficient time, language, or space to explain the nuances of their conclusions. The result is a partially formed narrative that brings the surviving victim and listeners together only on limited points. Testimony is inherently fragmentary because a complete narration of the events is simply not possible. The surviving victim must select what to include and omit in order to best construct a meaningful narrative for the perceived audience. Audio-visual testimony is a work of performance, storytelling, self-editing, and audience-based curation.

Audio-visual testimony is typically constructed around a series of cycles built around chronology, themes, and episodes. For example, the surviving victim might use phrases like "Before the war" (chronology), "I had a happy childhood" (theme), or "Every Friday night I would go to synagogue with my father" (episode). Their language then changes as the narrative progresses and they say, "When the Nazis arrived in 1939" (chronology), "everything changed" (theme), or "my father was beaten in the street" (episode). Such structures follow predictable patterns. Rarely does a testimony refer to the period prior to the Nazi period as being typified by deprivation and poverty, although for some it was. Rarely does testimony suggest that when the Nazis arrived, nothing changed, although for some little did change initially. Neither do surviving victims suggest that the displaced persons camps were squalid, degrading places where the overwhelming confusion of having survived presented a terrible and traumatic ordeal for many, even though for most that was true.

Testimony is always given in service of narrating the existential threat of inevitable death:

> Every survivor memoir must be read at least partially as a work of the imagination, which selects some details and blocks out others for the purpose of shaping the reader's response—indeed, for the purpose of organising the author's own response too. . . . An axiom of the narrative mode, from which survivor memoirs are not exempt, is that all telling modifies what is being told.
> (Langer 1982, xii)

Testimony is a reorganized and juxtaposed set of themes and episodes, best understood as "a series of narrated fragments wherein survivors share with us their own human reactions and thereby modify the unadulterated evil they experienced" (Davidson and Charney 1992, 214). Reorganizing themes and episodes for an audience does not mean that the message is incoherent. When I observed Pinchas Gutter deliver his personal testimony to 300 schoolteachers in Cape Town, South Africa[5] in 1999, he avoided the most traumatic episodes of his experiences. He did not mention the murder of his twin sister, horrific scenes from the Warsaw Ghetto, or his separation from his father at Majdanek, which were typically a part of his testimony (Gutter 1998). Pinchas' audience that day was a group of young people who had experienced racial persecution as young children during apartheid in South Africa. Paradoxically, *because* of their own experiences living in an apartheid state, the audience understood the meaning of his words in the present, without needing a traumatizing, detailed account of the atrocity he experienced.

Gutter appeared to understand that the detail of his testimony was *less* significant to his audience than the fact that he was speaking to people who had been persecuted themselves. They were already in an empathetic I-Thou relationship with him, without either side needing to fully reveal the source of their pain. I observed that the audience was not afraid to ask Gutter unusually frank questions, including those about his role as a white person living in South Africa during the apartheid era. Gutter responded that he had learned just how hard it was to react and resist oppression, and he was ashamed not to have done more. The honesty he showed toward them helped Gutter gain a deeper level of trust with the audience, who gave him a standing ovation. The juxtaposition of a white Jewish victim of genocide talking to an audience of largely Black South African victims of white racial persecution illustrates how testifying is conditioned and challenged by context. The audience changed Pinchas' testimony. Testimony is an extension of a seen or perceived relationship with the audience. The assumed posture of that audience thereby conditions what is said and sayable by the surviving victim.

Witness as Authentication

According to Maurice Blanchot, "If there is, among all words, one that is inauthentic, then surely it is the word 'authentic'" (1986, 60). Benzion Dinur, writing in 1957 about memoirs written during the Holocaust, states that:

> These memoirs must be treated in the same way as any other testimony and must, of course, be properly examined. The plain and unvarnished character of the narration and the presence of the narrator on the spot at the time, constitute in themselves no guarantee of the authenticity of such memoirs. The reason need not be any desire to 'amend' or 'improve' upon actual events for any ulterior purpose. It is difficult for the individual to liberate himself from his own personality. He has the propensity to see the past, and his own experiences, from the vantage point of the present.
>
> (Benzion and Esh 1957, 19)

Benzion suggests that authors writing in the moment need close examination, even when it may be assumed that proximal narratives are untainted by later interpretations and represent authentic witness. Des Pres posits the exact opposite; whether written at the time or later, there is no apparent motivation for a victim to report anything other than their lived experience:

> [It] is given in memory, told in pain and often clumsily, with little thought for style or rhetorical device. The experience [surviving victims] describe, furthermore, resists the tendency to ictionalize which informs most remembering.
>
> (Des Pres 1976, 29)

Barrington Moore developed a concept that he described as the "unity of misery" (Moore 1972). After extreme events, people with common experiences express them with almost documentary similarity. Yet, human suffering is *not* identical. Such unity would deviate from lived experience, creating shared meta narratives rather than shared experience. There is always the danger that such mythologization will take place, but that is not the purpose of testimony, which points to the individual experience rather than collective myth. Whatever the "unity of misery" of Jews who had lived under German genocidal policy, achieving a single voice from the experience would only serve to undermine its complexity. The "unity of misery" concept resonates because there is unanimity on the *kind* of narrative that might be expected based on the *type* of events and the *identity* of the people who survived it, not on the specificity of the facts. The question becomes: if the unity of misery is not enough, what constitutes "authentic witness?"

"I cannot imagine . . . someone writing about the Holocaust who was not a part of it," stated Aharon Appelfeld (Lewis 1984, 16). If he is correct, the only way to write testimony is if an author was there. That said, George Steiner (1967) does not agree with Appelfeld, suggesting that "poets get it right in a way that even the witness and historians don't" (Lewis 1984, 53). He recites the poetry of Homer on Troy, stating, "I can see him listening to the distant surviving victims and saying, 'I know better.' And, in fact, he did" (53). Likewise, William Styron "balked at the idea that someone who was not there was incapable of dealing with it" (Lewis 1984, 176), when referring to his own authorship of *Sophie's Choice*. Nevertheless, Henry Greenspan who has listened closely to testimony like Appelfeld, makes the case that only those who experienced the Holocaust can retell it:

> Perhaps only those who actually endured the destruction can retell it: the survivors and those who left some record—a letter, a diary—but did not survive. Their accounts invested with the authority of direct experience, may then become chapters of a new inviolable text to be reread and retold.
>
> *(Greenspan 1998, 5)*

An inviolable version makes testimony untouchable and contributes to both its sacralization and relativization. Just because it comes from an authentic source, does not mean it can be read uncritically or re-used for narrative purposes. James Young identifies "the rhetoric of fact" (Young 1993, 62)—a rhetorical device used to authenticate events by drawing on eyewitness accounts within the narrative. Examples of this form of authentication may be found in Anatoly Kuznetsov's documentary novel *Babi Yar* (1967). In his book, Kuznetsov interrupts the narrative with conversations with the reader. For example, in the section "A Necessary Explanation by the Author" (Kuznetsov 1967, xiii–xv) he states:

> Everything in this book is truth . . . the word "documentary" in the subtitle of this novel means that I am presenting authenticated facts and documents and that here you will find not the slightest literary invention.
>
> *(Kuznetsov 1967, xiii)*

Kuznetsov's insisted on the documentary nature of his text, while also introducing it as a novel. This incongruity creates literary tension, because historical fiction involves imaginary invention. Written and published in the Soviet Union, his book is sufficiently infused with anti-fascist rhetoric to politicize the entire narrative. Even if the events he described are based upon real events, his claim to authenticity is further undermined by Kuznetsov's interjection, "The Author Speaking" (Kuznetsov 1967, 47). Here he provides a disclaimer for his personal lack of knowledge of the events by stating, "There was a great deal that boy [Kuznetsov himself] did not see and even more that he did not understand. He was only twelve years old" (93). James Young points out that Kuznetsov formed the basis of his narrative over the mass shootings at the ravine using testimony of surviving victim Dina Pronicheva (Young 1993, 54). Kuznetsov's sources were both testimonial and documentary.

When D.M. Thomas later wrote *The White Hotel*, he relied on Kuznetsov's account and repeated the section relaying the testimony of Dina Pronicheva almost verbatim. Although Thomas has been accused of plagiarizing the piece from Kuznetsov, he stated that "imagination . . . is exhausted in the effort to take in the unimaginable, which happened" (Kenrick 1982, 24). In this way, he justifies his use of Pronicheva's eyewitness account as the only way to bring the reader closer to the events. In the text of *The White Hotel*, Thomas takes pains to make his readers aware of the rhetorical device. Even though his story is about the death of Lisa Erdman at Babi Yar, he acknowledges Dina Pronicheva's testimony. He writes, "Dina survived to be the only witness, the sole authority for what Lisa saw and felt" (Thomas 1981, 251).

In conversation with Stephen Lewis, Thomas confirmed the decision he took was to "bring my fictional character closer and closer to Dina Pronicheva, the actual survivor . . . they move step by step with each other and fiction becomes dissolved for a few moments in history" (Lewis 1984, 78). In the same passage he also states, "nor can the living ever speak for the dead." In this context, "the dead" are the tens of thousands for whom Thomas says his narrative warrants special sensitivity. Literary artists as "secondary witnesses" bring authenticity to their work by drawing on primary source material. But such reliance on the "authentic voice" is challenged by what constitutes authenticity. The question becomes whether such re-representation serves the testimony or vice versa. Surviving victims and those who again witness their testimony create an informal hierarchical witness chain. The surviving victim, as the most authentic voice of experience (other than the dead), allows the interested reader or listener to come closer to what the experience was like. To the ears and eyes of the observer, the surviving victim is the authentic voice and image. Unlike the secondary witness, they are authentic because they *experienced* it.

A definitive, singular voice that most correctly depicts the Holocaust experience is not possible, given there were many ways that the German authorities applied their persecutory policies. For example, Auschwitz is a defining symbol of the Holocaust. It prominently occupies the public imagination as a death camp or concentration camp of enormous scale and cruelty, making testimony related to

Auschwitz particularly prominent. But does a voice from someone who survived Auschwitz make other voices (say from Sachsenhausen or Stutthof) less "authentic"? Is it possible that there is a hierarchy to authenticity? If an Auschwitz testimony is deemed to be a "more authentic" Holocaust experience than a surviving victim who witnessed the mass killings of Ponary or Babi Yar, does that diminish the meaning of deaths in other places? The murder of complete families and communities shot at close range in unmarked graves is the very definition of genocide. There is no "authentic" voice from Bełzec, because other than the published testimony of Rudolf Reder (1946), no one survived to be witness. Yet, even within the Auschwitz experience, a hierarchy might well create many competing versions of Auschwitz. Some surviving victims of Auschwitz survived selection, went to quarantine, and were dispatched to other work camps that were sub-camps of Auschwitz. Are they less an "authentic voice" of Auschwitz than an internee working in the SS office, worker digging ditches, or a *sonderkommando* working in the crematoria?

If the definition of the "authentic voice" is driven by an iconology or hierarchy of suffering, it creates an exclusive and objectified form of authenticity. By this measure, a person who did not have a particular experience (such as surviving Auschwitz) is not deemed to be the kind of person (object) that satisfies a testimonial voyeurism that puts the worst experience as being the most meaningful. Desire to get closer to what is deemed the most authentic experience maps testimony to the I-It construct. The authenticity of the witness is determined by the listener based on which type of object they are evaluated to be, by the type of experience they had. By comparison, in the I-Thou construct, the onus is on the listener to inquire of *any* surviving victim and discover who they are and how the experience of the existential threat to their life affected them.

In 2012, I interviewed Sara Shapiro in Detroit Michigan for USC Shoah Foundation (Shapiro 2012). Her Holocaust history was not marked by death camps, and on the surface, she had a "lucky escape"—her parents paid for her safe passage just before the liquidation of the Korets ghetto. Sara spent over two years working as a maid under a stolen Ukrainian identity. And yet, her testimony was one of the most traumatic interviews I have conducted. During her ordeal, the 12-year-old Sara dared not to speak or sleep, lest she be found out by the antisemitic family. She left her circumcised brother alone to later be found and killed, and turned away a Jewish girl only to learn she was later raped and murdered by the master of her own household. All these experiences left her irreparably traumatized. There was nothing iconographic about her testimony. She wasn't present during big historical moments, and she delivered no remarkable insights into the nature of life. Yet, rarely have I felt as close to raw and authentic pain as I did while interviewing Sara.

I recall attending a teachers' conference in Johannesburg in the 1990s, and listening to a testimony by Donald Krausz, a surviving Holocaust victim from the Netherlands. He described his life in Holland prior to German occupation—the changes that took place after the invasion, life in the Jewish quarter, and the deportation of the family to Westerbork. As expected, he described the trains coming into Westerbork to take Jews to the East, and inevitably he and his family being loaded onto one. I knew enough about the family experiences of Dutch Jews holding foreign passports (the family had Hungarian citizenship) to know that they were likely to be held for future exchange, and *not* sent to the death camps of Auschwitz, Treblinka, or Sobibor, the typical weekly destinations from Westerbork. He told the story of how the family was loaded onto the train and the expected scene of overcrowding and insanitary conditions. When the cattle wagon doors opened he described the scene at Auschwitz-Birkenau—in the third person. He described the scene at the *rampe*, the selection for life or death, shower rooms, delousing, and gassing. His description of the camp included daily routines, work *Kommandos*, and finally, the liquidation of the camps and the death marches.

The audience was unaware that Donald had deviated from his *own* experience to give them a more "authentic" version that he thought they had come to hear. After he finished giving his talk he opened up to questions. I raised my hand while he was still on stage and thanked him for describing what had happened to Jews that were sent to Auschwitz and asked him what had happened to *him* after he had been in Westerbork. Without showing surprise that the deviation from his own experience had been revealed, he proceeded to describe his time in Ravensbrück and Sachsenhausen. After the presentation to the teachers ended, I privately asked him why he had not told his own story. He replied that his Holocaust experience was "not really typical" and that he "wanted the audience to know what happened to Jews during the Holocaust."[6]

I have subsequently reviewed Donald's USC Shoah Foundation (Krausz 1995) interview during which he gives a detailed description of the cattle car journey. After the description of the journey is over the interviewer has the presence of mind to clarify whether he personally was in the cattle wagon that he describes in some detail.

DONALD: . . . [A]bout 1000 people left in that train. The trains were cattle trucks . . . In Holland they used to pack in 60–70 people. . . . The journey tool about 3 days. There was a bucket in each truck to use as a latrine. There a was a bucket for water. Not very much. There were small apertures . . . so you could get not get out. There were no seats, there were no beds. Everything went into those trucks, the young, the old, the sick, the dying. So, these people had no light, they had no water, ultimately, they had no hope. I have been told by people who did that journey that . . . with the first 24 hours of that three day journey that the latrine that was in the corner was overflowing, after which these people for the remaining days and nights either stood or sat or lay in their own dirt . . . that's as far as we knew. About the destination we knew nothing at that stage [pauses 3 seconds] That was the story with the trains.
NT: How did you know that? Were *you* on one of those trains?
DONALD: Not at the time . . . Hungarians were exempt from those transports.

(Krausz 1995 Seg. #67–71)

It is noteworthy that Donald does not use the first person in this description, and therefore is not lying. However, he uses the description of the journey in the cattle wagons to leave the impression that it was an experience with which he is personally familiar. Had the interviewer not clarified with him whether it was indeed his own first-hand experience, it leaves the impression that he witnessed it personally. Much like his description of arrival at Auschwitz during the presentation, Donald used the broadly understood experiences of others to authenticate his own experience. Further review of his audio-visual testimony reveals a well-told first-person testimony of great relevance to understanding an atypical trajectory of a Jewish family of Hungarian citizenship who were sent to concentration camps without gassing facilities, because of their immigration status. His experience in those camps was horrifying nonetheless.

I surmised that Donald had come to consider himself an artefact of history, and so he told a story based on what he *thought* the object his audience had come to hear should say. He conceded in personal conversation afterward that he had a low sense of self-esteem as a Holocaust survivor because he had not been through "the worst of it." Society had conditioned him to represent something he had not experienced, to become someone he wasn't.

The I-Thou framework does not privilege one over another. If the audience is curious to learn about *all* experiences, every surviving victim knows that she or he can speak from their own authentic perspective and be fully heard for who they are.

Marvelous But Fallacious

Primo Levi describes memory as "a marvellous but fallacious instrument" (Levi 1988, 11)—its fallibility being a part of its marvel. Historical documents record their truth once and do not change, objects of a fixed past. My argument throughout this book is that testimonies are human documents that change over time as subjects in the present. First-person human documentarians help create primary sources while translating facts into meaning. This translation ensures that within the genre "factual errors do occur from time to time" (Langer 1991, 15). There are facts that happened to the experiencing self, and how the facts are remembered, recounted, and recalled by the remembering self. Sometimes the facts *are* the meaning, as when Michael Podchlebnik describes the discovery of his murdered wife and children. Often the facts support an altogether different meaning, as we encountered with Victoria Vincent and the hanging scene. Where factual errors do become part of the narrative, either because the testifier does not remember correctly or because they reimagine the past to support their narrative in the present, they should be read as a part of medium.

Knowing that there will be flaws in memory recall is not a reason to suspend the collection of testimony or dismiss the content collected, "as testimony is important in many more ways than collecting and verifying historical data" (Young 1993, 32). Memory itself is fallible on several levels. What several individuals remember about the same event is subject to who they were in that moment, the perspective they had of that moment, and the consequence of that specific event on their own life, and the way in which that experience is shaped over time. Testimony, as an extension of memory, is not carved in stone. Not only can it be erased, but it can also evolve by taking on new features, as we learned from Paul Oppenheimer. Testimony is also replete with omissions.

Henry Greenspan reported that surviving victim Victor S. recounted, "what is not told is also true; what is not in the book is also true" (Greenspan 1998, xix). The insight provided by Victor that not everything has been said that could be said helps us see the subjective nature of testimony. Memory contains many elements that are constrained by testimony. They could be edited to fit the story that they want to tell, may be too personal to reveal to a general audience, or are subject to subconscious "forgetting." Primo Levi notes that "the further events fade into the past, the more the construction of convenient truth grows and is perfected" (Levi 1988, 23). He also suggests that the gap between things as "they were 'down there' and things as they are represented by the current imagination fed by approximative books, films and myths" (157) grows wider over time.

This fallibility of human memory is not unique to the Holocaust. How our bodies process memory continues to be studied by scientists, who draw the same conclusion: memory is not the experience itself, but is shaped by experience and the context in which the remembering is happening:

> [H]uman memory (mainly what neuroscientists call episodic memory) is filtered as much as constructed. It is selective; it leaves things out, whether as a result of the kind of trauma that makes it harder for men and women to reconcile their past experience with a continuous sense of self, or because what is remembered is framed—perhaps in unconscious ways—by social and political needs in the present.
>
> *(Tumblety 2013, 4)*

Our memory becomes "more 'susceptible to distortion,' as it sucks up other facts and convinces itself that they were part of the memory" (Fernyhough 2013, 14). Human memory is fluid and changes over time, during which "obfuscation, degradation and crystallisation all help to shape a stylised form of the original event" (Levi 1988, 11). Mediations happen in many forms, and how the story is initially told affects how it is used afterward (Young 1990, 32). Charlotte Delbo writes that, "today, I am not sure that what I wrote is true. I am certain it is *truthful*" (Delbo 1995, 1). Like many of these examples, Delbo demonstrates self-awareness of how to provide self-verification to her readers when confronted with intersecting boundaries of truth and historical fact. She is aware that memory has limits, and therefore her testimony is prone to historical faults and she may well be criticized for failing to tell a historically correct story. But she does not doubt her intention to be *truthful*.

When Ella Lingens-Reiner refers to "my own side of the truth" (1948, ix) she is not implying that her text contains lies. Rather, she is conveying that she can be held to account for giving her readers her own perspective and experiences. Her personal identity (an Aryan in Auschwitz) and her intended readership (English-speaking British public) limit and condition what she can say. She recognizes that others might write "vastly different things" and "tell what was true for them . . . creating a picture that would complement mine" (Lingens-Reiner 1948, x). If it is true that "Holocaust literature is more impressive in the sum of its parts than as separate statements" (Rosenfeld 1988, 34), then Lingens-Reiner's "version" is just one of many complementary ones. Applying many accounts to a collective body of testimony creates a single meta-story made up of layered points of view, which aligns with Hegel's dialectic method of understanding the something-others to be a part of the Being-in-itself. The value in comparing apparently contradictory testimony is not to identify inaccuracy. Rather, through synthesis, we might understand a "single" set of events through multiple individual truths.

Time also affects how memory is shaped as an extension of being, to the "temporal axis of personhood" (Antze and Lambek 1996, xxv). Witness as an extension of memory is also shaped in relation to life at any given point because what is said about the past is invariably conditioned by the present. The present is always changing, affected by the age and life cycle of the individual and their social cultural and political milieu. It can be expected that memory, witness, and testimony will change with it. Oral historian Philip Maisel discussed how time affected the testimonies of several surviving victims he interviewed twice, more than a decade apart:

STEPHEN: How have attitudes of Holocaust survivors changed over the last thirty years since you have been interviewing?
PHILP: A lot. . . . We interviewed some people for a second time, especially to find out, how did things change. And what we did we find out? They mellowed . . . people got softer. Certain facts they mentioned before they did not mention the second time . . . they didn't think it was [still] important enough . . . their values changed.
STEPHEN: Did the story change?
PHILIP: [T]he story didn't change. The description of the story changed.

(Maisel 2021)

When Maisel refers to the description of the story, he is not suggesting that the basic facts of the history changed, only that the facts were presented differently over time. He goes on to say further that:

PHILIP: First their memories are not hurting them so much. The person is more mature and the basic changes are, I would say [they are] more reasonable. The person has learned something during this period . . . There is a possibility that certain events have been forgotten, but this I cannot vouch for. . . . the person is more at peace with himself. He learned to accept things in life that previously were too difficult to accept.

STEPHEN: Do you think . . . personal circumstances change their attitude?
PHILIP: Definitely . . . sometimes the [spouse] is not alive anymore, . . . children grow up [and] with different views from themselves . . . they suddenly realize that there are any things that they misjudged in the past. It's a process of growing.

(Maisel 2021)

Change may well occur in unexpected and devious ways. Primo Levi is sympathetic to what he describes as "the drifting of memory" among victims of Hitler's "war against memory" (Levi 1988, 18). We should not confuse the alteration of memory with pure fabrication or the need to exculpate guilt, whereby the surviving victim may be ashamed of certain events, and so "filters out the most painful memories" (19). Levi does not suggest that the surviving victim forget the experience or consciously remember it. Instead, due to the difficulty of communication, the surviving witness may not want or isn't able to tell their story. There are at least three forms of identifiable "forgetting" or shaping: 1) time erodes the ability to remember specific details, 2) the surviving victim chooses what they wish to remember in public and in what form, and 3) they shape memory to make it more pronounceable, palatable, or comprehensible in the present:

> Even as we recall the past our memories reshape it until it is hard to tell if we remember original experiences or only earlier memories of them. At the same time, the process of memory is interpretative, and creates new self-understanding, so that we change ourselves through our recollections.
>
> *(Bromberg 1980, 6)*

The process of remembering always includes a set of mnemonic options in which the surviving victim gets to choose from within their memory recall what to say, to whom, and in what context, in symbiosis with their often-unseen audience.

Surviving witness Sim Kessel demonstrates his awareness that he might not have remembered everything due to the pressures of survival. However, he assures his readership that "on the ground of truth or sincerity I could not, I think be reproached. But on many points I wanted to be more precise" (Kessel 1975, 11). His honesty is admirable although his admission of inaccuracy is startling, particularly when the text confidently describes beating, torture, and murder. His confidence, coupled with an absence of family or personal reflection (the text begins with his arrest by the Gestapo in July 1942), exudes an aura of one man's struggle with the Germans, rather than a complete memoir. When read empathetically in the context of Ella Lingens-Reiners' argument for a "perfectly valid part of the truth," Kessel's text helps us understand the nature of Nazi persecution. However, it is not meant to be read in isolation. The surviving victim's memoir "selects some details and blocks out others for the purpose of shaping the reader's response" (Langer 1982, xii). It is always necessary to read, contrast, and juxtapose testimonies, including reading of the same surviving victim's testimonies over time. When read, listened to, or watched in a critical analysis based in I-Thou curiosity, one testimony will not de-value another. Instead, it will reveal ways that one testimony might enrich our understanding of another.

Oral historian Bill Williams described an oral history in which the surviving victim narrates a "selection" scene. Men and women were separated in a school playground, giving the impression of a selection in a concentration camp. Using the trope of impeding death, she included what she perceived her audience— Williams, the interviewer—expected to hear. What Williams observed was her reshaping testimony using language instantly recognizable to the audience, though there was no threat of death in the situation she was describing.[7] Surviving victim Margaret Kagan expresses concern about how the accuracy of testimony is compromised when simplified stereotypes are used to describe a phenomenon that was more complex in lived reality. Specifically, she observes that when Jewish Police are mentioned in testimony it is almost always in a negative context:

> Well, like the [Jewish] Police were bad in the ghetto, and they were [always] criminal. It depended on what sort of day it was that one was talking about . . . [and] how responsible the ghetto management were for misleading the ghetto population.[8]

Margaret's complaint focuses on how memory loses part of its historicity through a need to form historical stereotypes, thereby losing the nuance of the circumstances. An outcome of the remembering self is supporting the idea that "in sum" the Jewish Police were on the wrong side of history, rather than allowing the experiencing self to explore the daily dilemma of how civilian rule (however egregious) was to be administered and who was to do it. As a surviving victim, Margaret demonstrates a keen interest in the nuances of testimony. She is convinced her that her peer's testimonies do not always accurately represent the facts as she experienced them, but has come to terms with what she calls "highlighting":

> MARGARET: I today am much more tolerant of what I call highlighting as opposed to lying. Highlighting. There is a lot of [that] going on. Every book that I've read . . .
> STEPHEN: So what do you mean by highlighting exactly?
> MARGARET: Well, omitting certain things and emphasizing others. I was very upset and that's why very often I couldn't find my way in participating in any of these discussions because to me they were not direct enough and accurate enough for me to be able to associate.[9]

Margaret was reluctant to testify because, since her arrival in England in 1946, she believed that testimony was not an accurate enough means of representation. However, she goes on to state that her intolerance of "highlighting" was moderated when she saw the film *Rashomon* in 1950. At this point, she thought, "it's just impossible to tell a story . . . there is no such thing as absolute truth, is there?" Once she discovered the possibilities of multiple narratives telling a single story, she was more able to accept the tropes of those she disagreed with. She accepted them not because she agreed with the stereotypes, but because she accepted that she could have her own version too—her form of the truth.[10]

Highlighting becomes more problematic when the surviving victim purposefully misinterprets or creates inaccuracies in their past. Fania Fénelon, author of *Playing for Time*, has been sharply criticized by fellow women's orchestra member, Anita Lasker-Wallfisch, author of *Inherit the Truth* (1996), and Auschwitz-Birkenau inmate doctor Ella Lingens-Reiner for willful inaccuracy. Lasker-Wallfisch states of Fénelon's text:

> She was a professional fantasist . . . [I] always admitted that everybody looks at the same event with different eye[s], [but] You cannot go to such aberrations as she did unless you have got a problem with yourself.[11]

Lasker-Wallfisch's anger stems from her taking personal offense at how she was portrayed in Fénelon's version of events. But she also expresses outrage on behalf of non-surviving members of the orchestra, whom she felt Fénelon had unjustly criticized and could not answer for themselves.[12] This accusation from one surviving victim of another may appear to be based on perspective. However, the professional historian can help us decipher what is based in fact and what is not—an important contribution to misstated testimony:

> Reading Fania Fénelon's book one has very mixed feelings—admiration for the author's lively and colourful language, but also astonishment and opposition to her overgrown fantasy, her free alteration of facts and expression of improbable ill-feeling toward her fellow sufferers.
> (Dunicz-Niwinska 1996, 65–67)

Lingens-Reiner, who was also an eyewitness to the Auschwitz-Birkenau women's camp, sounds a more cautionary note, but remains critical of Fénelon. Concerned that her account enables Holocaust denial, she states,

> there is a danger that I see some descriptions which are not right because they exaggerate. They exaggerate because they think it's more impressive . . . I don't know whether you have ever read the music (sic) of Madame Fénelon . . . I read it. It's also a bit not quite true.[13]

The issue of exaggeration that Lingens-Reiner refers to implies falsification.[14] Lawrence Langer states unequivocally, "sometimes they lie!"[15] A distinction must be drawn between memories that shape a narrative seeking a particular outcome, and those promoted by people who consciously distort the past at the expense of historical accuracy. In the future, the risk is that when co-witnesses such as Anita Lasker-Wallfisch challenge the facticity of misrepresentative testimonies such as that of Fania Fénelon, such accounts will nevertheless become history.

Returns to Auschwitz

Kitty Hart-Moxon has made several documentaries on location, returning to sites of the Holocaust over time with different documentary filmmaking crews (Morely 1979; Nelson 2002; Purcell 2015). While making the documentary *Death March, A Survivors Story* (Nelson 2002),[16] I accompanied Kitty re-tracing the steps of her death march, over three months and two separate filming trips.

As a part of the re-tracing of her journey we visited Dzierżoniów (known as Reichenbach during the Second World War) where she had spent several months in this small town working in a Telefunken factory after being evacuated from Auschwitz-Birkenau. In *I am Alive*, Kitty describes the walk they took through Reichenbach each morning. They went from the barracks where they were housed, to the Telefunken factory where they worked: "We all especially looked forward every day to passing one house, a bakery from which came the most wonderful smells of freshly baked loaves of bread" (Hart 1962, 91). Without prompting, as we walked through the town during filming, Kitty indicated that we were about to walk down a street where there used to be a small bakery on the left-hand side of the Street. She had not been there for 57 years, and exactly where she indicated there once was a bakery, there was *still* a small family bakery. In her 1961 account she recalls, "our hunger was indescribable, for there were no facilities for 'organizing' of any sort" (91). By "organizing" she meant that none of the girls were able to acquire a loaf of bread from the store. On her return in 2002, Kitty entered the store from the same street she had walked along in 1945, greeted the owner in German, and then bought her own loaf of bread in a spontaneous act of revenge. Her "marvelous" example of accurate memory recall was followed shortly thereafter by a more "fallacious" moment.

While filming at the former Telefunken building, on entering the building I asked her,

STEPHEN: If we go inside . . . do you think you would recognize it?
KITTY: I would recognize the lavatories!

(Nelson 2002)

Once inside the building Kitty affirmed that they were the lavatories that she and her mother had used. We then entered a large hall.

KITTY: This was a large hall with machines.
STEPHEN: Do you recognize it?
KITTY: [Hesitates] It was a room like that.

Kitty's initial confirmation that the room had contained machinery, followed by her clarification that it was a "room like that," was only elicited when I asked her to confirm it was the exact room. Only when she exited the rear of the building did she recognize the structures where she had *actually* worked. She knew there was something not quite right with the first large hall. The mnemonic prompt of *seeing the physical space* changed her recall. It is quite understandable that the imposing brick façade of the building as seen from the road would have triggered the memories of what had happened in that complex, but the workshops were not in that brick building. Nevertheless her overall memory of the work she did in that complex did not change even when she realized she had been in a different location on the site.

Being on location with surviving victims has often confirmed their narrative testimony, and even added previously unknown details to it. During the making of *One Day in Auschwitz* (Purcell 2015) with Kitty Hart-Moxon, she demonstrated the "marvelous" nature of memory at the former *Kanada* section of Auschwitz-Birkenau, where she had sorted the belongings of murdered Jews in 1944. During her stay in *Kanada* she tried to save diamonds and other precious stones discovered in the lining of clothes she was sorting. In *Return to Auschwitz* she describes hiding diamonds and jewelry she had requisitioned (Hart-Moxon 1997, 142) During filming she said that she had hidden them in the latrine outhouse near the women's barracks. An Auschwitz-Birkenau State Museum senior guide expressed doubt about her account, as there was no record of a latrine. Insistent that there had been a latrine there, Hart-Moxon paced approximately 20 meters from the edge of the barracks foundation in the direction of Crematorium IV, turned around and confidently pronounced "Here!" The guide retrieved the aerial photographs of Auschwitz-Birkenau captured by American reconnaissance aircraft in the summer of 1944. On the image was a small black square at the exact spot where Hart-Moxon had been standing. What had appeared to be a missing pixel or speck of dust on the photograph was in fact the roof of a minute, one-meter-square latrine where Hart-Moxon had hidden the diamonds.

FIGURE 4.3   Auschwitz-Birkenau aerial photograph August 23, 1944. The image clearly shows a small square building near to the women's barracks where Kitty recalls she hid diamonds and jewelry

Source: 60 Squadron SAAF, Sortie No. 60/PR288. Public domain.

106 The Crisis of Witness

Hart-Moxon's penchant for both marvelous and fallacious memory on location was also illustrated during a film shoot near Porta-Westfallica, where she had worked underground in a Phillips Factory. Her memory of distance was hazy. In 1961 she said that they walked on a "winding path that led through the woods"

FIGURE 4.4 During the making of the documentary, *Death March, A Survivors Story* (BBC), Kitty visited Gross Rosen Concentration Camp

Source: Photo Courtesy, David Nelson.

(Hart 1962, 110), which is exactly how we rediscovered the route from the accommodation to the factory during the making of *Death March*. She also writes that, "after about two hours we started to descend [where we saw] a huge entrance cut into the rock" (110), which was the entrance to the underground shaft. In 2002 we walked the same route in approximately 15 minutes. Her memory may not have been entirely mistaken, as it is likely that it could have taken them as long as two hours to assemble the workers, count them, and slowly march them to the factory. The journey would have taken longer walking with weary workers, then transporting them on primitive wooden elevators to their station. Nevertheless, I had expected a much longer physical distance based on her description, from which I learned that distance is not always related to time as we understand it. Her memory about the architecture of the underground workshops was remarkably accurate. In *I Am Alive* she describes the lifts shafts that "took us underground going deeper and deeper into the mountain" (Hart 1962, 111). Hart-Moxon was not aware that documentary filmmaker David Nelson had acquired archival photographs and diagrams of the same shaft and workshop that she described on location, which included a description of a wooden elevator platform used to take prisoners down to the workshops cut into the mountain. The photographs confirmed the accuracy of her recall.

Christopher Browning discusses the need to treat testimony sources critically (Browning 2003, 84). Ideally, testimony is triangulated with other testimonies or other archival sources to build a more nuanced understanding of historical circumstances. One confirms or challenges the other. In the case of Kitty and her descriptions of Westfalica-Hausberge, the testimony reveals new insights about the work she did and how she felt in the claustrophobic space, which the documents do not show. In turn the photographic evidence and diagrammatic illustrations, provide visual documentary proof of her account. Over time I have come to trust the source of testimony, then verify with evidence.

The Value of Rutabagas

As further illustration of how to trust the source of testimony, then use other sources to verify, we now turn our attention to a pile of rutabagas outside the camp kitchen at Bergen-Belsen on April 15, 1945. As we shall see, the existence of the rutabagas are in and of themselves sufficient to give any information about the liberation of the campo, but like many other observable facts that day, they are part of the picture.

In a recent personal conversation with surviving victim Sonia Warshawski, she described to me the day she was shot in the chest on the day of liberation at Bergen-Belsen. She explained that she was working at one of the kitchens, and in the excitement of the highly anticipated liberation on the morning of April 15, 1945, some of the prisoners rushed to the piles of rutabagas for much-needed nourishment. As she returned from the latrines and ran toward the kitchen to break the news of the arrival of the British Army, she was shot at close range in the chest.

SONIA WARSHAWSKI: So when finally, I was working in one of the kitchen[s], in the peeling. You know, we peeled not potatoes but rutabagas ("swedes") . . . We already knew that something is going on because . . . the Nazi[s], . . . in charge of us, they didn't come [to the kitchen]. I went out to the latrine, and I stared. From far I could see tanks coming, and I was so excited I wanted to come back and tell the girls what I'm seeing. And meanwhile, across from us was the men's camp and they just start[ed] running because in front of this kitchen we had piles [of] rutabagas and everyone wanted to just grab the rutabagas . . . you don't know what hunger can do . . . And the guards were still standing there and they start shooting . . . and the bullet came through [me] . . .
INTERVIEWER: They were shooting because [the inmates] were taking the rutabagas?
SONIA WARSHAWSKI: Yeah. They were shooting just [into] the crowd . . .
INTERVIEWER: They could see the tanks coming too? They knew, they knew . . .
SONIA WARSHAWSKI: Yes, they [were] already sure. You could hear the tanks coming.

(Warshawski 1999)

Warshawski's testimony describes how she was wounded in the chest and taken inside while swallowing blood from her internal injuries. Unable to stand because of her wounds, as the armored vehicles entered the camp, a Russian POW helped her see and celebrate the moment of liberation that followed the shooting:

This Russian fellow picked me up and he took me to the window to see . . . he said [in] Russian to me, "Look out and you see." And on the platform of a big truck was an old SS, you know, three men and the men they were standing up with their hands up and also the one who was in charge of Bergen-Belsen and gosh, I forgot his name. You probably would know the name of the one who was . . . he was first in Auschwitz.

(Warshawski 1999)

In this section of her testimony Sonia identifies (although cannot name) camp Kommandant Josef Kramer, who had been brought to the scene of the shooting by the British. In her 1996 USC Shoah Foundation testimony, Sonia was able to name Kramer and add that the SS women were also rounded up:

The English were there, and they surrounded all the SS women . . . and in one truck . . . the man Kramer [who] was in charge, the SS man of this camp in Bergen-Belsen.

(Warshawski 1996, seg. #111)

An article "Bergen Concentration Camp" in *The Lancet*, published several weeks later on May 12, reports the same episode in Sonia's testimony:

On April 15 . . . the commandant Kramer was interviewed . . . while this interview was proceeding, a runner arrived to say that the SS were firing on prisoners. It was found that famished prisoners were trying to take potatoes from a heap near the cookhouse and the SS were shooting them. Kramer made no attempt to stop his men. Nor was any attempt made by the Germans to help the wounded and the dying.

(The Lancet 1945)

Sonia's sighting of Kramer while being held in the arms of a Russian POW also provides a visual symmetry that might seem more poetic than true. But Lt. Colonel Leonard Berney, who was there during the interrogation with Kramer, confirms that Kramer was taken to the site of the shooting:

> While we were talking to Kramer, we heard shooting coming from the camp. (We could not see into the camp from where we were.) Kramer explained that some of the prisoners were rioting and trying to raid the food stores and that the guards were trying to keep order [Colonel] Taylor decided to enter the camp to investigate. Taylor, Kramer and I together with the Intelligence Office (a Lieutenant Sington), who had arrived with his loud-hailer van, and two army photographers, drove into the camp.

(Berney 2015)

Derrick Sington recalls the liberation of Belsen in his 1946 memoir *Belsen Uncovered*, in which he describes a German Army captain telling Kramer and Col. Taylor that "The kitchens are being stormed" (Sington 1946, 21). He confirms that Kramer was taken to the site of the shooting and started removing bodies (23). He also states that women were caught in the crossfire, describing the death of a Slovak woman who had been shot through the eye while walking near the kitchen (23). Sonia was unaware of any sources corroborating her experience of being shot. Her conversational report to me and the testimonies she has given in the past were not extensive, but there were details that demonstrate truthful recall.

It is important to note that Sonia was more accurate than the British soldiers, notwithstanding their greater access to information. Without prompting she clarifies that the vegetables were rutabagas, and not potatoes. Sonia had no idea that another (inaccurate but more authoritative) account would identify them as potatoes, thereby cementing her position as a trustworthy source. The SS personnel were not on duty that day in the kitchen, because most SS left the camp before the arrival of the British on April 15. Only her trip to the latrine confirmed that there were tanks in the vicinity of the camp, which would have been audible and clearly visible from the two main arteries that ran through the camp. Her description of the rioting and the ravenous men fits the description from British officers who were on the spot. She also confirms that the shots were not meant for her. She was trying to get back to the safety of the kitchen and got caught in the crossfire as the guards fired into the crowd.

Reports of the details of the liberation of Belsen have largely come from British military personnel (Sington 1946; Berney 2015). They described the incident as having a profound impression on the military (Shephard 2005), but give no further detail. A map of Belsen shows the main entrance where Lt. Sington's loud hailer

FIGURE 4.5 British Tank drives parallel to the Bergen-Belsen Concentration camp on April 15, 1945, its engines and tank tracks would have been clearly audible to recently liberated inmates. Lt. Derrick Sington's loud hailer vehicle referred to by Lt. Leonard Berney is clearly visible at the gate

Source: Photo BU-3928–1 used with permission of Imperial War Museums.

vehicle and the Commet tank (Figure 4.5) were photographed prior to entering the camp. This is also presumably where discussions were taking place with Josef Kramer, if as reported, the British were yet to enter the camp. The possible site of the shooting incident is marked opposite the men's camp, as described by Sonia Warshawski. From that vantage point she would have been able to hear and see the Comet tank as she walked on the Main Highway or the central path of the camp on the way to or from the latrines.

Sonia's testimony helps us better understand the incident and demonstrates that detail can be accurately retained over a long period of time. A photograph taken on the same day (Figure 4.4) clearly shows the tank and the loud hailer vehicle

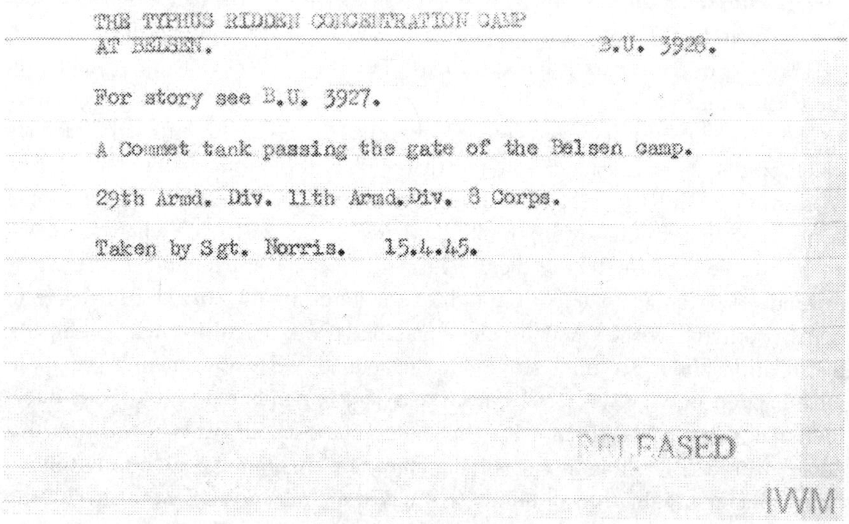

THE TYPHUS RIDDEN CONCENTRATION CAMP
AT BELSEN.   B.U. 3928.

For story see B.U. 3927.

A Commet tank passing the gate of the Belsen camp.

29th Armd. Div. 11th Armd.Div. 8 Corps.

Taken by Sgt. Norris. 15.4.45.

RELEASED
IWM

FIGURE 4.6 Photographer Sgt. Norris's index card indicates that the Commet tank passing by the gates of Belsen on April 15, 1945, was a part of the 29th Armoured Division, 11th Armoured Division, 8 Corps

Source: Photo BU-3928-2 used with permission of Imperial War Museums.

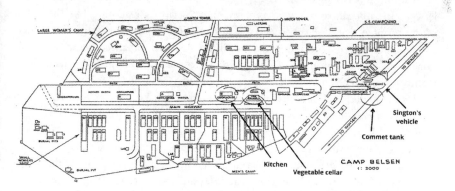

FIGURE 4.7 Plan of Bergen-Belsen dated May 1945, as presented to the first Belsen Trial, in October 1945. It shows possible location of kitchen with vegetable store, which is in proximity to the perimeter fence and front gate where British troops arrived, which Hela Goldstein would have been able to see from her vantage point if she was moving around the camp in search of the latrine (Original plan, source unknown, first used in the Belsen Trial, first published by Sington (1946).

near the camp, which Sonia would have been able to see and hear. These sources corroborate Sonia's testimony with Sington's description. In turn, Sonia provides proof—including the physical scars on her body—of the shooting event.

The I-Thou construct is based on trust. For the encounter to be meaningful, the witness and listener enter the encounter with good intentions and respect for each other. The unspoken agreement is that the witness will tell the truth as they understand it, and the listener will hear that truth without judgement. The I-Thou relationship with Kitty at Kanada did not result in a conflict about accuracy, only curiosity about why she would think that there had been a latrine where there was no prior record of one being there. The result was a confirmation that memory can indeed be quite "marvelous," and a contribution to historical knowledge in which both the witness and listener benefitted from a trusting relationship. In that relationship, it was understood what happened, what was remembered about what happened, what was recalled from what was remembered, and how we interpret what was recalled about what happened. These are all layers of memory that emerge through retelling in an evolving conversation. This approach to testimony yields greater insight than doubting it. Only once testimony is heard in full can the marvelous be disentangled from the fallacious, both of which are a part of the wonder of human memory—unless memory has become an outright lie.

(False) Testimony

The publication of Binjamin Wilkomirski's account *Fragments: Memories of a Childhood, 1939–1948* (1996) raised a particularly problematic question about the nature of testimony. Following the international success of the book, Israeli journalist Daniel Ganzfried began to doubt its veracity, and described "reading it like [it was] a movie script."[17] Facts began to emerge that cast doubts on Wilkomirski's identity and whether he was a surviving victim of the Holocaust. Ganzfried posed the question about "how fiction and factuality, the two components of every recounted memory, are to be differentiated from each other" (Ganzfried 1998, n.p.).[18] Ganzfried concluded that Wilkomirki was "never confined to a concentration camp" and was in fact Bruno Grosjean born in Biel, Switzerland in 1941 (Maechler 2001, vii).

The book itself is a disorienting mosaic of fragmentary "memories" that are confusing and horrific. As a piece of would-be literary fiction, its imagery of "dead women . . . giving birth to rats" (Wilkomirski 1996, 86) and descriptions of the "grey uniforms" of the guards (35) present haunting images. As testimony, its potency is unbearable, as rarely are surviving victims able to combine such vivid literary deftness in memoirs. Wilkomirski succeeds in synthesizing fragmented memories of a small child, weaving "experiences" of the camp into his post-Holocaust nightmares. The interchange between modes of remembering sufficiently elides potential inconsistencies that otherwise might have emerged. The jacket cover of the English edition sums up the impression that the book creates for the unsuspecting reader:

> In piercingly simple scenes he gives us "fragments" of his recollections, with a child's unadorned speech and unsparing vision, so that we too become

small again and see that bewildering, horrifying world through child's eyes. No adult interpretations intervene. From inside the mind of a little boy we experience love, terror, friendship and above all survival, and the final arduous return to the "real" world.

(Wilkomirski 1996, n.p.)

Many Holocaust scholars and literary experts initially failed to recognize the flaw in his work (Karpf 1998) or did suspect it was flawed but felt uncomfortable confronting it (Maechler 2001). They missed his falsification because, as the work of a child's memory, it is devoid of identifying details. It is not possible to critique on historical grounds, as it does not contain historical material. However, it was reported that, at an international conference at which Wilkomirski was speaking, historian Raul Hilberg questioned whether his text was "fact or fiction," to which he replied that they were "recollections" (Scharf 1999, 45). Holocaust scholar and writer on Polish-Jewish relations Rafael Felix Scharf was asked to serve on the jury of a literary prize for which *Fragments* had been nominated. Having read the text he asked to be relieved of the role, saying:

> That child's voice behind which the author is hiding disarms the potentially sceptical reader. At the same time one realises that these are not the perceptions of a child, but projections of an adult mind (for instance a remark like: this is not real peace, this is their peace, the peace of the victors . . .).
>
> *(Scharf 1999, 45)*

Scharf ultimately concluded that Binjamin Wilkomirski is a "figment of the author's imagination, a wilful deception" (Scharf 1999, 45). Within his book, Wilkomirski is adamant about his identity. Perhaps to cover any queries that should arise, he declares in his afterword that,

> the document I hold in my hands . . . gives the date of birth as February 12, 1941. But this date has nothing to do with the history of this century or my personal history. I have now taken legal steps to have this imposed identity annulled.
>
> *(Wilkomirski 1996, 154)*

Scharf summarizes that "had [Wilkomirski] warned his readers before that this was a 'story' and not insisted on calling it a 'memoir,' nobody would have raised an objection" (Scharf 1999, 45). Should Wilkomirski have chosen to disclose the book's possible fictional nature, it may nevertheless have been appreciated as a novella. His own publishers stated of the fraud, "It would have been a very clever piece of writing if it wasn't so fraudulent" (*The Guardian* 1999, para. 16). It investigates the fragmentary nature of memory in a similar vein to Cynthia Ozick's *The Shawl* (1991). However, Wilkomirski assumed the identity he created and remained adamant about his identity as a child survivor. Scharf suspected this was cover for "yet another layer to that story . . . that will ultimately emerge" (Scharf 1999, 45).

In 1997, Wilkomirski gave a three-hour testimony to USC Shoah Foundation recounting his life story (in German). His testimony posed an unusual problem, because the Foundation does not remove a testimonial recording unless an interviewee admits that it was falsified. For example, one interviewee who gave testimony as a surviving victim later admitted that they fabricated their identity. They asked that their recording be removed based on her falsification of witness testimony and the testimony was duly removed. Wilkomirski has made no such confession nor made such a request. His testimony thus remains a part of the collection, with an advisory note that "the authenticity of the content of this interview has been called into question." The reason for this policy is that if USC Shoah Foundation becomes the arbiter of authenticity for testimony, there is a slippery slope wherein any testimony containing an inaccuracy (which is many) could be determined to be unrepresentative of the actual facts and thereby removed. As this chapter has discussed, parts of any testimony could be accused of being inaccurate or fabricated. It is the view of the USC Shoah Foundation that the Visual History Archive is populated by testimony based on human memory. Because human memory is inherently fallible, user discretion is always advised. That said, user-generated notes as well as archival staff notes were recently introduced, which had been a part of the Fortunoff Archive's methodology for many years. Using notes, more advice can be given to users of the testimony through historical notes in cases like that of Wilkomirski.

We have been discussing the crisis of witness throughout this book. The falsification of testimony adds another dimension to a crisis unfolding at the borders of testimony and the imagination. Testimony *is* shaped by the imagination, but it is not the work of the imagination. Anne Karpf was taken aback by the Wilkomirski revelation, stating, "It almost felt blasphemous, as if being a Holocaust survivor was a costume you could don."[19]

Hoaxers like Wilkomirski so believed their own story that they were prepared to go on camera and give personal testimony. One such person is Misha Defonseca, who claims in her book *Surviving with Wolves* (Defonseca 2005) that during the war she had lived with wolves during her fantastical journey in search of her deported parents. Her parents, who were not Jewish, were a part of the Belgian resistance and were deported to German concentration camps where they died. It was first revealed in 2008, after she and her co-writer Vera Lee won a copyright court case against her publisher Mt. Ivy, that she had fabricated the story about her search for her missing parents. The publisher appealed and was able to provide evidence that her identity was in fact Monique de Wael. During the appeals process, De Wael admitted the falsification, stating, "it's not the true reality, but it is my reality" (Flood 2014, n.p.). De Wael's identity was further established when school friends recognized her and placed her in a classroom in Brussels in 1943. In a statement from her lawyers in 2008 she says, "there are times when I find it difficult to differentiate between reality and my inner world" (Waterfield 2008, n.p.).

The question of whether she should claim her falsified "inner world" character returns us to the complex relationship between memory and testimony. Virtually all surviving victims struggle with how to turn the traumatic events as remembered by the experiencing self into the remembering self that reports those events. The benefit of audio-visual testimony format is that they can "relive" the events through the experiencing self. They explain what happened through a step-by-step process, while also reflecting on what their experiences meant "in sum." The balance between the remembering and experiencing self working is left to the individual, but there is a tacit assumption that the factual data of the experiencing self is as accurate as possible. The reflection of the remembering self is entirely at the discretion of the interviewee.

In her USC Shoah Foundation pre-interview, Misha Defonseca confirms her name to camera, but also gives Monique de Wael as a name she had been "given" during the war (Defonseca 1997). She also identifies herself as being a part of several "experience groups," which is a term the USC Shoah Foundation uses to classify the identity of an individual by their experiences. Under "Ghettos" she confirms herself as having been in the Warsaw Ghetto. Under "Hiding or Living Under False Identity" she writes: Brussels (Belgium), Germany, Grenoble (France), Otwosk (Warsaw, Poland), Romania, Ukraine, and Yugoslavia (Defonseca 1997). When the data is entered into the pre-interview questionnaire, the interviewee attests to the facts with a trained interviewer. I have filled out this multi-page document many times with surviving victims and know how intimate and clearly focused on historical data the process is. Monique de Wael knowingly lied to her interviewer. Providing detailed background information that was knowingly false breached the trust of the interviewer and the audience, who come to archives to learn about actual events. In the previous section I referred to how important trust is with the surviving victim. The hoax testimonies undermine that trust for all surviving victims.

De Wael indicates how she constructs her fantasy version of history when describing the disappearance of her mother to the concentration camp system:

> I have always think (sic) that after the war my mother was taken away by the Russians because she speak very well Russian. . . . I prefer this idea that she has survived for a while even if she has made another life without me, [rather than] died miserably in the camps. She probably [did . . .] but I prefer dreaming something else, that's for sure.
>
> *(Defonseca 1997, seg. #4)*

Her admission that she would "rather dream something else" is the underpinning reality of this account. What the testimony reveals which the book does not is that de Wael was not only writing about a fantasy past—which could be deciphered as a mislabeled work of fiction—she is also living the life of Misha Defonseca, which can only be revealed through the first-person interview to camera. At some point she transitioned from a daydreaming Monique de Wael to the fully formed character of Misha Defonseca, who can talk to the camera. When referring to songs she heard her mother sing at home, she refers to having recently heard the song Kalinka, which she says reminded her of her childhood. But then

116 The Crisis of Witness

FIGURE 4.8 Misha Defonseca wears a large "Chai" necklace during her interview for USC Shoah Foundation despite not being Jewish (1997). Her interview has not been deaccessioned as testimonies are only removed from the archive when requested by the interviewee. Defonseca has never asked for her testimony to be removed, although she has publicly acknowledged that her story was false

Source: Used by permission of USC Shoah Foundation.

she clarified that she cannot say for certain she heard it at home. She frames the childhood memory, stating that:

MD: I am so afraid to say things [just] because I want it [to be that way]. You know? In place of what is really true. You know what I mean?
INT: Well, could you explain?
MD: Er, well, when I hear this music now, I think it is the song of my mother. But I don't know if I want to remember that because my heart wants to remember that, or if it's real.

(Defonseca 1997, seg. #5)

The interviewer tries to get her to clarify, but she states that her memory is hazy. She wants things to be in a way that may not have been true to real life. Shortly after stating this, she describes her parents being arrested for their work with the resistance. She has much clearer memories of the "foster home" she was sent to and the e Wael family, who made her change her identity for her safety. In reality, she was with her grandparents. She explains that it was there that she was given the name de Wael, and states, "unfortunately I got [given] this name for [an] identity . . . it was very difficult for me to accept this name" (Defonseca 1997, seg. #6), a name that was her real identity.

De Wael, lonely and traumatized following the removal of her parents, was understandably uncertain about the world that adults had made for her. Although she says that she was seven at the time, she was in fact just four years old. Like many children who fell victim to war atrocities, she was collateral damage of her parents' work in the resistance. Later it was discovered that her father had cracked under interrogation. She not only had to live with losing her parents, but also the stigma of being a "traitor's daughter" (Mitchell 2021, n.p.). She experienced the world of humans through loss and shame from a very early age.

De Wael sets out on a fantasy journey of over 835 miles across Europe in search of her missing (non-Jewish) parents. Apart from the impossibility of a seven-year-old making such a journey, she states that "In Poland I follow people who were wearing [yellow] star. . . . I saw people with a star I look always [to see] if this is my parents" (Defonseca 1997, seg. #10). She follows the people with the stars to the entrance of the Warsaw Ghetto, where she hopes to find her parents. "All the Jewish people go there, might be my parents are there. That was my obsession" (#10). This she says despite knowing her parents were not Jewish, thereby stealing the identity of the Jewish victims of the ghetto for her Catholic parents. The interviewer asks de Wael to describe the ghetto. In the ten seconds of hesitation before she begins her description, de Wael shows several body movements. She shields her face with her hands, and then shifts her eyes right and left as she looks for words, which research shows is body language linked to lying (Glass 2014). During her description of the ghetto, she recreates images that she likely gleaned from archival photos of the ghetto, including "dead bodies covered in newspaper" (Defonseca 1997, #10). She creates a fantasy scene of a pregnant woman being shot and other Jews scattering "like flies" (#10) and then leaving the ghetto in one of the carts used to move corpses to the cemetery.

De Wael is publicly remembered for her description of living with wolves. She describes sitting in the forest and feeling like she was being watched, "and I saw what for me was a *huge* dog . . . it was marvellous" (though it was entirely fallacious). She goes on, "and it was a wolf. It was a beauty (sic) wolf." Entirely comfortable with the lie she is telling on camera her eyes gleam as she looks the interviewer directly in the eye confidently:

> I was happy. I was the kid . . . it was my mommy wolf . . . I needed a mommy desperately . . . and I was accepted [by the wolf and her mate] It was like a family . . . I hope people understand it was something marvelous . . . as my friend said, "You have God on your shoulder."
>
> *(Defonseca 1997, seg. #13)*

118 The Crisis of Witness

In the vein of the Roman foundation myth about the twins Romulus and Remus who were sheltered and suckled by the she-wolf, de Wael creates her own myth. Although she does not go so far as to say she was sheltered and suckled, the wolf becomes her surrogate mother and the wolves provide nourishment. In her version as she says, "I ate what they ate," referring to their imaginary prey (#12). The Shoah Foundation interviewer does *not* ask clarifying questions or put de Wael on the spot about what a clear fabrication. Instead she moves asks incredulously, "did you meet anyone else in the forest?" (Defonseca 1997, seg. #13).

Once de Wael parts from the first set of wolves, she uses an antisemitic stereotype to describe her the journey of her assumed character Misha DeFonsenca:

MD: I continue[d] my wandering you know like, er, how [do] you call that, er, the Jewy wandering? The Jewish . . .
INTERVIEWER: Wandering Jew.
MD: Wandering Jew. I was really that. I was really that. [PAUSE 2 seconds]. I don't wish to be that. [PAUSE 2 seconds]. But I was. [PAUSE 4 seconds].
INTERVIEWER: So where did you wander to next?

Her use of a stereotype as a non-Jewish person while pretending to be Jewish is jarring and antisemitic. De Wael was not only profiting from the story that she had published, but in her interview with USC Shoah Foundation reiterated stereotypes that had been promoted by propaganda minister Josef Goebbels as a part of his anti-Jewish propaganda. *Der Ewige Jude* (the "eternal" or "wandering Jew") was a 1940 film directed by Fritz Hippler, head of the propaganda unit's film division.

De Wael's interview includes a detailed description of a rape scene, in which she describes seeing a German soldier first raping a young virgin, then shooting her. When he discovers that Misha had seen him, he comes over to where she was hiding. The nine-year-old Misha has a dagger, and successfully overwhelms the armed adult soldier and kills him, in what is clearly an impossible scenario.

Finally, de Wael gets to the root of her story. When describing her drive to continue her search she states, "I missed my parents terribly . . . still now" (Defonseca 1997, #14). Because she ultimately admitted her hoax in public, when reviewing the interview this statement stood out as the defining sentence. The story and her transmogrified identity were produced within her imagination for the parents she lost and was seeking in her mind. The fantasy world of the four-year-old child who was thereafter in constant search of her parents eventually transformed into an adult with an entirely new persona. Not only did she create a new identity, she rejected her own identity in the de Wael family, who provided for her after her parents were arrested. Describing her next family wolf pack, she says of her search and the protection the fantasy wolves provided for her: "I needed that for my soul" (Defonseca 1997, #14).

Defonseca lost her case on appeal. Judge Kantrowitz recognized that "under oath, Defonseca averred that . . . her story was true."[20] He also drew the conclusion

FIGURE 4.9   D Mjölnir [Hans Schweitzer], poster for the film *Der Ewige Jude* (The Eternal or Wandering Jew), directed by Fritz Hippler, 1940

Source: Photo used with permission from United States Holocaust Memorial Museum.

that whether "Defonseca's belief was reasonable or not, the introduction in evidence of the actual facts of her history . . . could have made a significant difference in the jury's deliberations." The development of a memory-based fantasy story in which her identity is subsumed within the life of another, is pathological. Like Wilkomirski, had she written a fictional story, it would have been an acceptable (if fantastical) form of creative art. The recent Amazon TV series *Hunters* takes fantasy Holocaust history to a similar level. I consider *Hunters* an egregious breach of sensibility, but it is clear that it has no historical connection. De Wael's "testimony" is an offense to all those who lived through the Warsaw Ghetto, children who were actually murdered, women who were verifiably raped and killed, and the many who suffered other experiences she describes. Her hoax, the subject of the documentary film *Misha and the Wolves* (Hobkinson 2021), has highlighted the need to verify. Verification asks demanding questions, which the USC Shoah Foundation interviewer did not do when the testimony did not feel right, even though it was clear she was very uncomfortable with what was being shared and moved the interview along to a swift conclusion. Such techniques did not serve either the purpose of history or memory. Had the right questions been asked in 1997, her hoax could have been exposed a decade before she was forced to publicly admit her falsehood.

False testimony is a very rare occurrence. There are only a handful of similar, examples, such as Donald Watt (1991, 1995a, 1995b) which was proved false by Konrad Kwiet (Kwiet 1997), and Herman Rosenblat (1995) and his wife Rosa (Rosenblat 1995) who fabricated their concentration camp love story. The I-Thou reading of testimony provides a safe way to navigate such erroneous accounts. There is no question that they are pure works of fiction, but behind them is a human being. They sought to find a new identity with whom they could identify through their own pain. Yet the incalculable damage they caused to history and to those who went through real pain is not easily calculated.

Notes

1. Kitty Hart-Moxon, interview with author, September 20, 1996.
2. The libel trial of David Irving against Deborah Lipstadt and Penguin Books did not use survivor testimony as evidence, and on a number of occasions Irving questioned the reliability of eyewitness statements. It is also interesting to note that, following the trial, when survivor Trude Levi was interviewed by Irving on Radio 4's *Today* (April 14, 2000), Levi was asked to remain at home and the interview was shown as a delayed live broadcast, in case Irving insulted or demeaned Levi's testimony.
3. I have decided not to cite denial sites and sources that call testimony into question in this volume. Due to the pernicious nature of these claims, I do not deem them legitimate sources for a scholarly volume, unless the volume itself was specifically dedicated to analyzing the phenomenon of denial itself.
4. I took a photograph of the painting and made it the home screen on my phone. Only then did I realize that his art had always intended to be his testimony. His painting is still my home screen.
5. Talk delivered at Cape Town Holocaust and Genocide Centre, August 13, 1999.
6. Paraphrase of a verbal discussion, which was not recorded.

7 Bill Williams delivered these comments in a presentation delivered at Keele University in 1995.
8 Margaret Kagan, telephone interview with author, February 6, 1999.
9 Ibid.
10 Margaret eventually did give her own audio-visual testimony on June 16, 1998. USC Shoah Foundation interview 46259.
11 Anita Lasker-Wallfisch, telephone interview with author, February 6, 1999.
12 Though Anita did not spell out the particular points of her criticism to me, her public condemnation of Fénelon's comments may have been responsible for certain changes to the reissue of *Playing For Time*. Her comments were also supported by Helena Dunicz-Niwinska (1996).
13 Ella Lingens-Reiner, interview, February 13, 1999.
14 The issue of "false" testimony will be discussed shortly under "(False) Testimony."
15 Comment given by Lawrence Langer during a keynote speech at "Emerging Questions in Holocaust Testimony Research" at the University of Virginia co-sponsored by USC Shoah Foundation Center for Advanced Genocide Research, November 2017.
16 For film synopsis, see: www.bbc.co.uk/pressoffice/pressreleases/stories/2002/05_may/14/landmark_survivor.shtml. Retrieved, January 17, 2021.
17 On BBC's *Inside Story*, November 3, 1999. Ganzfried, an Israeli journalist was based in Switzerland where *Fragments* was written and first published.
18 Ganzfried, Daniel, "Die Geliehene Holocaust-Biographie" (Translates as: "The Purloined Holocaust Biography"), *Die Weltwoche* (August 27, 1998).
19 *Inside Story*, BBC, aired November 3, 1999.
20 Details of the judgment were delivered on April 29, 2014 at the Appeals Court of Massachusetts, Middlesex. https://caselaw.findlaw.com/ma-court-of-appeals/1664766.html.

References

Alterman, Nathane. 1997. *Interview by USC Shoah Foundation* (Interview 33586). Los Angeles, CA: Visual History Archive.
Antze, Paul, and Michael Lambek, eds. 1996. *Tense Past: Cultural Essays in Trauma and Memory*. New York: Routledge.
Ariav, Nimrod. 2016. *Interview by USC Shoah Foundation* (Interview 55570). Los Angeles, CA: Visual History Archive.
Bauman, Janina. 1991. *Winter in the Morning: A Young Girl's Life in the Warsaw Ghetto and Beyond*. London: Virago Press.
Benzion, Dinur, and Shaul Esh, eds. 1957. *Yad Vashem Studies: On the European Jewish Catastrophe and Resistance*. Jerusalem: Publishing Department of the Jewish Agency for Yad Vashem Remembrance Authority.
Berney, Leonard. 2015. *Liberating Belsen Concentration Camp: A Personal Account*. Self-published.
Blanchot, Maurice. 1986. *The Writing of the Disaster*. Lincoln, NE: University of Nebraska Press.
Bromberg, Pam. 1980. "Lillian Hellman's Uncertainties." *New Boston Review* 5 (August/September): 6.
Browning, Christopher R. 2003. *Collected Memories: Holocaust History and Postwar Testimony*. Madison, WI: University of Wisconsin Press.
Davidson, Shamai, and Israel Charney, eds. 1992. *Holding on to Humanity*. New York: New York University Press.
Defonseca, Misha. 1997. *Interview by USC Shoah Foundation* (Interview 25354). Los Angeles, CA: Visual History Archive.
Defonseca, Misha. 2005. *Surviving with Wolves*. London: Portrait.

Delbo, Charlotte. 1995. *Auschwitz and After*. New Haven, CT: Yale University Press.
Des Pres, Terrence. 1976. *The Survivor: An Anatomy of Life in the Death Camps*. Oxford: Oxford University Press.
Dunicz-Niwinska, Helena. 1996. "Truth and Fantasy." *Pro Memoria* 3–4: 65–67.
Felman, Shoshana, and Dori Laub. 1992. *Testimony: Crises of Witnessing in Literature, Psychoanalysis and History*. London: Routledge.
Fernyhough, Charles. 2013. *Pieces of Light: How the New Science of Memory Illuminates the Stories We Tell About Our Pasts*. New York: HarperCollins.
Finkel, Ben. 2015. *Interview by USC Shoah Foundation* (Interview 55580). Los Angeles, CA: Visual History Archive.
Flood, Alison. 2014. "Author of Fake Holocaust Memoir to Return $22.5m to Publisher." *The Guardian*, May 12. www.theguardian.com/books/2014/may/12/author-fake-holocaust-memoir-to-return-22m.
Fried, Eva. 2006. "The Stockholm International Forum Conferences (2000–2004)." www.government.se/contentassets/66bc8f513e67474e96ad70c519d4ad1a/the-stockholm-international-forum-conferences-2000-2004.
Ganzfried, Daniel. 1998. "Die Geliehene Holocaust-Biographie: The Purloined Holocaust Biography." *Der Weltwoche*, August 27. Translation: https://www.stopbadtherapy.com/experts/fragments/ganzfried.shtml
Glass, Lillian. 2014. *The Body Language of Liars. From Little White Lies to Pathological Deception: How to See Through the Fibs, Frauds, and Falsehoods People Tell You Every Day*. Pompton Plans: Career Press.
Greenspan, Henry. 1998. *On Listening to Holocaust Survivors: Recounting and Life History*. Westport, CT: Praeger.
Gutter, Pinchas. 1993. *Interview by USC Shoah Foundation* (Interview 54192). Los Angeles, CA: Visual History Archive.
Gutter, Pinchas. 1995. *Interview by USC Shoah Foundation* (Interview 534). Los Angeles, CA: Visual History Archive.
Gutter, Pinchas. 1998. *Interview Transcript. Tape Numbers CTHC 9, 10, 11, and 12*. Cape Town: Holocaust Centre Archive.
Halter, Roman. 2007. *Roman's Journey*. London: Portobello.
Hart, Kitty. 1962. *I Am Alive*. London: Corgi.
Hart-Moxon, Kitty. 1997. *Return to Auschwitz*. Revised ed. Newark, NJ: Beth Shalom Holocaust Centre.
Hegel, Georg Wilhelm Fredrich. 2010. "First Subdivision of the Logic: The Doctrine of Being §§ 84–111." In *George Willhelm Friedrich Hegel: Encyclopedia of the Philosophical Sciences in Basic Outline*, edited by Klaus Brinkmann and Daniel O. Dahlstrom. Cambridge: Cambridge University Press.
Hobkinson, Sam. 2021. "Misha and the Wolves." Netflix video, 1:29:48. www.netflix.com/watch/80226649.
Holocaust Educational Trust (HET). n.d. "Lessons from Auschwitz." www.het.org.uk/lessons-from-auschwitz-programme.
International Holocaust Remembrance Alliance (IHRA). 2000. "Stockholm Declaration." www.holocaustremembrance.com/about-us/stockholm-declaration.
Karpf, Anne. 1998. "Child of the Shoah." *The Guardian*, February 11, 2–3.
Kenrick, D. A. 1982. "The White Hotel." *Times Literary Supplement*, April 2, 383.
Kessel, Sim. 1975. *Hanged at Auschwitz*. London: Coronet Books.
Krausz, Donald. 1995. *USC Shoah Foundation Interview 5163*. Los Angeles, CA: Visual History Archive.

Kuznetsov, Anatoly. 1967. *Babi Yar.* New York: Dell Publishing.
Kwiet, Konrad. 1997. "Anzac and Auschwitz: The Unbelievable Story of Donald Watt." *Patterns of Prejudice* 31, no. 4: 53–60.
Langer, Lawrence L. 1982. *Versions of Survival: The Holocaust and the Human Spirit.* New York: New York University Press.
Langer, Lawrence L. 1991. *Holocaust Testimonies: The Ruins of Memory.* New Haven, CT: Yale University Press.
Lasker-Wallfisch, Anita. 1996. *Inherit the Truth; 1939–1945.* London: Giles de la Mare Publishers.
Levi, Primo. 1988. *The Drowned and the Saved.* London: Abacus Books.
Lewis, Helen. 1992. *A Time to Speak.* Belfast: Blackstaff Press.
Lewis, Stephen. 1984. *Art Out of Agony: The Holocaust Theme in Literature, Sculpture and Film.* Montreal: CBC Enterprises.
Lingens-Reiner, Ella. 1948. *Prisoners of Fear.* London: Victor Gollancz.
Lyotard, Jean-François. 1988. *The Differend: Phrases in Dispute.* Manchester: Manchester University Press.
Maechler, Stefan. 2001. *The Wilkomirski Affair: A Study in Biographical Truth.* New York: Schocken Books.
Maisel, Philip. 2021. *Interview with USC Shoah Foundation* (Interview 58612). Los Angeles, CA: Visual History Archive.
Mitchell, Molli. 2021. "Misha and the Wolves: Who Is Misha Defonseca? Where Is She Now?" *Newsweek*, August 11. www.newsweek.com/misha-wolves-who-defonseca-where-now-documentary-netflix-holocaust-1618332.
Moore, Barrington. 1972. *Reflections on the Causes of Human Misery and Upon Certain Proposals to Eliminate Them.* Boston, MA: Beacon Press.
Morely, Peter, dir. 1979. *Kitty: Return to Auschwitz.* Leeds: Yorkshire Television.
Nelson, David. 2002. *Death March: A Survivor's Story.* London: BBC. YouTube video, 1:02:08. www.youtube.com/watch?v=2_kSjRxB9Q0.
Oppenheimer, Paul. 1996a. *From Belsen to Buckingham Palace.* Newark, NJ: Beth Shalom Holocaust Centre.
Oppenheimer, Paul. 1996b. *Interview with USC Shoah Foundation* (Interview 13469). Los Angeles, CA: Visual History Archive.
Ozick, Cynthia. 1991. *The Shawl.* London: Jonathan Cape.
Purcell, Steven, dir. 2015. *One Day in Auschwitz.* New York: Discovery Channel.
Reder, Rudolf. 1946. *Bełżec.* Kraków: Centralna Żydowska Komisja Historyczna.
Rosenblat, Herman. 1995. *Interview by USC Shoah Foundation* (Interview 781). Los Angeles, CA: Visual History Archive.
Rosenblat, Rosa. 1995. *Interview by USC Shoah Foundation* (Interview 779). Los Angeles, CA: Visual History Archive.
Rosenfeld, Alvin Hirsch. 1988. *A Double Dying: Reflections on Holocaust Literature.* Bloomington, IN: Indiana University Press.
Scharf, Rafael Felix. 1999. "Fragments of Truth: A Crisis of Memory and Representation." *Perspective* 2, no. 2: 45.
Shapiro, Sara. 2012. *Interview by USC Shoah Foundation* (Interview 52105). Los Angeles, CA: Visual History Archive.
Shephard, Ben. 2005. *After Daybreak: The Liberation of Bergen-Belsen, 1945.* New York: Schocken Books.
Sington, Derrick. 1946. *Belsen Uncovered.* London: Duckworth.
Smith, Stephen D. 2001. *The Void in Search of Memory Lost.* Film.

Steiner, G. 1967. *Language and Silence; Essays on Language, Literature, and the Inhuman.* New York: Atheneum.
The Guardian. 1999. "Fragments of a Fraud." October 14. www.theguardian.com/theguardian/1999/oct/15/features11.g24.
The Lancet. 1945. "Belsen Concentration Camp." *The Lancet* 245, no. 6350 (May 12): 604–605. https://doi.org/10.1016/S0140-6736(45)90413-2.
Thomas, D. M. 1981. *The White Hotel.* New York: The Viking Press.
Tumblety, Joan, ed. 2013. *Memory and History: Understanding Memory as Source and Subject.* London: Routledge.
United Nations. 2010. "'Generations' Video Exhibition Opens at United Nations Headquarters on 25 January as Part of Holocaust Remembrance Activities." January 20. www.un.org/press/en/2010/note6240.doc.htm.
Warshawski, Sonia. 1996. *Interview with USC Shoah Foundation* (Interview 11740). Los Angeles, CA: Visual History Archive.
Warshawski, Sonia. 1999. Testimony for Midwest Center for Holocaust Education, Kansas.
Waterfield, Bruno. 2008. "Wolf Woman Invents Holocaust Survival Tale." *Daily Telegraph*, February 29. www.telegraph.co.uk/news/worldnews/1580357/Wolf-woman-invents-Holocaust-survival-tale.html.
Watt, Donald. 1991. *I Was There Too: The Story of an Australian P.O.W. Sent to Auschwitz for Trying to Escape.* D. J. Watt.
Watt, Donald. 1995a. *Stoker: The Story of an Australian Soldier Who Survived Auschwitz-Birkenau.* East Roseville: Simon and Schuster.
Watt, Donald. 1995b. *Interview with USC Shoah Foundation* (Interview 5041). Los Angeles, CA: Visual History Archive.
Wilkomirski, Binjamin. 1996. *Fragments; Memories of a Childhood, 1939–1948.* London: Picador.
Wilkomirski, Binjamin. 1997. *Interview with USC Shoah Foundation* (Interview 29545). Los Angeles, CA: Visual History Archive.
Young, James Edward. 1990. *Writing and Rewriting the Holocaust: Narrative and the Consequences of Interpretation.* Bloomington, IN: Indiana University Press.
Young, James Edward. 1993. *The Texture of Memory: Holocaust Memorials and Meaning.* New Haven, CT: Yale University Press.

PART II
The Origins of Holocaust Witness

> It's like the sun. You cannot look at the sun, the temperature is too high. The Holocaust is a kind of temperature you cannot speak, you cannot utter, you cannot feel.
>
> —*Aharon Appelfeld*

5
WITNESS WITHIN THE STORM

An Audience of Strangers

Encounter is possible, even with the dead. Victims trapped in ghettos, camps, and hiding places were able to write within the storm of the Holocaust to those who would one day follow. Their faded words were scribbled—sometimes in great haste—in notebooks, diaries, letters, and scraps of paper, buried for posterity. These documents are not artefacts or objects of the past—they too are subjects. They were written by people who tried to convey the agony of their circumstances for their own personal peace of mind, engage those who might help, or simply left traces of their humanity for those not yet born:

> They tried to stave off the fear that nothing would remain of their lives and worlds by rendering their experiences meaningful to themselves and to future readers . . . As they wrote, diarists often kept in their heads the image of an audience of strangers from the outside world reading their diaries.
>
> *(Garbarini 2006, 163)*

We are that audience of strangers.

The origins of Holocaust testimony predate the Holocaust itself. First-person accounts of persecution in Nazi Germany and the concentration camp system were available in English as early as the mid-1930s. *The Yellow Spot: The Extermination of the Jews in Germany* (ANON 1936) detailed the impact of antisemitic laws on the Jews with 287 pages of evidence drawn from Nazi sources and first-person testimony. As early as 1933, an observer reported that

> in September 1933 a few S.S. men brought a Jewish businessman and his two sons into Sonnenburg camp . . . the news spread among the guards: "Three

new Jewish pigs! Let's finish them off!" . . . During that night all three . . . tried to commit suicide.

(264–266)

This lengthy eyewitness passage describes the treatment of the Jews to explain the atrocity that was unfolding across the Third Reich. Another unnamed source gave "testimony on oath" that described conditions in Dachau for Jewish prisoners in 1933, writing

> I have seen this with my own eyes—they had repeatedly to crawl through the puddles near the entrance until they had a crust of mud all over. Those who did not crawl sufficiently flat on the mud would be jumped on by S.S. men who would kick them from behind, and beat them with bayonets and whips.
>
> *(264)*

The publication of such wide-ranging and detailed accounts in English in 1936 demonstrates a growing general knowledge about the nature of the growing violence. The subtitle of the book, *The Extermination of the Jews of Germany*, makes clear that the authors believed the policies of the Third Reich were genocidal even if that term had yet to enter the lexicon. What sets titles like this apart is that most analyses of the Third Reich were written from the outside, looking in through political and foreign affairs. *The Yellow Spot* provides an inside-out perspective that only victims can give. To this day, pre-genocidal situations pay scant attention to the victims of exclusionary ideologies, even when these victims' experiences and fears are the best way to understand the nature of the ultimate intent. Victims feel the intent behind the policies affecting their lives long before symptoms are seen externally. The authors of *The Yellow Spot* drew the conclusion that Nazi ideology was exterminatory, because the evidence of its devastating impact on the Jews could lead to no other conclusion.

Konrad Heiden—like the authors of *The Yellow Spot*—"gives a clear and careful interpretation of the Nazi blueprint for ultimate extermination of the Jews of Germany" in his 1939 publication, *The New Inquisition* (Heiden 1939), which was written in response to the November Pogrom in Germany, November 9–10, 1938. He used, among other sources, lengthy passages of testimony from Jews who experienced the pogrom and its aftermath, including the incarceration of thousands of men and boys in concentration camps. In an attempt at objectivity, Heiden writes of his subjects, "they have been selected because the character and the very inflection of their authors reveal an attempt at presenting a description with as much calmness and objectivity as possible" (Heiden 1939, 96). Detailed descriptions by former Jewish prisoners about conditions in Dachau, Buchenwald, and Sachsenhausen include:

> Drill began the next day. It was tolerable for us younger men, many of us frontline veterans. Elderly men simply dropped and got kicks, blows from

rifle butts, slaps and punches in the face... But the worst was still to come...
We had to remain standing for nineteen hours in the camp.

(Heiden 1939, 99–100)

Before the outbreak of the Second World War, Heiden was certain that the authentic voice of the surviving victim of the concentration camp system should be heard. Accordingly, he uses first-person testimony extensively throughout his damning account.

In *I was Hitler's Prisoner*, Stefan Lorant (1935) shares his entire diary, written in 1933 while he was a political prisoner in "protective custody." Lorant, who was a publisher by profession and not of Jewish origin, managed to keep a detailed diary during his incarceration. His diary documented his daily experiences, in which he states, "I noted down everything I saw, heard and experienced" (vii). In the diary, he also expresses disappointment in his compatriots who were carrying out the atrocities stating, "they are living in a dream. Their awakening will be a terrible one" (viii). Like Lorant, several political prisoners who had been released from concentration camps in the 1930s also published prior to the outbreak of the Second World War, largely to warn the world of the perils of National Socialism.

Erika Mann—daughter of the 1929 Nobel laureate for literature Thomas Mann—had left Germany through a marriage of convenience to W.H. Auden in 1935 (Snyder 1976). As a German-Jewish refugee she drew on her first-hand knowledge about the Nazi education system of indoctrination and published *School for Barbarians, Education Under the Nazis* (Mann 1938). In the preface to her book, which details why she believes the Nazis will be successful in raising an entire generation of brainwashed Nazis, Erika Mann describes meeting a "Mrs. M." clandestinely in Switzerland. Mrs. M. and her husband Dr. M. were both "Aryans" who did not want to bring up their child in Nazi Germany, and were looking for a way to leave. In the book, we learn that Mann is trying to alleviate their predicament by passing on their papers. Mann describes the conversation the women had through an eight-page dialogue: "Of course, Dr, M. is a member of the party and the Reich Medical Association and the *fachschaft* (the Nazi professional union)" (Mann 1938, 12). She describes Mrs. M. as a "semi-official personage" who was the "perfect brood-mare, recommended by the state" (13). She had been photographed for the Board of Health calendar as the perfectly proportioned "Aryan" woman. "And now you want to leave, after all this time? Why?" Mann asks Mrs. M., who responds by showing her images of her fourteen-month-old son Franz. Mrs. M. is concerned that it is only a matter of time before Franz "comes home saluting with his hand up" and eventually will "denounce me" (15). Mrs. M. describes what happened to her friend's child Wolfgang, who was half-Jewish. Wolfgang looked forward to days when "the sun did not shine" so that he did not have to miss out on playing with the "Aryan" children outside. Determined to protect her child from Nazi propaganda, she asserts that he "must never pass on the way to school, those newspaper stands, where the *Stürmer* is up with all its obscenities" (Mann 1938, 17).

As the women part company, Mann agrees to pass Mrs. M.'s papers to people who might help. She then reports:

> Three weeks later I read that a physician and his wife have been arrested. Dr M. of Munich has been placed in the concentration camp Dachau; Mrs. M. in a Munich prison. . . . The son of this pair, Franz M. aged fourteen months—the paragraph concludes—has been committed to the State Children's Home. In this manner it is too be hoped, it may still be possible to make a good National Socialist out of the boy.
>
> *(Mann 1938, 18)*

Erika Mann was *not* reporting atrocity, nor describing the persecution that she and her family experienced prior to their departure from Germany. Instead, she was using her personal experience with Mrs. M. as a type of testimony. She provided an English-speaking audience with timely insights about the nature of the danger—a warning from a direct witness to Nazi persecution that was not understood or heeded in time. In the context of our memory-witness testimony construct, Erika turned memories that were immediate into a real-time form of witness testimony, using it in the present as a form of real-time advocacy.

Testimony is not confined to retrospective reporting. If victims were encountered more often in emerging violent societies and their testimonies listened to in advance of the worst excesses, the voice of the victim could help mitigate genocide. With all of the access we have to technology and social media, real-time testimony is no further advanced now than it was in the 1930s. There was no shortage of first-person reports, but no audience in policy circles prepared to listen or mount interventions. The early Chroniclers of Nazi atrocity, the harbingers of what was to come, delivered messages that fell on deaf ears.

Once the Second World War was underway and the German occupation of Europe solidified, the first personal accounts to document the experience of mass murder were written by victims who did not survive to testify to their experiences retrospectively (Flinker 1965; Kaplan 1973; Ringelblum 1974; Tory 1990; Adelson 1996), and those who wrote final letters to loved ones who were trapped under occupation or overseas (Dafni and Kleiman 1991). Those who wrote during the ordeal did so facing inevitable death. They had a front-seat view of the storm of violence swirling around them and had to summon the sheer will to survive every day, let alone document it. The maelstrom they lived everyday made it difficult to tell their stories. Fearing the worst, though the dire conclusion of the Holocaust was not yet known, they struggled to convey what they could see from the vantage point they occupied.

Chroniclers—diarists, historians, letter writers in the camps and ghettos—documented their own destruction. Virtually none of these works were published or distributed at the time. Despite their obscurity, Chroniclers give detailed insight into the lives and struggles of the Jews living under genocidal conditions. The highly organized work of the *Oneg Shabbat* (or *Oneg Shabbes*) Chroniclers (Lewin

1989) was written by individual diarists working as a group determined to tell their own story and that of the ghetto as a whole. The attempts of the *Sonderkommando* to document crimes made them all witnesses to their own suffering and death:

> We find chronicles . . . written by the sondercommandos [sic]. . . . While they were burning their families, their communities, they managed to keep diaries. I can tell you, with all the strength and faith that I have, that no book equals theirs.
>
> *(Elie Wiesel in Lewis 1984, 157)*

The traces left by Holocaust Chroniclers serve several roles. First, these physical testimonies—the paper on which they were written—are historical artefacts, and objects that need to be preserved and treasured. Second, the words Chroniclers wrote are memorials to the authors who wrote them, and to those to whom they refer therein. Virtually none of the authors have a final resting place or a *matzevah* (memorial stone). Just as a headstone attests to the life of an individual that bears their name, Chroniclers' writings attest to their life and their humanity. Third, they are acts of defiance, contravening the Nazi attempt to silence and eviscerate every trace of their existence in anonymity. Finally, these writings are subjects to be encountered in an ongoing dialogue about their present (now in the past). At the time, their own sense of selfhood was being subjected to atrocity, which they overcame by making themselves into the subject of their own version of history, rather than that of their oppressors. Writing was one of the few ways to counter the dehumanizing and destructive ideology that was pushing them into oblivion. Alexandra Garbarini observes that,

> the distinction that scholars draw between "selfhood" and "subjectivity" is not merely academic. Diarists' references over the course of the war to their sense of self indicate that they moved from feeling like unified individuals to being the subjects of forces that determined their experiences of subjectivity.
>
> *(Garbarini 2006, 164)*

The documents that the Chroniclers left behind are more than just observational reports. They are documents of personal struggle, in which the life and increasingly likely death of the individual are embodied through the traumatic events they convey and in the silence that ultimately follows. The crisis of witness during the period constrained the narrative in much the same way we have previously discussed. However, their central crisis was witnessing the death of individuals, families, community, and ultimately, one's self (Ezrahi 1980; Young 1993; Horowitz 1994).

Jack Kugelmass observed that "during the Holocaust, myth was transmogrified into history." That is, the "camps and related experiences of capture, imprisonment and escape were literal rather than symbolic descents into Hell" (Antze and Lambek 1996, 207). Kugelmass makes a compelling point, but era documentation made no attempt to create a mythic narrative, nor was the historical reality "a transmogrified myth." The circumstances of "Hell" were created by people, inflicted upon others, and had nothing to do with Hadean myths. The terror that befell them was a real-life nightmare in slow motion. Because we now know the outcome, we have the tendency to look back through time, knowing what would occur. What the Chroniclers provide us with is a real-time insight into the agony of not knowing where or when it would end. Because we know that Jews would ultimately die, we take little time to understand how they lived, but the Holocaust was a human experience to be lived through daily, until death or until atrocity finally ended.

Maurice Blanchot's concept of "the disaster" is a "deferred death" (1986, 146), in which the "writing of the disaster" represents the work of the Chronicler inscribing their own impending death. Among the many Chroniclers who documented and commented upon their own destruction during "the disaster" of the Holocaust, many chose to focus their narrative on seemingly everyday things. Adam Czerniaków's nine notebooks detail his daily activities as Chairman of the Jewish Council in Warsaw, and their contents at times appear mundane (Hilberg et al. 1979), even in the maelstrom of emotions they must have been going through. The Chroniclers "allow us to move from the broad and often overly simplified picture of the Holocaust and its victims to dozens of individual snapshots" (Garbarini 2006, 162) that detail their daily existence. Blanchot's observation that "were you in anguish you wouldn't be" (11) helps us understand the understatement of many accounts and is complemented by his comment that "they do not think of death, having no other relation but with death" (40). Together, these observations reveal that the inevitability of death meant there was less necessity to reflect upon its significance. The Chroniclers, with few exceptions, choose to focus on the plight—they did not have the luxury to reflect on its meaning.

The Chroniclers created a set of testimonial narratives that remain in tension with post-Holocaust survivor testimony. The former speaks from within the events, and *projects* the struggle of living through unimaginable circumstances onto a post-Holocaust world they never get to experience. The surviving victims, on the other hand, speak of the past and narrate the process of survival, *reflecting* on their death that might have been, but was not. The surviving victim, by dint of their continued existence after the Second World War, has the perspective of hindsight. Where the two modes of testimony intersect is through the mandate from the dead. Both the Chronicler and the surviving victim meet the demands of the dead by recording the dying of those who did not survive, which in the case of the Chroniclers includes themselves.

When the writing of the Chroniclers is encountered through a subject-to-subject, I-Thou relationship, a closer and more personal reading of their text becomes possible. Much as with any other testimony, the Chronicler is a subject, as well as a textual object. The diaries and chronicles of the period are by default historical artefacts, so the tendency to treat them as objects alone is natural. But more than any other genre of testimony, the words and experiences of the Chroniclers bring the reader closer to the lived experiences of those who did not survive. Unlike the surviving victims there is no remembering self that has the luxury of being able to reflect in sum, only an experiencing in the moment.

Janusz Korczak, Chaim Kaplan, and Emmanuel Ringelblum all had written journal entries just days before they were murdered, placing the reader at the nexus of the Holocaust as it unfolded. Czerniaków's notes end abruptly and without explanation on July 23, 1942—on the day the deportations to Treblinka began, as detailed in his entry the day before. His last paragraph gives a clue to the impossible task he faced: "It is 3 o'clock. So far 4,000 are ready to go. The orders are there must be 9,000 by 4 o'clock" (Hilberg et al. 1979, 385).

Mary Berg was the child of an American citizen, and therefore was given a level of protection in the Warsaw Ghetto: "The American flag on her lapel and another on the door of her apartment protected her like a talisman against the enemy" (Berg 1945, 9). She was one of the few diarists in the Warsaw Ghetto to survive along with her diary. At 17 years old she knew about Czerniaków's decision to end his own life as the order for the deportations began. She writes:

> July 24 1942.
> President Adam Czerniaków has committed suicide. He did it last night on July 23. He could not bear his terrible burden . . . His closest collaborators, who saw him shortly before his death, say that he displayed great courage and energy until the last moment.
> *(Berg 1945, 172)*

As they struggle with the reality of what is unfolding, these texts do not have an external persona, as encountered in post-Holocaust testimony. In their pages, there is only the individual, their observations, and their fate. As such, the Chroniclers who wrote from within their experience were narrators and documentarians of their own imminent deaths. On July 22, 1942, the day before his suicide, Czerniakow received news of the deportations, as he writes in his notebook:

> We were told that all Jews irrespective of sex and age, with certain exceptions, will be deported to the East. By 4.00 pm today a contingent of 6,000 people must be provided. . . . The most tragic dilemma is the children in the orphanages, etc.
> *(Hilberg et al. 1979, 384)*

Czerniaków did not leave his final words to his notebooks, but in two suicide notes. One was written to his wife, the other to the Jewish Council. Both were discovered by his personal assistant Leon Tyszka immediately after his death. In these notes, Czerniaków explains his decision to end his life his colleagues:

> Werthoff and his associates (the resettlement staff) came to see me and demanded that a transport of children be prepared for tomorrow. This

overfills my cup of bitterness for I cannot deliberately deliver defenseless children to death. I decided to leave. Do not treat this as an act of cowardice or an escape. I am powerless, my heart breaks with pain and sorrow, I cannot bear this any longer. My deed will show the truth to everyone and perhaps lead to the proper course of action. I realize that I leave you a heavy heritage.

(Lichten and Krzyżanowski 1984, 88)

The substance of the text is not about the act of dying, but of the conditions that led to his impossible dilemma. Even in this document of departure it is possible to approach the testament of Czerniaków with empathy. I included this passage about Czerniaków because when I re-read his notebooks and suicide notes with an I-Thou perspective I discovered that I was much more able to understand his decision than 25 years ago, when I had read the same words from an objective perspective. Seeing the text from the author's point of view changed the text itself. Czerniaków was no longer an object of history to me—he had become a subject facing an impossible struggle to save his people.

Educator and orphanage director Janusz Korczak briefly kept a diary (May–July 1942) while in the Warsaw Ghetto. Written in the orphanage he ran at 16 Sienna Street in the ghetto, it displays a style of writing characterized by a conspicuous silence about the events he was going through. Part diary, part social commentary, and part philosophical reflection, Korczak takes personal refuge from the ravages of the ghetto through his journal. For the avid historian eager to find day-by-day insight into the life and death of the ghetto, it is disappointingly clear that Korczak had no intention of providing an historical or testimonial account for the benefit of a later reader of history. Rather, he reflects on his past and the future, self-aware that "like digging a well, you do not start at the deepest end" (Korczak 1980, 106). The desperate time of trouble he was going through produced an incoherent and cynical narrative, providing insight into the confusion he faced during the last months of his life. Chilling metaphors infuse the text, drawn from what was happening around him:

> 1 August 1942: Whenever the stems of potato plants grew excessively, a heavy roller would be dragged over them to crush them so that the fruit in the ground could ripen better.
>
> *(Korczak 1980, 205)*

On the day he wrote this, the deportation of Warsaw's Jews had already been underway for ten days, yet he never mentions the deportations directly. Five days later he was to be deported to Treblinka, along with the 200 children from his orphanage. When he does refer to the deportations, it is indirectly. On one occasion he recalls a conversation he had with a third party, writing that, "you say you cannot go east—you will die there. So, choose something else. You are on your own, you must take the risk" (Korczak 1980, 201). The insight we gain through his journal is not about what happened, but what events meant in the life of the individual.

As such, raw data about the ghetto is only found through allusion and reflection, making Korczak difficult to decipher. One of his surviving disciples, Joseph Arnon, commented that his writings are "suffused with a surrealistic atmosphere" though combined with the "realistic regard for exactitude" (Arnon n.d., 3). Korczak's notes were written for his own benefit. In his diary we encounter him as an individual, the person cocooned within his narrative refuge. The silence he leaves is a part of who he is. His diary was never intended for an audience of strangers.

As with Korczak's diary, throughout the texts of the Chroniclers there are notable silences in which significant events are not reported but the pain they apparently cannot express still remains. The silences—in themselves expressions of trauma, despair, and confusion—are not textualized because, like the crisis of witness previously discussed, they resist language. There was a practical reason for silence, engendered by the consequences of being found, not to mention the psychological denial of the grim reality of the circumstances. Such witness narrative was documented in secrecy, creating an unseen and unheard narrative within the private world of the individual. Whatever the silence and secrecy that surrounded it, the creation of these documents was either an act of psychological resistance, personal survival, or an attempt to communicate to a future they would not occupy with historical foresight. Each of these possibilities resisted the intent of the German authorities to erase all traces of the Chroniclers through total silence, who unbeknown to them were secretly testifying to future generations.

The Diary of a Young Girl (Frank 1952) is poignant not because the content of Anne Frank describes the act of her death, but precisely because it *does not*. Even in hiding, Anne Frank was either unaware of the lethal threat or chose to ignore it. The air of normalcy she inscribed into her narrative during what the reader now knows was a time of unprecedented abnormality is compounded by the sometimes-precocious nature of her text. She had a clear sense of how abnormal her circumstances were, even though its end point was still unimaginable to her, unlike her counterpart Moshe Flinker (1965), who sensed an impending apocalyptic doom. The most significant part of Anne Frank's diary, for all its eloquence, is when the silence begins. The abrupt and final disruption to her text creates the silence in which the mandate—the imperative to listen—then speaks. As Blanchot put it, "when all is said, all that remains to be said is the disaster" (Blanchot 1986, 33).

S.L. Schneidrman, editor of Mary Berg's *Warsaw Ghetto* diary, appeared to know about the activity of the Chroniclers in 1945, long before evidence surfaced. He states in the preface to the diary's first edition:

> At some future time, we hope, chronicles hidden by writers in the ruins of the Warsaw ghetto will be discovered. Oher survivors may be found to give additional testimony to this heroic episode of the war- heroic not only because of the death of so many martyrs, but because of their stubborn will to live a dignified life against the odds.
>
> *(Berg 1945, 9)*

Victims created words that would not remain silent even after they themselves had been silenced. The Chroniclers may have hoped that their documents would be found and read, but there was no certainty that their documents would survive longer than their creators. At times, the diary is there for the diarist alone, as Chaim Kaplan makes clear. His motivation for keeping his diary can be seen in his entry for November 15, 1941, in which he states that "the important thing is that in keeping this diary I find spiritual rest" (Kaplan 1973, 16). Even so, Kaplan does not lose sight of his diary's historical significance; he asks, "if my life ends—what will become of my diary?" (400) That Kaplan intended his diary to survive him is evidenced by his attempt to smuggle his diary out of the ghetto to the safekeeping of Mr. Wojcek, a Polish acquaintance on the Aryan side of the ghetto wall. From his desire to preserve his words, we can intuit that Kaplan was consciously narrating the experience for a future reader. It *is* his testimony.

While Mordechai Kaplan actively gave voice to his experience, many silently awaited death. Still, I argue that the absence of their texts does not indicate an absence of their experience. Their silence—which we interpret as words left unspoken—are part of the landscape of testimony itself:

> The language of awaiting—perhaps it is silent, but it does not separate speaking and silence; it makes of silence already a kind of speaking; already it says in silence the speaking that silence is. For mortal silence does not keep still.
> (Blanchot 1986, 59)

The language of waiting for death is a mortal voicing of experience that is most often expressed through silence. For many there was no possibility of finding their voice in the debilitating circumstances, or the text was lost. Nevertheless, it is surprising how many in the ghettos and camps did manage to summon the strength to communicate beyond their own lifetime and secretly wrote what they could as they awaited their impending fate. Their actions—of writing and speaking—show a need to become witnesses to their own dying. The Chroniclers bring us into the world of those who were awaiting and witnessing their own deaths. The daily struggle to leave fragments of memory provides insight about the *experiencing self* rarely found, even in the most raw and unmediated perspectives of those who did survive. The Chroniclers never had the luxury of having a *remembering self*, to reflect "in sum." Their trajectory of Holocaust memory was to have the presence of mind to give from to witness in the moment to bring us closer to the intimacy of the experiencing self—memory, witness, and testimony—from within.

Historiographical Defiance

Jewish historian and Holocaust victim Simon Dubnow is reported to have "over and over again to his companions in the Riga ghetto: '*Yidden, shreibt un fershreibt*' (Jews, write it all down)" Wiesel 1986, n.p.; Gutman 1990, 408). Whatever

Dubnow actually said, which itself was never written down, he was known to be of the view that Jews should document experience to capture history-in-the-making. Elie Wiesel, who quoted Dubnow in his Nobel Peace Prize acceptance speech, observed that,

> his words were heeded. Overnight, countless victims become chroniclers and historians in the ghettos, even in the death camps. Even members of the *Sonderkommandos*, those inmates forced to burn their fellow inmates' corpses before being burned in turn, left behind extraordinary documents. To testify became an obsession. They left us poems and letters, diaries and fragments of novels, some known throughout the world, others still unpublished.
>
> *(Wiesel 1986, n.p.)*

He also expressed disappointment that post-war historians such as Hilberg, Dawidowicz, and Ainsztein could only write history with the benefit of hindsight. To Wiesel, they did not sufficiently appreciate the immediacy and insight of Dubnow's contribution, who wrote history in circumstances that the situation defied.

Heinrich Himmler is quoted as saying, of the mass murder of the Jews: "In our history, this is an unwritten and never-to-be-written page of glory" (Dawidowicz 1976, 134). Holocaust perpetrators were aware of their own historical destiny. Dubnow's demand to write it down was a form of historical resistance intended to overcome the historiographical distortion that would have taken place in the event of a German victory. Wiesel underscores the need for the writing of history by those who lived it:

> There are all the reasons in the world for us who were there not to believe in knowledge or words or history . . . But we do just the opposite.
>
> *(Wiesel 1985, 121)*

Elie Wiesel does not write that the victims "*did* just the opposite" but places the action in the ongoing present tense—"we *do* just the opposite." Dubnow was one of the few with the courage and foresight to do so at the time. His words—and the actions of all Chroniclers—directly defy the German plan to murder them and re-write or obscure the history of their deaths.

The duty to record in defiance of the Germans was understood by the Chroniclers. Abraham Lewin describes a meeting of the *Oneg Shabbat* team of historians meeting inside the Warsaw Ghetto:

> We gather every Sabbath, a group of activists in the Jewish community, to discuss our diaries and writings. We want our sufferings, these "birth-pangs of the Messiah," to be impressed upon the memories of future generations and the memory of the whole world.
>
> *(Lewin 1989, 120)*

Oneg Shabbat was the codename given to the team of professionals from a variety of walks of life who, while incarcerated in the Warsaw Ghetto, recorded what the community was going through. *Oneg Shabbat* literally means "rejoicing in the Sabbath" and is typical of gatherings to celebrate the Sabbath, for example those that take place on Friday evenings in Jewish homes. The codename and timing gave Ringelblum and his fellow archivists cover to gather, collate, and discuss their writings. The language Lewin uses to describe their work is striking. When he uses the terms "Sabbath," "activists," and "diaries and writings" in a single sentence, it indicates the highly charged and symbolic environment they had created for their documentary work. Recording what was happening to them in the ghetto took on sacral and apocalyptic resonance. It was a form of premeditated and *active* resistance.

Saturday was probably the most convenient day on which to work, but the substitution of Sabbath observance with recording the destruction of the Jews of Warsaw takes on its own sacral meaning in Lewin's reporting; the Sabbath became the day to fight back with words and historical data, so that Jews in the future could return to the Sabbath as it was meant to be. Similarly, referring to being part of a group of "activists" who were chronicling the events reinforced their act of defiance as an intentional attack upon the *intent* of the German occupiers to permanently silence them. They intended for their work to outlive them and the Nazi regime. Lewin's use of a terminology such as "the birth-pangs of the Messiah" symbolizes an apocalyptic era with indelible significance for the future of the whole world. His entry is tinged with overarching despondency, written in the hope that the work they were carrying out would one day contribute to the memory of future generations. Reading Lewin as I-Thou—taking the perspective of the subject—gives insight into the human sacrifice, hope, and grit that was needed to document atrocity in the face of overwhelming odds.

The defiant witnesses of the period were not limited to the ghettos, although the opportunity to write and to keep writings in the camps was severely restricted. The few texts that remain from within the camps represent a rare and important source of information. They too demonstrate defiance by virtue of their secrecy. By writing and then burying the texts to hide them, members of the *Sonderkommando* at Auschwitz-Birkenau hoped that, despite their impending deaths, their writing would preserve information about what had happened there. *Sonderkommando* chronicler Salmen Gradowski, while working in one of the crematoria at Birkenau, cites his motivation as wanting "to leave this as also other numerous notes as memento for the future world of peace, so that it may learn what happened here" (Bezwinska and Czech 1973, 77). His sense of duty to the "future world of peace" is accompanied by an explanation belying the guilt of working in the crematoria:

> We the "*Sonderkommando*", had long since wanted to put a stop to our horrible work . . . we had wanted to do great things . . . May the future judge us on the base of my notes.
>
> (Bezwinska and Czech 1973, 77)

The "great things" to which Gradowski alludes was the planned uprising, which occurred on October 7, 1944. The uprising was unsuccessful, but Gradowski is credited with being one of its five Polish-Jewish leaders (Piper and Swiebocka 1996, 233). His defiance extends not only to physically attacking his captors—he was a writer and a fighter—it also conveys the impossible predicament he faced to his later imagined readership. The importance of these manuscripts to this book is that they reveal just how much the victims understood the role of witness testimony, and the significance that the events they were experiencing would one day have on history. They correctly assumed that part of the intent of Auschwitz-Birkenau was to preclude eyewitness testimony. In response, they bravely acted to defy that intent and create a victim testimony voice from within.

The five manuscripts of the *Sonderkommando* were discovered around the crematoria at Auschwitz-Birkenau between 1945–1962, and another manuscript was handed to the museum at Oswiecim in 1970 (Bezwinska and Czech 1973). A manuscript of particular interest bore the initials J.A.R.A. and written by Salmen Gradowski was discovered near Crematorium III. The author's awareness of his task as a Chronicler of the camp is witnessed in his final statement:

> I ask [sic] to collect all my various relations and notes . . . they are to be found in various boxes and jars on the terrain of the yard of crematorium III . . . I ask to have them all put jointly in order and publish them under the title "Amidst a Nightmare of Crime."
>
> *(Bezwinska and Czech 1973, 122)*

The rest of the text was never found, but it was clear from the part of Gradowski's text that was recovered that these *Sonderkommando* writers viewed themselves as historians:

> I am writing these words in a moment of the greatest danger and excitement. May the future judge us on the base of my notes and may the world see in them, if only one drop, the minimum, of this tragic world amidst which we have lived.
>
> *September 6, 1944*
> *(Bezwinska and Czech 1973, 77)*

Gradowski's awareness that his text would be of value to future readers is demonstrated by how he takes into his personal confidence an anonymous future reader, whom he leads through the story of his experiences:

> You see, my friend, how people stand at the small window of the carriages as if rooted and look out into the free world [and] Have a look at this my friend. Here goes a group composed of over two hundred men selected from among that large human mass. . . . They are walking with their heads bowed low, full of heavy worry.
>
> *(Bezwinska and Czech 1973, 96)*

While the texts of the hidden *Sonderkommando* remain relatively obscure, the *Sonderkommando* and their activities have been given adequate attention in more recent historiographical examinations (Greif 2005). *Anatomy of the Auschwitz Death Camp* (Gutman and Berenbaum 1994) thoroughly describes the role and function of the *Sonderkommando*. This comprehensive text introduces the Auschwitz complex and salient points of its history, paying particular attention to the *Sonderkommando* texts and their role in the uprising of October 7, 1944. It also names prominent *Sonderkommando* who either wrote or survived to tell their own story (Piper and Swiebocka 1996). Still, we know relatively little about their role and activity outside of scholarly works on the death camps and the machinery of destruction. The texts of the *Sonderkommando* are not definitive historiographies, as they had little access to information and were writing in constrained circumstances. Due to the small numbers of *Sonderkommando* that survived there are also relatively few survivor narratives written by or about former *Sonderkommando*. The exception are works such as *The Holocaust Odyssey of Daniel Bennahmias, Sonderkommando* (Fromer 1993).

However, those who did write and hide their reports were engaged in documenting some of the most unique events from within the Holocaust experience. These too are acts of testimony. In this regard, the generally limited treatment and exposure these texts have had since their initial publication in the early 1970s is surprising. The *Sonderkommando* played a pivotal role in affirming the presence and the process of genocidal murder at Auschwitz-Birkenau.

Gradowski's manuscript, written under dangerous circumstances, switches between a personal encounter beckoning the reader to experience the camp, to a more detached narration in the first-person plural. He is the knowing interlocutor, ensuring that whoever reads his text will "see" what he saw and become its witness too. The purpose of his report is to tell what was happening to all Jews that arrived in the crematorium complex, and who died in his presence daily. He knew when he wrote his testimony that he too would become one of the dead. His text is more than that of a defiant historian—it is part of the mandate from the dead.

Whether the Chroniclers were recording for the purpose of history, documenting their private impressions, or writing to a loved one, their survival invites the attentive reader to encounter them where they were: in their personal struggle, with all of their fear, hope, confusion, sorrow, and human resilience. They invite the listener to experience an I-Thou encounter with them in the midst of hell.

References

Adelson, Alan, ed. 1996. *The Diary of David Sierakowiak: Five Notebooks from the Łódz Ghetto*, translated by Kamil Turowski. New York: Oxford University Press.

ANON. 1936. *The Yellow Spot: The Extermination of the Jews in Germany*. London: Victor Gollancz.

Antze, Paul, and Michael Lambek, eds. 1996. *Tense Past: Cultural Essays in Trauma and Memory.* New York: Routledge.
Arnon, Joseph. n.d. *Who Was Janusz Korczak?* Melbourne: Federation of Polish Jews, Australian Council.
Berg, Mary. 1945. *Warsaw Ghetto, a Diary by Mary Berg.* New York: L.B. Fischer.
Bezwinska, Jadwiga, and Danuta Czech, eds. 1973. *Amidst a Nightmare of Crime: Notes of Prisoners of Sonderkommando found at Auschwitz.* Oswiecim: Państwowe Museum.
Blanchot, Maurice. 1986. *The Writing of the Disaster.* Lincoln, NE: University of Nebraska Press.
Dafni, Reuven, and Yehudit Kleiman, eds. 1991. *Final Letters from Victims of the Holocaust.* New York: Paragon House.
Dawidowicz, Lucy S. 1976. *A Holocaust Reader.* New York: Berman House.
Ezrahi, Sidra Dekoven. 1980. *By Words Alone: The Holocaust in Literature.* Chicago, IL: University of Chicago Press.
Flinker, Moshe. 1965. *Young Moshe's Diary: The Spiritual Torment of a Jewish Boy in Nazi Europe.* Jerusalem: Yad Vashem.
Frank, Anne. 1952. *The Diary of a Young Girl.* New York: Bantam Books.
Fromer, Rebecca C. 1993. The *Holocaust Odyssey of Daniel Bennahmias, Sonderkommando.* Tuscaloosa, AL: The University of Alabama Press.
Garbarini, Alexandra. 2006. *Numbered Days: Diaries and the Holocaust.* New Haven, CT: Yale University Press.
Greif, Gideon. 2005. *We Wept without Tears.* New Haven, CT: Yale University Press.
Gutman, Israel. 1990. "Dubnow, Simon." In *Encyclopaedia of the Holocaust.* New York: Macmillan.
Gutman, Yisrael, and Michael Berenbaum, eds. 1994. *Anatomy of the Auschwitz Death Camp.* Bloomington, IN: Indiana University Press.
Heiden, Konrad. 1939. *The New Inquisition,* translated by Heinz Norden. New York: Modern Age Books.
Hilberg, Raul, Stanislaw Staron, and Josef Kermisz, eds. 1979. *The Warsaw Diary of Adam Czerniaków: Prelude to Doom.* New York: Stein and Day.
Horowitz, Sara. 1994. "Voices from the Killing Ground." In *Holocaust Remembrance: The Shapes of Memory,* edited by Geoffrey H. Hartman, 42–58. Oxford: Blackwell.
Kaplan, Chaim. 1973. *The Warsaw Diary of Chaim A. Kaplan.* Revised ed., edited by Abraham Katsh. New York: Collier Books.
Korczak, Janusz. 1980. *The Ghetto Years.* Tel Aviv: Ghetto Fighters' House.
Lewin, Abraham. 1989. *A Cup of Tears: A Diary of the Warsaw Ghetto,* edited by Antony Polonsky. Oxford: Basil Blackwell.
Lewis, Stephen. 1984. *Art Out of Agony: The Holocaust Theme in Literature, Sculpture and Film.* Montreal: CBC Enterprises.
Lichten, Joseph, and Ludwik Krzyżanowski. 1984. "Adam Czerniaków and His Times." *The Polish Review* 29, no. 1/2: 71–89. www.jstor.org/stable/25778050.
Lorant, Stefan. 1935. *I Was Hitler's Prisoner: Leaves from a Prison Diary.* Harmondsworth, Middlesex: Penguin Books Limited.
Mann, Eirka. 1938. *School for Barbarians: Education Under the Nazis.* New York: Modern Age Books.
Piper, Franciszek, and Teresa Swiebocka. 1996. *Auschwitz: Nazi Death Camp.* Owiecim: Auschwitz-Birkenau State Museum.
Ringelblum, Emmanuel. 1974. *Notes from the Warsaw Ghetto: The Journal of Emmanuel Ringelblum,* edited by J. Sloan. New York: Schocken Books.

Snyder, Louis L. 1976. *Encyclopedia of the Third Reich*. New York: McGraw-Hill.
Tory, Avraham. 1990. *Surviving the Holocaust: The Kovno Ghetto Diary*. Cambridge, MA: Harvard University Press.
Wiesel, Elie. 1985. "Knowing and Not Knowing: In the Footsteps of Shimon Dubnow." In *Against Silence: The Voice and Vision of Elie Wiesel*, edited by Irving Abrahamson. New York: Holocaust Library.
Wiesel, Elie. 1986. "Nobel Peace Prize Acceptance Speech." www.nobelprize.org/prizes/peace/1986/wiesel/lecture/. Accessed February 19, 2022.
Young, James Edward. 1993. *The Texture of Memory: Holocaust Memorials and Meaning*. New Haven, CT: Yale University Press.

6
THEY WERE NOT SILENCED

The Need to Talk

In December of 1947, just two-and-a-half years after the end of the Second World War, the first conference about documentation of the Holocaust was convened in Paris under the auspices of the Centre of Contemporary Jewish Documentation (CJDC) (*Centre de Documentation Juive Contemporaine*) with 32 delegates representing 13 nations attending (Jockusch 2012). Its successor organization in Paris, now known as the *Mémorial de la Shoah*, was founded by Isaac Schneersohn in his apartment on April 28, 1943 in Grenoble. Its aim was to create an archive to document the Holocaust in France, to "bear witness and demand justice" in real time (Mémorial de la Shoah n.d., para. 4). The CJDC, much like the *Oneg Shabbes* movement in the Warsaw Ghetto, was a documentary project set up as an act of resistance by those facing genocide to overcome the obfuscation and denial they predicted would follow. At the opening of the 1947 conference, Schneersohn reminded the delegates of "the difficult . . . and onerous task of unmasking and decrying . . . the true face of the monster of Nazism" by collecting, preserving, and organizing "materials of truth" as a testimony to the Jewish catastrophe (Jockusch 2012, 4). Schneersohn's rallying cry to document the devastation of European Jewry was part of an emerging movement.

That same year in July, Yad Vashem had held a conference in Jerusalem (Ceserani and Sundquist 2011, 18). A similar organized effort to that of the CJDC had been established in Munich Germany on November 28, 1945, which described itself as the Central Historical Commission and was founded by Israel Kaplan and Moshe Yosef Feigenbaum. Eventually there were 47 commissions and 60 staff collecting documentation, including 2,250 testimonies of surviving victims across Germany (Ceserani and Sundquist 2011, 16). In August 1944, five surviving victims including Philip Friedman had set up the Jewish Historical Commission (*Centralna*

Żdowska Komisja Historzcyna) in Lublin, Poland: "These survivors felt driven to document what had happened to their community" (Aleksiun 2008, 74).

At its height, the Jewish Historical Commission had 25 branches and 100 staff (Ceserani and Sundquist 2011, 16). In Hungary, The National Relief Committee for Deportees had 30 interviewers who collected 3,600 interviews with Jews who had been subjected to forced labor, ghettoization, and deportation (17). There were also documentation programs in Austria and Italy. Laura Jockusch summarizes why these endeavors succeeded in her extensive review of the immediate post-war historical commissions, writing that

> [their] claim to historical significance rests with their overt agenda as activists seeking to commemorate the dead; gain legal retribution, material restitution, and moral redress for survivors; promote political education to combat antisemitism and fascism and foster democratic values; and prepare a foundation for further historical scholarship.
>
> (Jockusch 2012, 186)

While these private commissions were being established, memoirs were printed, war crimes trials statements produced, *yizkor* books compiled, and oral history projects initiated. Memoirs were published by surviving victims in the immediate aftermath of the Holocaust, including *The Ghetto Fights* (Edelman 1946), *Bełzec* (Reder 1946), *Five Chimneys* (Lengyel 1947a), *Prisoners of Fear* (Lingens-Reiner 1948), *I was a Doctor in Auschwitz* (Perl 1948), and many other narrative non-fiction titles that predate the Eichmann Trial of 1961. At the same time David Boder of the Illinois Institute of Technology was carrying out his oral history project in 1946 (Boder 1949; Niewyk 1998; Rosen 2012). In addition to the testimonial narratives, surviving victims of the Holocaust were worked daily at Yad Vashem World Holocaust Memorial in Jerusalem, which was conceived in 1942 and founded formerly by the State of Israel in 1953 (Gutter 1993, seg. # 232) as well as actively leading Holocaust memorial reunions and services from the mid-1940s (Helfgott 2013, seg. # 423). But for some, the attempt to be a witness in public was re-traumatizing, as Pinchas Gutter relays: "The first time I spoke publicly was in 1967 on Yom Hashoa [sic] in East London [South Africa]. I was so upset and I began to have horrific nightmares. . . . I did not speak about my experiences till 1992."[1]

Much existing scholarship rebuts the myth that surviving victims were "silent" in the years immediately following the Holocaust (Niewyk 1998; Ceserani and Sundquist 2011; Rosen 2012; Jockusch 2012; Cohen 2014; Rossoliński-Liebe 2020a, 2020b). That said, after an initial flurry of testimony documentation and publications, there was a period in the 1950–1960s when publication was less prevalent. Despite their best efforts, witnesses were silenced by a world recovering from its own trauma and distracted by the Cold War. When Edith Birken began to write her personal testimony in 1948, she chose to write a novel rather than a testimonial memoir. In so doing, she was able to subsume her identity into that of principal character Judith. It is hard to imagine the fear that she still experienced just three years after the end of the genocidal violence. She had just turned 18, after surviving the Łódz ghetto and Auschwitz-Birkenau alone at just 15 years old. The trauma was still real to her.

She knew that her fictional character Judith would always be safe, unlike Edith (herself), who was still vulnerable. *Unshed Tears* (Hofmann 2001) details her experience of being deported from Prague to the Łódz ghetto; her unrequited love affair with an older man with whom she stayed after her family had died in the ghetto; her incarceration in Auschwitz; and her unsuccessful search for the man she loved after the war was over. Edith tried to find a publisher through a literary agent. Edith received complements about her writing style by a publisher in 1950, then he asked whether she could "choose a different topic, as no one is interested in the War anymore" (Hofmann 2001, n.p.).[2] Following countless rejections, Edith's manuscript lay silent in her closet for 50 years until she brought it to my attention in 2000, after which point it was published for the first time. Edith had not been silent. She had *been silenced*.

The lives of the surviving victims were bifurcated into two worlds: one that had existed before in which they had a clear identity, and the post-liberation environment, described by Pinchas Gutter as his "rebirth."[3] The two choices they had were either to recede into the past, or remain in the post-liberation world in the hopes of "psychic restoration and moral reconciliation, which may be simply impossible" (Rosenfeld 1988, 53). Testimony helps bridge the gap between the past and present. Survivors did not only need to survive so that they could tell their story; "they also needed to tell their story in order to survive" (Felman and Laub 1992, 78). There are those who say that a survivor who is not a witness is not a survivor (Brenner 1980, 2). However, such a definition imposes an obligation that cannot be fulfilled based on the debilitating trauma that the individual endured, for whom silence may be a necessary state of being.

Victoria Vincent explained that she disguised her identity during her career teaching French and Italian language students.[4] She told the French students that she was born in Brussels (where she had once lived as a child), and she told the Italian students that she was born in Milan (where she had lived as a teenager). She was able to disguise her identity this way until one of the students opted to study both French and Italian. At that point, she had to disclose to her students that she was born in Jerusalem and grew up in the two cities (Brussels and Milan) prior to her incarceration in Auschwitz—the one time she revealed her identity outside of her immediate family. The question that her revelation precipitated is not whether surviving victims can be classed as "survivors" if they do not witness, but rather *why* surviving victims were so reluctant to talk about or analyze their experiences in public, since they had not forgotten the experience itself. Primo Levi suggests that, notwithstanding the trauma, forgetting that which happened was not only impossible, but that such events instilled a heightened sense of personal memory:

> Of my two years outside the law I have not forgotten a single thing. Without any deliberate effort, memory continues to restore to me events, faces,

> words, sensations, as if at the time my mind had gone through a period of exalted receptivity, during which not a detail was lost.
>
> *(Levi 1986, 11)*

The period of "exalted receptivity" that Levi refers to implies that his confrontation with mass murder enhanced the detail of what he remembered above other memories. He is confident that his recounting will be detailed and accurate, although this contradicts his statement that over time memory becomes blurred or obfuscated (Levi 1988, 11). Still, he does broadly recognize that surviving victims do not have a problem with remembering the details of what happened to them, so why would they choose not to speak?

It has been commonly stated that surviving victims shared little about their experiences because they wished to remain silent (Ceserani and Sundquist 2011). Judith Hassan, a psychotherapist working almost exclusively with Holocaust surviving victims, observes that surviving victims indicated another reason for their long-term reticence to revisit their past. She notes that shortly after their liberation, surviving victims of the Holocaust reported that they "found a world unwilling to listen to the atrocity of what they had been through" (Hassan 1998, 103). Recognizing that the inability to speak about the past is a symptom of trauma, therapists like Hassan have worked with surviving victims later in their lives to find their own private voice through an ongoing healing process. Carol Kidron observes that such "pathological silence and redemption through verbal articulation has overshadowed the phenomenon of silent, material and visceral lived experience of genocidal pasts" (Kidron 2012, 7), in which,

> trauma discourse, in general, and Holocaust and genocide literature, in particular, have consistently mystified the trauma survivor's experience either as one of constant pathological failure to mourn, integrate and separate from what could not be fully owned or as one that has been therapeutically redeemed and disentangled from the oppressive past through testimonial voice and/or ritual commemoration.
>
> *(Kidron 2012, 17)*

Her point was that making memory public should not be seen as an outcome of personal trauma therapy, and public silence does not mean there is no private memory. She identifies that some memories of the past may not be articulated through words at all, such are those uncovered through material mnemonics. Kidron describes how a surviving victim kept a spoon they used in Auschwitz and used it to feed her children breakfast daily in her home. As a silent daily reminder of her past life, no words needed to be exchanged for the spoon to have mnemonic meaning.

Involuntary trauma-informed silence and the voluntary choice to not publicly give words to experiences is the right of every individual, but that is not the same as being silenced by a society unprepared to listen. Notwithstanding the willingness of a few publishers to print memoir literature in the 1930s, the broad lack of reception to eyewitness testimony began before the war period. Before the outbreak of hostilities in 1939, refugees from the Third Reich had arrived in Britain, particularly after the November Pogrom of 1938. This group of individuals had not experienced the worst excesses that were to follow. Nevertheless, they encountered a British public reluctant to recognize what they had been through, leaving them without ways to express their experiences. Lisa Vincent, a refugee who came to England at the unusually old age of 17 on one of the *Kindertransports* in March 1940,[5] said that at that time she would have liked to have talked to "anybody who would listen to it. But everybody was so busy with their own lives . . . actually, I wanted to talk to soldiers and to people I knew, but it just, it wasn't possible."[6]

With the onset of war and her peer still regarding her identity simply as German, Lisa chose to remain silent and assumed an identity focused on "making a living, wanting to be English [and] wanting to merge into life" in England. Her desire for normalcy was in tension with her lingering feelings about the war and the fate of her family and friends in Germany. She describes the reaction of her new English friends to her experience:

> I was told "Lisa, don't be so involved in your personal life with the past. You are in Britain now and this is a free country and you [should] start a new life." So, I can remember making attempts to talk about my life without being listened to, or anybody really wanting to hear.

Saul Friedlander, himself a refugee from Nazi Germany, observes that with notable exceptions—such as Theodore Adorno, Hannah Arendt, and Salo Baron—Jewish intellectuals, including refugees from Nazi Germany (Friedlander 1994, 259), wholly avoided confronting the Holocaust. A similar charge is levied by rescuer Charles Fawcett. As a young American courier operating between France and Spain, he escorted several prominent individuals and intellectuals to safety under the direction of his American colleague Varian Fry. Fawcett observes that,

> at that time some of them were not very courageous and some of them were not very co-operative, and some were very arrogant . . . Well, they were starting a new life. They probably had friends back there that they didn't want to have problems and something about the nature of people. I suppose you might say that once they're safe, once they're starting a new life, they forget a little bit the problems of other people and all.[7]

Fawcett stops short of saying that these Jewish refugees had a moral obligation to witness what they had been through. He does question the motive behind their silence, particularly as the majority were prominent individuals who were given refuge in America. These included Heinrich Mann, Marc Chagall, Hannah Arendt, and some 2000 other people who had been listed by the Americans as significant enough to warrant the rescue operation Fawcett had volunteered for

(McClafferty 2008). From their geographical viewpoint in occupied France, they would have known little of the death camps and *Einsatzgruppen* killings happening in Central and Eastern Europe. That said, they were fully aware of the imminent mortal danger posed to any individual who was Jewish living in German occupied territories and their proxies. Early refugees who had left Germany in the 1930s included Lion Feuchtwanger, Thomas Mann, Franz Werfel, and Vicki Baum. Like the *Kindertransport* youth, they had not been subjected to the atrocities of the German camp system. It has been noted that "many of the famous émigrés . . . did not view themselves as exiles *from* Germany, rather as immigrants *to* the United States" (Schenderlein 2016, 134), perhaps explaining why they were relatively silent. One notable exception was Nobel Prize-winning physicist Albert Einstein, who was an outspoken critic of the German authorities in the 1930s. In November 1938 shortly after the November Pogrom, the cover of *Colliers Magazine* bore the title "Einstein Comforts the Jews" in which he wrote a piece entitled, "Why do people hate the Jews?" In his article he explains the long history of antisemitism, although he avoids directly confronting the ongoing Nazi threat to the Jews or the November Pogrom itself (Einstein 1938; Rowe and Schulmann 2007).

The imposition of silence post-war did not mean that surviving witnesses did not talk about their experiences at all. Paul Oppenheimer claimed that he did not speak to anyone about his experiences until much later in his life, although his wife Corrine recalled that she learned about his wartime experiences from one of his friends who had heard him speak about it in a classroom presentation prior to their engagement in the early 1960s.[8] Paul also insisted that he didn't knowingly speak to his children about his experiences, but similarly his wife confirmed in conversation, "Paul does not accept that they knew anything about it, but they did. We never told them the whole story. They asked questions and we answered their questions."[9] Oppenheimer's denial of the existence of his past within the close circle of his friends and family is not due to a poor memory or a hidden present that he struggled with, but rather of how he understood his memory. His past experiences were a persistent memory that shaped his internal identity but had not found external expression except through fragments of disjointed information. He was interviewed by USC Shoah Foundation (Oppenheimer 1996b) and wrote his memoir (Oppenheimer 1996a). In these, he makes clear that he did not knowingly speak about his past and that anything he did have to say was informal storytelling or family banter with his brother and co-surviving victim, Rudi. There was a part of him that just wanted to be "more British than the British," and merge into society without being defined by Bergen-Belsen. At the point he decided to formally become a public witness, his testimony took on narrative form. He only took on a formal public speaking role at the point when he had established himself and become a public figure for a different reason (automotive engineering) and published his memoir, *From Belsen to Buckingham Palace* (Oppenheimer 1996a).

In his formal presentations later in life, Paul described how his interest in talking about his own experiences in Westerbork and Bergen-Belsen developed after being awarded Member of the Order of the British Empire for his contribution to industry. Upon receiving the award, journalists asked him about his prior life, and quickly discovered his experiences as a Jew living in Nazi Germany. He explained that their insistent curiosity gave him renewed confidence to speak about his past. Since he was retiring after a successful career, he decided to dedicate his time to sharing his experience for the benefit of education. His trajectory of his memory allowed him to move from a phase of self-imposed silence to the successful present he enjoyed, largely unconditioned by a society that was now eager to hear his personal history.

Writing a generation after the end of the Second World War, Elie Wiesel grapples with whether silence or speaking out is the better option for surviving victims. He writes that "had all of them remained mute, their accumulated silences would have become unbearable: the impact would have deafened the world." However, he concludes that "still the story had to be told" (Wiesel 1982, 9). His admission that silence is preferable, but speaking is necessary confirms a central tension within the narrative process. The unwillingness of society to listen may have imposed silence upon the surviving victims, but there was also safety in silence. Michael Lee reflects on how he coped with the emotional and psychological challenges imposed by surviving such traumatic events:

> Probably by forgetting. Erasing a lot of things from my mind . . . there are one or two people [I know personally] who cannot cope with this even today. I mean one particular friend cannot talk about it. Another friend when she sort of talks about it . . . She suffers from nerves.[10]

Michael was not referring to the slippage of memory in respect of historical details, but to the submission of memory to trauma-induced forgetfulness. "Forgetting" was his coping strategy to hide the traumatic events of the past behind a veneer of normality. Lee is explaining what it means to live with an internalized dual existence in with a hidden present in which, "I don't live with it. It lives with me" (Langer 1991, 23). Whatever the surviving victims were coping with internally, their external story was largely about social shame in an ongoing conditioned present. Saul Friedlander reflects upon "the shame of telling a story that must appear unbelievable, and was, in my case, entirely out of tune with surrounding society" (Friedlander 1994, 259). Expressing how out of tune her experience was with her own family, surviving victim Kitty Hart-Moxon relates her arrival in England:

> My Uncle was waiting at Dover. The moment we got into his car he staggered us by saying firmly: "Before we go off to Birmingham there's one thing I must make quite clear. On no account are you to talk about any of the things that have happened to you. Not in my house. I don't want my girls upset. And I don't want to know."
>
> (Hart-Moxon 1997, 1)

Her disappointment is further illustrated when describing her first Christmas holiday season in England in 1946. Due to a series of circumstances, she spent three nights sleeping in Birmingham's Snow Hill railway station. She states that "what hurt most was that nobody, anywhere, cared about me" (Hart-Moxon 1997, 3). When I asked her recently about her motivation to break her silence, in 1961 she responded,

> I think everyone had the same obvious thoughts that whoever survives must tell the world, and I think many people were disappointed to learn that actually the 'world didn't really care' or perhaps it all took a long time to sink in what went on- especially [with] Auschwitz being behind the Iron Curtain.[11]

The silencing imposed by society was not always put as bluntly as Kitty heard it from her Uncle as "I don't want to know." Still, their underlying feeling was that society indeed did not want to know.

For some surviving victims, the pain of survival and its associated trauma turned to despair. While suicides among surviving victims have been demonstrated to be lower than peers who had earlier escaped persecution (Lurie et al. 2021), the incidence of those who survived atrocity only to terminate their own lives is striking. Elie Wiesel reflects that the decision of surviving victims such as Tadeusz Borowski, Joseph Wulf, Paul Celan, and Benno Werzberg to kill themselves was carrying out the task the killers did not have time to complete (Wiesel 1979, 219). He lays no blame on the surviving victims themselves, save for being "too numb, too weak and perhaps too timid to object" (220). Richard Glazar, who survived Treblinka, was an interview subject in *Shoah* (Lanzmann 1985) and published his memoir *Trap with a Green Fence* in 1995 (Glazar 1995), which is when I became acquainted with him. He struck me as a quiet, poised, and thoughtful man with a unique understanding of the death camp system. Two years later he committed suicide the day after his wife died of natural causes. Alvin Rosenfeld questions whether the suicide of surviving victims is "an inevitable outcome of their work, a final and desperate conclusion to it?" (Rosenfeld 1988, 18). The trauma, which was a constituent part of their self-inflicted deaths, not only claims the life of the individual. It brings a final silence to their past.

Surviving victims speak *for* someone, but also *to* someone (Des Pres 1976). Even with the wall of silence that greeted them, surviving victims wished to convey their past to anyone who would listen. As they began to communicate through personal eyewitness testimony, the onus was on them to find the strength to speak into the void of non-recognition they faced. As much as they may have wished to dialogue with society, until the 1960s, while some surviving victims had begun public witness along their trajectory of memory, there was not so much as an I-It relationship with society. Surviving victims were so absent from public discourse that they were not yet objects of history, let alone a subject of public discourse. That transition would take time.

The Awakening

In *The Awakening*, a short descriptive piece on post-Holocaust survival, Aharon Appelfeld describes his experience following the Second World War as "a desire to forget, to bury the bitter memories in the bedrock of the soul" (Hartman 1994, 152). He goes on to call his burying of memory "a marvellous oblivion . . . a latent protest against suffering and fate." What followed a few years later was a shocking emergence from that profound experience of forgetfulness. He felt exiled from himself by "unknown enemies" who had forbidden contact with even his own secrets. Appelfeld's description mirrors the experiences of many surviving victims who slowly emerged to tell their stories and those of the victims who did not survive. Describing the emergence of surviving victims from the confusion of silence, Appelfeld outlines his concept of "awakening":

> Just as our oblivion was profound, so our awakening from it was shocking . . . Only now did it seem clear for the first time to what vast distances we had exiled ourselves, as though we had been imprisoned all those years by unknown enemies, who had forbidden us any contacts with our own secrets.
> *(Appelfeld in Hartman 1994, 152)*

Elie Wiesel states that he imposed a ten-year silence upon himself before he began to write, to convey and analyze his experience (Wiesel 1996, 151).[12] Wiesel states in one interview that, "these survivors have waited thirty years to speak, because they did not want other people to cry" (Lewis 1984). Nevertheless, he writes that the surviving victims ultimately had to testify because "they were placed in the position of having to defend their [honor] and that of the dead" (Wiesel 1979, 243). There may well be much to be admired in the "determined stance of voicelessness" (Brenner 1980, 2). But such voicelessness is not total silence, rather the restraint of narrative until such time as its voicing becomes possible. The witness needs first to be willing and psychologically, linguistically, and cognitively able to present a coherent narrative. And if the intended audience is not willing to hear or unable to comprehend the gravity of the subject, then such voicing will not penetrate their conscience or that of wider society. There is also an element of fear for the witness. What would the consequence of rejection be? Would it mean that "the dead" are insulted as well as being forgotten? Would such rejection further obscure memory?

Aharon Appelfeld describes the past awakening an entire generation after the Holocaust, but there is significant evidence that surviving victims were willing to speak about their experiences in its immediate aftermath. Olga Lengyel, Ella Lingens-Reiner, and Gisella Perl wrote and published their experiences of the camps within three years of the liberation. Edith Birken and Thomas Geve are surviving victims who wrote manuscripts, but either did not seek or could not find publishers at the time.

Olga Lengyel's opening words of *Five Chimneys* are: "Mea culpa, my fault, mea maxima culpa!" (Lengyel 1947a, 1). In print by 1947, Lengyel's account is among the first post-war accounts to be published in English. Her line demonstrates the clear sense of guilt she feels at having survived. Her parents, husband, and two children did not. Lengyel relates her arrival at Auschwitz-Birkenau. In a bid to save her mother and elder son from work, she asks that they might be sent "left" during the selection which determined life and death. "How should I have known. I had spared them from hard work, but I had condemned [them] to death" (Lengyel 1947a, 16). She states that while it was impossible to react any differently, the feeling "persists that I could have, I might have, saved them" (1). Lawrence Langer describes Lengyel's situation as an example of a "choiceless choice" (Langer 1982, 72) not of her own making. Realizing this, Lengyel's opening remarks are also a challenge to her readership. Her personal feelings of guilt are balanced by her outrage at what happened to and around her during her year of incarceration at Auschwitz-Birkenau:

> I know that the world must share the guilt collectively. The Germans sinned grievously, but so did the rest of the nations, if only through refusing to believe and to toil day and night to save the wretched and dispossessed by every possible means.
>
> *(Lengyel 1947a, 210)*

In a later 1947 edition of Lengyel's account—the title of which had changed from *Five Chimneys* to *I survived Hitler's Ovens*—the publishers use a quote from Nobel Prize-winning physicist Albert Einstein, who wrote a letter to her: "You have done real service by letting the ones who are silent and most forgotten speak" (Lengyel 1947b, n.p.). Einstein's comment on Lengyel's text highlights the desire of many surviving victims to bear witness for the dead.

Ella Lingens-Reiner is less certain of her role as a witness because she was an Austrian incarcerated for resisting the Germans. Throughout *Prisoners of Fear* she protests the moral degradation of the German and Austrian masters of the camp. While Lingens-Reiner can come across as being detached and analytic, Terence Des Pres feels the rage ringing through every page (Des Pres 1976, 155). Lingens-Reiner does not explicitly describe her as driven to anger, but she does describe several distinct motivations for her to write, particularly her perspective as a non-Jewish survivor. She indicates that after the liberation, accounts of the camps started to emerge. While she states that "this is what we wanted to be known," she also recognized "something was missing and therefore something was wrong" (Lingens-Reiner 1948, ix). What was missing was, in her words, "the background which made [it] possible . . . if only sensational horrors were registered, there was a danger that . . . the whole system would not be understood." By "the whole system," she was referring to the daily events of concentration camp life, which she attempted to analyze in *Prisoners of Fear*. Her approach in her book is to undertake a dispassionate examination, which she indicates would be a "final condemnation," as it would contain the "half tones" in addition to the "black or white of extremes" (ix). While Lingens-Reiner evaluates her own actions with caution, Terrence Des

Pres characterizes Lingens-Reiner's moral choices as courageous and intelligent (Des Pres 1976, 152), a perspective that is not supported by Lawrence Langer, who believed her analysis of camp life was pointless because the frames of morality experienced in everyday life did not apply in the camps (Langer 1982, 83). I fundamentally disagree with Langer on this point, as Lingens-Reiner gives a unique and insightful breakdown of prisoner categories and how their lives differed, while living under the same roof. My own personal conversations with Ella Lingens-Reiner in Austria in 1999 revealed a woman of considerable commitment to memory. She had continued her own trajectory of memory long after her book was published presiding for many years as president of the Osterreichische Lagergemeinschaft Auschwitz (Austrian Auschwitz Camp Survivors Association). She also testified at the first Auschwitz Trial of 1964, and was made Righteous Among the Nations by Yad Vashem in 1980 (Yad Vashem n.d.).

Another non-Jew who published immediately after the liberation of the camps was David Rousset, formerly a professor of philosophy in Paris prior to the war. During the Nazi occupation of France, Rousset distributed information obtained from Allied sources. He was eventually arrested and spent the last 16 months of the war in Buchenwald Concentration Camp. Rousset's response to his incarceration was almost immediate. He completed his unfinished manuscript of *L'Univers Concentrationnaire*[13] in August 1945. His motivation to narrate his experience appears to be both political and humanitarian. Describing the concentration camp world as a "dead star loaded with corpses" (Rousset 1951, 109), he indicates the lasting impact he expects the history of the Holocaust to have on human activity in the universe as a whole. "The existence of the camps is a warning . . . under a new guise similar effects may appear tomorrow," he states, and warns that "it is the gangrene of a whole economic and social system" (Rousset 1951, 112). As a French resistance worker, Rousset's analysis is partly an act of verbal political revenge. Although he viewed Germany's occupation of Europe to be in keeping with its prior history, he also recognized that other nations might equally carry out such act, universalizing the behavior.

If a few surviving victims were able to react to their survival with such immediacy, the question remains why most did not. Charlotte Delbo's anthology *Auschwitz et Après* (Auschwitz and After) expresses the split between Auschwitz and post-liberation life in its title. In conversation after the war, she related that a fellow deportee said to her, "I died in Auschwitz, but no one knows it" (Delbo 1995, 267). In fact, Delbo once attended a commemoration at which her own name was read out among those who died in the camps. In response, she raised her hand and murmured, "*non monsieur: prèsente*" (xviii).[14] In the life after her experience of Auschwitz, which Delbo describes as "floating in a present of reality" (237), she describes the disorientation of the survival experience. Delbo links her physical experience of being stripped naked at Auschwitz, metaphysically stripping her of memory and her identity. "Memory peels off like tatters, tatters of burned skin" (255), she states to describe the debilitating nature of such an experience on the human conscience.

Delbo describes her disorientation after her return, in which she "was no longer open to imagination or explanation" (239). Attempting to explain the phenomenon, she states: "This was the part of me that died in Auschwitz." Delbo's struggle with the "useless knowledge" of Auschwitz is balanced by her insistence on witnessing to it. Hence, she only begins to witness her own experience at the point at which what she describes as her "insoluble dilemma" (239) starts to find a solution in her own mind. Until that point, she was unable to rediscover her own memory and identity, and hence did not relate her experience. The "awakening" in Delbo's experience relied on being able to give voice to her memory. However, she states her own skepticism about the possibility of such wounds ever fully healing:

> There is no wound that will not heal
> I told myself that day
> And still repeat it from time to time
> But not enough to believe it.
> (Delbo 1995, 241)

The hope of healing or—perhaps more significantly—the hope that such memories would dissipate may be reason for the surviving victim to share the experience with a wider audience, even if memories are doomed to remain disrupted narratives (Langer 1991, xi). Whatever the form in which they are shared, their disruptive nature continues to create confusion and despair in the lives of surviving victims.

The disruptive nature of the events can be seen in the psychological upheaval that surviving victims experienced. Following the initial period of post-war disinterest in the experiences of surviving victims, mental health professionals noticed pathologies associated with experiences of concentration camp survival. In 1964, psychiatrist and German-Jewish refugee William Niederland published a paper on his observations of surviving victims. He saw that a series of symptoms—including anxiety, fear of persecution, depression, nightmares, certain psychosomatic disorders, social withdrawal fatigue, and hypochondria—led to what he called "Survivor Syndrome" (Niederland 1964; Hass 1995, 2). In the same year, Holocaust survivor and psychiatrist Leo Eitinger published a book, *Concentration Camp Survivors in Norway and Israel*, in which he outlined a similar pathology that leaves the surviving victim unable "to live in a normal way" (Eitinger 1964, 190). The belief that surviving victims were displaying pathological tendencies continued throughout the 1960s in articles submitted to mental health journals (Kren 1989).[15] However, not all mental health professionals saw this development as being as valuable for the patient as for the field.

Judith Hassan was critical of the medical and psychoanalytic field, which compounded the silence that already existed. She states that surviving victims were viewed as "sick, suffering from syndromes and symptoms . . . the survivor was seen as having been damaged irreparably by his experience, and conveyed a very pessimistic view concerning healing" (Hassan 1998, 104). The link between trauma and the voicing of testimony is pertinent to surviving witnesses. I have had extensive conversations with surviving victim Pinchas Gutter about his mental health treatments. During the late 1940s, he was seen by a child psychologist in London, and in late 1960s South Africa he underwent a series of psychological treatments. He relays how difficult it was to find psychiatric and psychological support, given the source of his trauma. In the 1950s and 1960s, mental health professionals were still not professionally prepared to comprehend the extent of the experience of surviving victims.[16]

Today, surviving victims of the Holocaust have become a psychological phenomenon. A literature has rapidly emerged that examines the psychological effects of survival during and after the event. Many surviving victims, such as those that attended by way the *Shalvata* counseling center in London,[17] may only ever have put words to their experiences within the confines of their counseling sessions. The research of mental health professionals has also shed light on the reciprocal benefits between the surviving victim and society at large that testimony provides. By way of example, psychologist Boaz Kahana, and sociologists Zev Harel and Eva Kahana, in an extensive survey of surviving victims, note "their triumph in coping . . . bears ultimate witness to the triumph of human endurance" (Kahana et al. 1989, 97–212). They found that some 92% of their sample indicated that their Holocaust experiences had adversely affected their emotional wellbeing (204), but that further indicators demonstrated that "survivors have an often-unheralded potential to find meaning in adversity and to share this meaning with others" (210). The sharing they discovered in surviving victims included lecturing, involvement in memorial centers, contributions to literature, creating music and art about the Holocaust, as well as involvement in a range of charitable activities (Kahana et al. 1989, 208), and this study was carried out before the proliferation of testimony-sharing projects.

Aaron Hass (1995) claims that "survivors *did*. They tried not to think or feel" (103). But there is an absence of evidence to demonstrate that surviving victims did things in an attempt *not* to think and feel. Their thinking and feeling remained limited to the privacy of their own homes. In many cases, it was confined to their own inner self, as introversion was part of their continuing act of survival (Kidron 2012). The "doing" to which Hass refers—and which presumably relates to them rebuilding their lives—other commentators regard as a suppression of traumatic memories. Work, raising families, and referring only generally to their experiences enabled them to wait for retirement, loss of health, or bereavement to trigger a re-emergence of more public display of memories (Hassan 1998, 104). Hass identifies a trajectory of memory and testimony rooted in mental health and wellbeing, stating that after,

> an initial period of emotional numbing or exhilaration, followed by a time of denial and the repression of disturbing feelings and memories as he focuses on rebuilding a life and family, and culminating in a stage characterized by the integration of past experiences and reactions as she reminisces and speaks more of her locked-away memories.
>
> *(Hass 1995, 104)*[18]

Hass asserts that survivors are individual people, not a phenomenon, which fits with the I–Thou concept of de-objectifying the surviving victim. He frames the psychology of "the survivor" as a singular pathological phenomena bound to be unsuccessful, as all survivors present their own unique pathology. However, identifying underlying patterns does seem valuable. George Steiner talks of a "predictable interval" between the event and its awakening through questions from the generation that did not experience it directly (Lewis 1984, 49). For all those who were later awakened, there were many for whom there was no time to wait. To understand the trajectory of memory and the role that testimony has played from the outset, we will turn to specific examples of early contributors to memory, witness, and testimony prior to the coming out of testimony at the Eichmann Trial in 1961.

No Traveler Returns

Dr. Henry Shoskes (Henryk Szoszkes) occupies two positions. He is an eyewitness to his own experiences, and an author of the experiences of others. Shoskes was in Warsaw in 1939 when the Germans invaded. After Warsaw fell on September 27, 1939, he and other members of the Executive Committee of the Jewish Community were considered to represent the Jewish community to the Germans starting on October 3, 1939 (Shoskes 1945, 5). For the following six weeks Shoskes was at the center of the rapidly deteriorating relationships with members of the SS, who were establishing policy in respect of the Jews in a country that had three million Jews and in the city of Warsaw, which had twice as many Jews as the entire country of Germany. Shoskes dealt directly with a SS Captain named Batz[19] and *Gruppenführer* Mende, and saw first-hand how quickly their brutality would take hold. In mid-November, Shoskes secured false papers for himself, his wife, and son, and left Poland with the memories of his short but powerful interactions with the Nazis hierarchy fresh in his mind.[20]

By early 1940, Shoskes was in New York and signed a sworn affidavit on January 14 describing what he had witnessed in Warsaw (Apenszlak 1943, 26). The contents of his affidavit were widely distributed in the April 5, 1940 *Jewish Telegraphic Agency* (1940) and published in the *Contemporary Jewish Record*. Shoskes was shortly thereafter appointed to be the National Field Director of the American Federation for Polish Jews (*Jewish Telegraphic Agency* 1940), the organization that published one of the first accounts of the Holocaust in Poland, *The Black Book of Polish Jewry* (Apenszlak 1943). He tried to sound the alarm about what was happening in Warsaw on several occasions, including writing in the *New York Times* on March 1, 1942 that Jewish "extinction [is] feared by Jews in Poland." He published an article about the Warsaw Ghetto Uprising in the Yiddish newspaper *Jewish Journal* in September 1943, and in 1944 published an account in Yiddish and English titled, *Pages of a Ghetto-Diary: An Authentic Document on the Tragic Events in Poland, from the Invasion to the Battle of the Warsaw-Ghetto* (Shoskes 1944).

In mid-August of 1944, Dr. Henry Shoskes spoke with war correspondent and author Curt Riess about the Warsaw Ghetto and particularly the Uprising. Riess had already published several mainstream books about the Third Reich by 1944. Shoskes went to Riess for help publishing his story of the Warsaw Ghetto Uprising. Riess admits that he "was not too eager to hear about it," making it clear that at the time there was daily news of "so many other performances of heroism" (Shoskes 1945, viii). Riess reports that Shoskes would "not take no for an answer" and so he listened to his detailed descriptions of life in the Warsaw Ghetto and of the Uprising. Riess, who was a student of the Third Reich, reveals that "the vast majority of what I have learned . . . I have never read." He clarifies that Shoskes' sense of detail and nuance resulted in "not merely one story; there were dozens, hundreds of stories" (ix). Due to his prominent position in Warsaw prior to the war, Shoskes knew who rose into the ghetto leadership after he fled Warsaw "for the greater part of his life."[21] In particular, he had close ties to the ghetto historians Dr. Mayer Balaban and his student Dr. Emmanuel Ringelblum, who were both concerned with chronicling the ghetto.

Riess was intrigued by Shoskes' verbal account, as he provided a nuanced unfolding of the history in such a way that "not all Germans were black villains; not all Jews were angels" (ix). Riess makes clear that there were many sources behind Shoskes' account, including Polish underground papers and witness statements. They confirm that Shoskes had been in Warsaw in person to witness "with his own eyes many of the things he told me about" (x). Riess' instinct on hearing Shoskes' report first-hand was that Shoskes should write an eyewitness testimony of his time in the ghetto in the first person. Shoskes refused to do so, stating, "I don't think this is the right approach. Leave me out of it. The story I have to tell is so much bigger than I am" (x). The two men agreed to collaborate on writing a book in which they played distinct roles. Over a period of many days and weeks Shoskes described in detail his accounts of the ghetto, supported by the documents and witness statements he had in his possession (xii). Riess listened and wrote up the stories that Shoskes relayed, creating a single narrative from the many independent elements he heard. What emerged was a narrative history compiled from many sources.

The resulting book was not written as a report, but as narrative storytelling that includes lengthy passages of dialogue between protagonists in the ghetto. Shoskes remains the author of the work, but never writes in the first person, including the episodes he describes in the first chapter of *No Traveler Returns*, which reflect his own direct experiences with the German authorities during the six weeks he was in Warsaw as a liaison. Henry Shoskes went to great length to remove himself from the history. *The Black Book of Polish Jews* describes an exchange between SS *Grupenfeuhrer* Wende and Shoskes about establishing two brothels in Warsaw, one for German officers and one for rank-and-file troops. The intent of the Nazis was to force Jewish girls into sexual slavery with the help of the Jewish Council (Apenszlak 1943, 25–27). The book also reports that Captain Batz relayed the same message to Jewish Community Council treasurer Adam Czerniaków, who would later be appointed President of the *Judenrat* (27).

Describing the exact same events in *No Traveler Returns*, Shoskes details the order given by the Germans but does not include his own conversation with Wende and his strong resistance to the order. He chose to only report the conversation between Batz and Czerniaków. Shoskes takes an *anti-testimony* role, even though his reporting is based on his own eyewitness experience. An anti-testimony role is also evident in his writing about a meeting at the office of the German command. Shoskes relays to his readers that Captain Batz had informed the Jewish Council on November 7, 1939 that they had three days to form the Warsaw Ghetto and move the Jewish population there (Shoskes 1945, 13). The Jewish Council were deeply concerned that it was an unachievable and undesirable goal, and presented their case to General von Neumann-Neurode (15). The meeting is described in detail, as is a subsequent meeting wherein General Neumann chastised Captain Batz in his office while the delegation from the Jewish Council waited outside. Shoskes writes: "through the closed doors the Jews in the outer room could hear the General's excited voice talking rapidly and shouting the word 'preposterous' at regular intervals" (16). These are details that *only* an eyewitness could know. He also describes how, after Czerniaków returned the following day to meet Batz, "a few of the other members walked with him," which implies that Shoskes was among them. Using descriptions only an eyewitness could report, he relays that after a successful meeting in which Batz "postponed indefinitely" the formation of the Warsaw Ghetto, the delegation walked back to the Jewish Community building three miles away:

> It was still raining hard when the Jews made their way from the Gestapo headquarters back to the Community Building. . . . They walked like men in a trance; they were happy beyond words.
>
> *(Shoskes 1945, 18)*

The disassociated voice of the narrator throughout the book is likely the decision of Curt Riess, who appears to have ghost written much of it from Shoskes' accounts and other documentary sources. The writing partnership was based on creating a narrative that would make the history of the ghetto mainstream. Upon hearing the detailed retelling of the ghetto history from Shoskes, Riess understood that the struggle for survival and the ultimate resistance mounted in the Warsaw Ghetto was an epic history that had yet to be told:

> I slowly began to realize that there were not really so many accounts, that there was just one account, one story, a running story, strange, singular, which had never happened before anywhere in the world and which therefore, had never been told . . . It was a new story and still an old one.
>
> *(Shoskes 1945, xi)*

The transformation of Riess, who was at first reluctant to hear about the tragedies of the Jews in the Warsaw Ghetto, occurred during personal conversation. The outcome of the meeting as reported is an I-Thou relationship, wherein Riess listens to Shoskes based on *being witness* to the events. This changes how he views the events, turning it from a harrowing story of untold misery to an epic fight "comparable only to the greatest exhibitions of courage in history" (Shoskes 1945, ix). Shoskes and Riess take up different roles in a subject-subject dialogue, as interlocutors of that history. The text that emerges is compelling and highly readable. But despite their best effort to bring the reader closer to the history, they created a non-testimonial (and therefore objectified) account. It is difficult to determine how Shoskes and Riess arrived at detailed conversational passages that neither of them was there for. Shoskes has admitted he drew on other published sources including *The Black Book of Polish Jewry*. For example, both books relay how the Germans described the ghetto. *The Black Book* provides almost a full page of verbatim text drawn from German journalist Walter Doering and published in the August 1941 edition of *Die Deutsche Polizei*, as documentary proof of how Germans described the ghetto (Apenszlak 1943, 44–45). In *No Travel Returns*, Shoskes quotes from the same passage, but refers to the author as "German newsmen." He quotes from a passage that appears in both books:

> "Here a couple of Jewesses haggled over a few potatoes. There some Jewish boys fought over a cigarette butt. Wherever we looked, we saw miserable fallen creatures."
>
> And the final word of these gentlemen of the press: "Let them choke in their filth . . . it's alright with us."
>
> (Shoskes 1945, 35)

In *The Black Book* the exact same passage appears differently:

> "There a couple of Jewesses are scolding over a few potatoes; here some Jew-boys fight over a cigarette butt. Wherever we looked, we saw miserable, fallen creatures." His final sentence is: "*Moegen Sie in Ihrem Dreck erstickedn! Uns soll es recht sein*" [Let them choke in their filth! It's all right with us].
>
> (Apenszlak 1943, 45)

The two books take different perspectives on how to communicate facts. *The Black Book* provides documentary sources and relays specifications. To describe the death camp of Treblinka, it details precise information about the size of the camp, how the gas chambers were laid out, and the method of gassing, then citing where it obtained its information:

> According to the report of an eyewitness the interior of the building is as follows: a corridor 3 meters wide runs through the middle; there are five chambers on each side; the height of each chamber is about 2 meters, the area about 35 square meters. The execution chambers are without windows, but they have doors opening on the corridor and a type of valve on the outside walls.
>
> (Apenszlak 1943, 142)

Shoskes also relies on the testimony of an unnamed eyewitness. Unlike the witness in *The Black Book*, he was not able to get into the inside of the killing apparatus. Instead Shoskes tells the story of the young man's journey to and from Treblinka, who was greeted by "Welcome to Treblinka," and he told them to "take it easy" (Shoskes 1945, 154). He realized the implication of the two groups of one hundred Jews each that had been taken to bathe before him did not come out of the "so called bathhouses . . . the young worker understood." When he returned to the trucks "he crawled into one of them and hid himself under the clothes" (154). The witness gets out of the truck when it stops about 20 miles from Treblinka and is taken in by local Poles. In the ten days that follow, he learns from the Poles, who have further information about what happened at the death camp. On returning to Warsaw, the young man is believed to have climbed back into the Warsaw Ghetto and reported what he had learned to Michael Klepisz, a former associate of Shoskes. Unlike *The Black Book*, which has the intent of providing the specifications of mass murder gleaned from testimony, *No Traveler Returns* uses the eyewitness as the means to explain how the Warsaw Ghetto population received reliable information about mass murder at Treblinka.

Shoskes did not use testimony as his genre even though he was a surviving victim. Nevertheless, he reported the facts of his experience and incorporated the testimony of others and ensured it was published in English on a mainstream imprint, *prior* to the end of the Second World War.

Dos Polyishe Yidntum

Mark Turkov had much in common with Henry Shoskes. He was a Polish Jew who loved to write, travel, and write about traveling. Like Shoskes, he authored stories in newspaper articles in Polish and Yiddish, such as his 1937 "*Ruzvelts amerike, ayndurkn fun a rayze iber di fareynikte shtatn*" (Roosevelt's America, impressions from a trip to the United States). Unlike Shoskes, Turkov emigrated to Argentina shortly before the German invasion and did not directly encounter persecution. Later, like Shoskes, he became a representative of Polish Jewry in the diaspora, becoming President of the South American Federation of Polish Jews. But it was in his capacity as a publisher that he contributed to documenting the life and death of Polish Jewry. A series of 175 books and pamphlets were published by *Dos Polyishe Yidntum* (Polish Jewry) between 1946–1966 in response to the destruction of Polish Jewry.

Jan Schwarz highlights that the introduction of the first book in the series, *Malke ovshyani dertseylt: Kronik fun undzer tsayt* (Malke Tells her Tale: Chronicle of our Time, 1946), makes clear that the "memoirs of famous Jewish personalities whose life and creativity were an intrinsic part of Polish Jewry will be the main themes of the books and pamphlets" (Schwarz 2008, 174). Whoever the "famous Jewish personalities" were intended to be, the first author "Malke" was a surviving victim and eyewitness to the Holocaust. The third book in the series, simply titled *Treblinke* (Treblinka) and published in 1946, is a 172-page report on the death camp. By 1947, *Dos Polyishe Yidntum* books were being distributed in 22 countries, many of them survivor narratives. Over 250,000 copies were in print by 1954. Many of the earlier volumes were testimonies, such as Mordechai Strilger's Yiddish memoirs, which describe his experiences in death camps and work factories. These books include 1947's *Maydanek* (Majdanek), about his incarceration in the death camp and concentration camp near Lublin, 1948's *In di Fabrykn von Toyt* (In the Factories of Death), and the book *Verk "ce"* (Workshop "c") about the HASAG ammunition factory at Skarżysko-Kamiena. This series was where prominent surviving victims were published for the first time, including Eliezer Wiesel, whose *Un di velt hot geshvign* (And the World was Silent) was published in 1956 (Wiesel 1956). Two years later, an abridged version appeared under the authorship of Elie Wiesel in French as *La Nuit* (1958a) and in English as *Night* (1958b).

Henry Shoskes also published as a part of the *Dos Polyishe Yidntum* series. He had returned to Poland for the first time after the Holocaust in 1946, a trip he details in *Polyn-1946: Ayndruken fun a rayze* (Impressions from a Journey) (Shoskes 1946). Later he published *A velt vos iz farbay: Kaptilen zichroynes* (A World that is Over: Chapters of Memoirs) (1949). While not strictly testimony memoirs, he uses his credentials as a surviving victim to provide a view into the destruction of Polish Jewry only possible from a survivor's perspective. The books in the series were "personal accounts, written in an intimate manner" and were "perfectly attuned to the needs of the Yiddish readership" (Schwarz 2008, 184). The personal nature of the text may raise concerns about their underlying historicity, but Jan Schwarz quotes Yiddish scholar Max Weinreich as saying of the series, "despite the fact that the books are not scientific writing, but information, we can rest assured that the scholar must turn to the books in researching the years of destruction" (Mitlberg 1947, 14).[22] In so saying, Weinreich identifies two significant points that relate to testimony as a whole. The first is that whatever its documentary deficiencies, testimony is a valuable source for historians. Second, the burden is not on the witness to prove the validity of their statement, but upon the professional historian to determine what is of value to historiography.

Weinreich unwittingly takes the position of co-subject in relation to the surviving victim. He does not objectify the text, and instead subjectifies the person who wrote the text. Subjectification is at the heart of the I-Thou relationship; the text (object) may or may not be accurate, but the person behind the text (subject) is communicating about the nature of the events. In that single sentence, Weinreich makes the point that historical precision is not the principal purpose—respecting the source is.

The use of the Yiddish language was not coincidental in the I-Thou encounter in *Dos Polyishe Yidntum* series, as it was the mother tongue of most authors. The readership needed to understand the experiences of their own fellow European Jews. In recent years, the Holocaust has been internationalized, published in many languages and made widely available in English. In the 1940s the Holocaust—then known as *der dritte hurban* (the third destruction) in Yiddish—was still being lived *within* the Jewish community. The subject-subject conversation was that of Jews giving witness to other Jews who had their own experiences of loss and suffering. When publishing in Yiddish there was no I-It, because *der dritte hurban* affected anyone who spoke the Yiddish language in a deeply personal and subjective manner. They were in conversation with the text because its contents profoundly impacted the life and identity of Yiddish speakers worldwide.

At the same time the *Dos Polyishe Yidntum* series of was being produced by the Yiddish-speaking Polish *landsmannschaft* in Argentina, there was feverish activity across many *landsmannschaft* to create *Yizcher Bicher*—memorial books, typically anglicized as "Yizkor Books." The purpose of Yizkor Books was to document and memorialize the communities that were destroyed and were primarily authored by Holocaust survivors in their countries of resettlement (Amir and Horowitz 2008). The number of Yizkor Books produced is unknown but could be as many as 1,200 (Schwarz 2008, 187). Each is considered a form of *matsyeve* (gravestone), because for those who survived and had no physical place to visit their loved ones, the Yizkor Books were a memorial representation of their loss (Amir and Horowitz 2008). Yizkor Books are neither testimony nor historiography, although they contribute to both. They are narrative memorials inscribed with the memory of people, places, organizations, traditions, photos, and maps, creating a permanent record of who the victims were and what their lives were like. The Yizkor Books documented lost communities and acted as a form of healing. Yosef Hayim Yerushalmi, in discussing modern dilemma of Jewish memory, describes the relationship between memory and healing within the modern Jewish tradition. He suggests that "Jewish memory cannot be healed unless the group itself finds healing, unless its wholeness is restored" (1982, 94).

Writers of the Yizkor Books were aware of the value of first-person testimony within the genre. Some authors explicitly state that eyewitness accounts are the best defense against future catastrophes (Amir and Horowitz 2008, 43). The problem was that, despite the proliferation of Yiddish literature related to the destruction of European Jewry, it was not representative of a wider interest within the Jewish world about Yiddish culture (Schwarz 2005) or history—including the history of the Holocaust. Notwithstanding the number of publications and the wide circulation of the Yiddish testimonies and Yizkor Books, most were never translated into English. The vast majority remain in their original languages to this day, as Shmulewitz observed in the early 1970s, "it is regrettable that this literature has not yet been translated from Yiddish into English. . . . This material surely constitutes one of the most important sources for the history of the destructiveness of the Second World War" (1973, 49). A study of 348 Yizkor Books in the New York Public library shows that 60% are in Hebrew, 24% Yiddish, 10% English, 2% Hungarian, and 4% written in other languages (Amir and Horowitz 2008, 45). The inaccessibility of the 175 published texts in *Dos Polyishe Yidntum* series continues to this day, Eli Wiesel's breakout book *Night* being a rare exception. The memoirs published by Mordechai Strigler were only recently published in German in 2017. Schwarz's analysis of the indifference of the wider Jewish community, let alone the wider world, still holds true:

> The issue was not that of 'silence' of the surviving remnants of Polish Jewry; rather, it was the contemporary world's ignorance of and, in the case of Israeli

and American Jewry, indifference and even hostility to the existence of a vibrant Yiddish cultural world in their midst.

(Schwarz 2008, 187)

That said, the surviving victims had not given up on their own sacred mission to tell the world, whether in Yiddish or other languages, as Strigler eloquently relays in *Maydenek*:

> What has been written about our historical period has only touched the surface. The essence has not yet been disclosed. And something must be told about the internal pain, the deep psychological struggle, and essential human sadness of a generation's terrifying death.
>
> *(Strigler 1947, 8)*

The Yiddish and Hebrew writers of the 1940s and 1950s amassed hundreds of thousands of pages of still-to-be-fully-understood pages of testimony that were not published for the wider world when they were originally written. For some their trajectory of Holocaust memory through testimony began and ended then. Their words remain worthy of widespread translation and dissemination, to help us get closer to those who were courageous enough to write in the immediate aftermath of the destruction. More than any others, these testimonial texts bring us into the world of the subject, who expressed their being, unmediated, through their mother tongue in the immediate aftermath. They were not attempting to "tell the world" through its most prolific language, in translation, but to express themselves in their own words, within their own community, to restore missing fragments of their lost families, countering the oblivion of forgetfulness.

To Tell the World

British Army Chaplain Leslie Hardman reports that on his arrival at Bergen-Belsen in April 1945, survivors of the camps—many of whom were still dying every day—asked him to take on the mantle of reporting what he had seen. He said,

> they kept on saying to me "tell the world, tell the world." They must know what happened. "Did you know it? Did you know what was happening to us? You won't be able to save us all, but those who can talk and will survive they must present all our suffering to the world." I know it's 50-odd years now, but nonetheless as long as you have it in writing, in books, in tapes and so on, so the generation of another 50 years' time will see what's happened.[23]

In the immediate post-war period, the context in which surviving victims were speaking changed dramatically from the circumstances in which the wartime chroniclers had been writing. Surviving victims weren't potential victims of imminent death but living remnants of their victimhood. They no longer faced a struggle to survive the daily threat of life living under Nazi oppression, and instead entered a struggle to survive their own survival. Alvin Rosenfeld observes that this remnant took "on an aspect of life-after-death . . . a life afflicted by guilt, absurdity and irreality" (Rosenfeld 1988, 53). Whether in fact life was absurd and irreal, and whether such absurdity prevented them from telling their story, it is true that most surviving victims either chose not to speak or could not.

Speaking was just not a priority over physical recovery, searching for family, finding a new home, grieving lost loved ones, and coping with the mental trauma of years of fear and abuse. It is remarkable that any found the strength to narrate their history, some as early as the end of the war. In many written and oral accounts, surviving victims reported that they were motivated to survive the Holocaust because they wished to become a witness. Waldemar Ginsburg says unequivocally that "the whole reason to survive was to bear witness."[24] It seems easy for surviving victims to give a rationale for their survival and to state after the fact that Jews wanted to live to tell the world. "The belief that they had been spared not by accident but in order to bear witness surely helped them cope with loss and feelings of guilt" (Jockusch 2012, 186), which was a remarkable intellectual and spiritual effort. If Ginsburg is to be believed, witness was the very purpose of their survival.

There is third-party evidence documented shortly after the Holocaust that appears to confirm the need to witness. Ella Lingens-Reiner reported in 1948 that "one of the sources of our determination to resist was the thought that we had to survive in order to tell the world what we had seen and endured" (Lingens-Reiner 1948, ix). This general statement about the will of all inmates to live to tell the story is more clearly defined when she later describes the attitudes of Jewish inmates of Auschwitz. In her writing, she divides them into two categories: those who were struggling to survive as individuals, and those who saw it as a struggle for the survival of the Jewish people. She observes that as the likelihood of survival among Jews was "twice as improbable as the survival of a non-Jewish prisoner . . . the Jewish prisoner's whole mind was filled with the struggle for mere personal existence" (Lingens-Reiner 1948, 118), which suggests that daily needs came before everything.

She contrasts those who saw existence through the immediate and urgent need for personal survival with the motivations of those who saw their fate in the context of the long arm of Jewish history. Describing the experience of mass murder under the Nazis as "the cruelest and most extensive persecution of their race in history," she notes that "the number of Jews who saw it there and then as the catastrophe of their race was relatively small" (Lingens-Reiner 1948, 118). Those who did recognize the Holocaust as a Jewish catastrophe, she writes, "no longer fought for their personal survival, but for the rescue of small groups of Jews who would have the mission of creating another, happier Jewish nation" (118). Lingens-Reiner's observation that some Jews victimized by the Nazis saw purpose beyond mere physical survival sheds light on the desire to "tell the world." Underlying it was a reason more compelling than writing a personal memoir. It was seen as the collective responsibility of Jews to speak for those who could no longer speak for themselves and to warn the world.

In *Five Chimneys*, Olga Lengyel relates an episode at Auschwitz-Birkenau in which the motivation to gather information to tell the wider world was an act of resistance. Her personal morale had reached a low point; she describes herself as having a "serious nervous depression" and being "mentally ripe for suicide" (Lengyel 1947a, 67). As a medical orderly, she had a position of privilege in Auschwitz-Birkenau, but realized that her parents and children had been murdered and the likelihood of seeing her husband again was remote. An elderly Frenchman whom she simply calls "L" (66) (members of the resistance never knew each other's names) invited her to become a vehicle of communication for the camp resistance. Her two functions within the camp resistance would be to verbally distribute information about events outside the camp as she received it, and to relay written communications between members of the resistance. In weighing the consequences of being caught, she considered the possibility of torture and death. Her contact in the resistance urged her to "observe everything that goes on here . . . when the war is over the World must know about this. It must know the truth" (68). In response to the challenge from "L," Lengyel writes, "from that moment on I had a new reason for living." The activities in which she engaged thereafter gave her access to information in the camp, which she did not witness personally, yet utilizes in her own testimony. She notes that "through these new contacts, I finally learned the minutest detail about the gas chambers and crematories" (68). Lengyel summarizes how she overcame her suicidal state of mind:

> I had then two reasons to live: one to work with the resistance movement and help as long as I could stand upon my feet; two to dream and pray for the day to come when I could go free and tell the world. "This is what I saw with my own eyes. It must never be allowed to happen again."
>
> *(Lengyel 1947a, 76)*

Gisella Perl was a doctor in Auschwitz-Birkenau. In her 1948 memoir *I was a Doctor in Auschwitz*, she outlines her motivation for writing:

> I offer this book as a monument commemorating the years 1940–45, commemorating Nazi bestiality, Nazi sadism, Nazi inhumanity and the death of their six million innocent Jewish victims.
>
> *(Perl 1948, x)*

Perl focuses her witness on exposing the perpetrators, although she indicates that each episode she recalls about the victims is "but a stone in that monument which will stand forever to remind the world of this shameful phase of history and to ask of it vigilance" (Perl 1948, 11). She makes no direct mention of the will to survive and suggests there was a certain inevitability about events.

Another Jewish woman doctor, Lucie Adelsberger, in *Auschwitz: A Doctor's Story*, writing much later than Perl, asks more demanding questions of her ordeal:

"what was the purpose of this hell we were living in if no one survived to open the book someday and tell the story of the victims of Auschwitz?" (Adelsberger 1997, 54). Adelsberger does not offer an answer to this rhetorical question, as the text of her book grapples with the answer. What she does not fully identify is that "the purpose of this hell" was to ensure the impossibility of such a "book" ever being written. Both Perl and Adelsberger identify with the purpose of surviving to bear witness almost 50 years apart.

To narrow the motivations behind surviving victims' narratives to a single purpose would undermine its complexity. Instead, several plausible interconnected motivations may exist, as described by Sidra DeKoven Ezrahi:

> For most of these writers, the compulsion to record their experiences could be attributed to several motives: the desire for some sort of revenge; the need to bear witness "so that the world will know what we suffered"; the desire to commemorate the dead; the impulse to absolve oneself or one's companions of aspirations of passivity or complicity; the sense of mission to warn humanity of its capacity for genocide. But the real victory which these documents attested was the very fact of personal survival.
>
> (Ezrahi 1980, 21)

Personal survival played a significant role in what was witnessed, but the fact that they had survived was itself insufficient motivation to write. For some authors, the higher purpose of bearing witness or surviving as a people may have motivated them. Others desired to provide information in a timely manner. In May 1946, Kitty Hart-Moxon, then the 18-year-old Kitty Felix, wrote a report for a Quaker relief team at the Bergen-Belsen Displaced Person's Camp. In the unpublished 3,000-word document, Felix writes "chapters" about the history and procedures of Auschwitz-Birkenau. The document has the following structure:

Title	Short Report on C. Camp 'Auschwitz-Birkenau'.
I	No title (overview of creation of camp and the numbering system)
II	Reception—(details the selection process on the ramp at Birkenau) The Arrangements in crematorium 1 and 2 in year 1942, 3 and 4 in 1943/4
III	The camp Brzezinki called 'Canada'
IV	THE LIFE IN "F.K.L." CAMP A&B. (WOMEN'S CAMP)
—	No title (details living conditions 1941–1943)
—	No title (details living conditions after mid-1943)
—	Experiments:- Blood taking
5.	No title (details food rations)
—	The Disinfections in November
X	Untitled final paragraph[25]

Kitty wrote this document in basic English—an interesting choice at the time, as English was her third language after Polish and German. She clearly wanted to communicate the information she had directly to the English-speaking staff of the relief organization rather than through translation from Polish. The structure of her report is significant for three reasons. First, she writes exclusively about Auschwitz-Birkenau, although she was in several camps at different points during her ordeal. Second, she shows awareness of historical details that might only come to light in the public domain later, following analysis of historical and statistical data (Czech 1989; Gutman and Berenbaum 1994; Piper and Swiebocka 1996). Third, her report contains no personal details or experiences. She wrote the text as a statement of facts, as if prepared for evidence in trial. The only indication that her motivation to write is driven by the *fact* of her survival appears in the opening words. She opens the document with the following statement:

> Described for a Relief Worker from RS/100/FRS—The first Relief Team in the liberated C.C. Belsen. I wish other people all over the world could have some understanding for these facts!
> From my own experience
> Ex-prisoner 39934
>
> (Felix 1946, n.p.)

An unidentified relief worker was responsible for safekeeping the document for 51 years before returning the document to the author in 1997. Felix's introductory comment indicates her desire for her witness statement to reach as many people as possible. Her insistence that the reader know that it came from her own experience is undersigned with her Auschwitz concentration camp number, 39934. The self-awareness she demonstrates about her identity as a surviving victim of Auschwitz is an early indication that survival itself would come to play a major role in motivating surviving victims to tell their story. Throughout her 1946 statement, Felix demonstrates a keen interest in historical data. For example, she spends considerable time attempting to present and clarify numbers and statistics. She confirms that "transports arrived about 2–3 a day and 2 or 1 at night." She notes in the same section I that "10% of people from each transport were brought to the camps, the rest had to go to the gas chambers," a statistic that is close to that verified through historical research, particularly in the latter stages of the gassing process.[26] She also goes to considerable length to explain how the numbering system worked in the camp and that "the tatoo (sic) numbers in the women's camp in the end of 1943 reached about 68,000—alive people always less than 20,000," indicating that at least 48,000 women had died or been moved to other concentration camps.[27] How she is able to provide such detailed statistical information so soon after the end of the war is unclear, as there is little doubt that an internee in her situation did not have access to accurate numbers during the Holocaust. It was clearly of importance to illustrate the scale of the Holocaust using whatever statistical data she could find.

Philip Maisel is a surviving victim of the Holocaust and an oral historian who has documented over 1,000 audio-visual interviews of surviving victims and witnesses to the Holocaust who settled in Melbourne, Australia. The Maisel testimonies—their methodology and scope—merit much deeper study than can be covered in this volume. Maisel himself related in a 2021 interview that I conducted with him for USC Shaoh Foundation's Visual History Archive remotely, that he had made a commitment to "tell the world" *during* his incarceration. The Philip Maisel Holocaust Collection at the Jewish Holocaust Centre in Melbourne was his way of fulfilling that promise. Maisel helped found the collection in 1992 at the age of 70. During an interview he stated:

PHILIP: When I was in the camp, I promised my friends, to promise one another, that if we survive, even for five minutes, we will tell the world what happened during the Holocaust.
STEPHEN: . . . can you confirm to me that those conversations actually did take place in the camps at the time?
PHILIP: Yes. Yes. You see the chance of survival at certain times was very Shoah small and it is human nature that you want people to know what actually happened during the Holocaust. There was a danger that nobody survives the Holocaust . . . I want to survive in order to tell people what happened.
STEPHEN: Do you see your work today as a fulfillment of that promise?
PHILIP: To a very great extent yes.

(Maisel 2021)

Anita Lasker-Wallfisch counters the idea that victims of the camps were thinking of the future, writing that "we were only occupied with the question of whether we would survive the next day. We did not have the luxury of reflecting on the future."[28] Pinchas Gutter was also not aware of any such imperative to "tell the world." He states that, "I never heard anyone saying that. What was often said was that with G-d's help we will outlive Hitler."[29] Jews had experienced suffering before. They had outlived Haman, who attempted to murder Jews, as described in the *Megillah* (book of Esther). They also outlasted Chmielnicki, who murdered tens of thousands of Jews across Europe (1648–1658). So their determination demonstrated that "humans can transcend tragedy and rebuild their lives, developing new ways to express their heritage and culture" (Hanover and Helmreich 1983, xiv–xv). As Yosef Hayim Yerushalmi observed, "even the most terrible events are somehow less terrifying when viewed within old patterns rather than within their bewildering specificity" (1982, 36). He delivers a message of Jewish continuity. History has shown that even in the most violent of times, Jews will survive.

Eva Schloss was also not aware of such imperative to "tell the world." "I never heard anyone talking about this . . . after we came back from Auschwitz the general mood was, never again" and that "survivors didn't speak about their experiences for around 40 years."[30] Eva is a prolific author and speaker who travels the globe to share her testimony. As the stepdaughter of Otto Frank,[31] Eva witnessed the process he went through to publish his deceased daughter's diary, which became a worldwide phenomenon. Eva waited until 1988 to publish her first book, *Eva's Story* (Schloss and Kent 1988).

Sonia Warshawski told me in personal conversation that, much like the hanging scene in Auschwitz described by Victoria Ancona-Vincent (1995), in Majdanek two women were about to be hanged. She reported:

> We had to stand in a square. We saw the rope. I saw two SS women and two girls of about my age. As the rope was put around their neck they said, "Never forget! Take revenge!"
>
> I asked her what that meant by "revenge." She replied, "there were many who were dying. They knew they were dying." Their last words were, "if you make it, tell the world what happened."[32]

That's How It Was

Dutch survivor of Westerbork, Bergen-Belsen Erich Marx, wrote his testimony *So war es: Ein Bericht über Westerbork und Bergen-Belsen* (That's How It Was: A Report on Westerbork and Bergen-Belsen) (Marx 2015, 72–101) in September of 1945. His 28-page summary of life in the two camps details information such how many inmates stayed in each barracks in Westerbork (1000), how many showers were in the bath house (40), and detailed camp intake and deportation procedures. Marx also provides insight into "exchange Jews," the approximately 3,000 mainly Dutch Jews with foreign connections such as a passport or significant business dealings abroad. They were sent to Bergen-Belsen as a future exchange for German prisoners of War (Oppenheimer 1996a, 84). Marx describes in detail the conditions and daily routines at Belsen. The level of specificity includes a roll call inventory from the exchange camp in Belsen on January 20, 1945, which he had managed to retain because he had worked as a camp clerk. It details those who were not fit for work by category or barracks (see Figure 7.4). It provides the startling information that of

TABLE 6.1 Roll call information detailing non-workers in Bergen-Belsen, January 20, 1945. This table was reconstructed from data recalled and documented by Erich Marx (Marx 2015, 83). The miscalculations in the table were part of the original document reconstructed by Marx

20 January 1945	Men	Women	Children	Total
Sick Barracks	158	78	15	249
Invalids Barracks	35	50		85
Other Invalids	85	150		235
Elderly Barracks	120	128		248
Medical Register	29	1		30
Mobile Sick	277	403	151	831
Pregnant women		12		12
Mothers with Children under 3			552	552
Diamond Group Ascher	10	14		24
Total	714	902	718	2,334

the 3,000 Dutch Jews held for exchange, 2,334 were unfit for work by that point, and that the group included 12 pregnant women and 552 mothers with children under three years old.

Marx rarely writes in the first-person singular, instead relaying facts using the third person plural, particularly when describing the conditions his fellow Jews experienced in the camps. He also rarely provides information that only an insider to the camp workings could know, such as the arrival of a little-known sub-group of Jewish prisoners from North Africa who were deported to Bergen-Belsen via Italy (Marx 2015, 85). Marx expresses concern about how they were affected by the cold and informs his readers that they were not compliant with the German authorities, and sabotaged the SS rules with "new tricks" (86) to avoid work. Marx provides statistical data on the influx of new inmates from other camps and shows the rapid expansion of the prisoner population through the autumn of 1944 and early 1945. He "saw all incoming and outgoing transports" and "had to 'log' the daily death lists and to put together the 'statistics' for Berlin" (87). These responsibilities not only gave him unprecedented access to information, it also meant he could move freely around the camp and could glean insights into the inner workings of the system.

His account is neatly divided into sections to allow readers to navigate topics such as "The Composition of the Camp," "Hygiene Conditions of the Camp," "News Service," "Activity," and "Punishments." In addition to gathering the information contained in his report, Marx was also able to use his access for humanitarian purposes by keeping "family members in touch with each other" (87) and being able to "pocket some food here and there" (87). He did these actions with full knowledge that he would have been "severely punished" had he been caught. He also provides insights into the knowledge and culpability of the camp guards, who were close enough to him that he could see them operating the camp. He describes as them as "SS bruisers" and specifically states that camp *Kommandant* Josef Kramer "permitted and encouraged all of these terrible things. He identifies more than a dozen specific perpetrators by name for specific acts, and whom he collectively describes as the dregs of mankind." By contrast, in a section entitled "The White Raven," Marx describes the actions of SS man Uscha Müller who, as head of the "grocery store," made sandwiches for prisoners. Marx calculates that "hundreds of prisoners owe their lives to him" (96).

For all his interest in providing accurate information, Marx's account has significant errors. For example, he uses the date "1948" at one point when describing the deportations (77), which is clearly a typographical error, as he was writing in 1945. His description of "the American troops who arrived on 12 April to liberate the camp" was not a typographical error, but an historical inaccuracy. It is worth noting by that point Marx was no longer at Belsen, as he had been evacuated on one of three trains that left the camp before the British arrived. So his reference to "American troops" is likely a general description of the Allied Forces. Later he uses the term "as the Allied troops approached," indicating he may have used "Allied" and "American" troops interchangeably. Notwithstanding the misstatement of facts, it is notable that he was aware that ahead of the liberation of the camp on April 15, 1945, an expeditionary force led by British Army Major Dick William had been part of a small reconnaissance mission to the camp on the April 12 (Williams 1997, seg. #111).[33]

Marx describes how he resisted. On April 7, 1945, he was ordered to burn all of the documentation from the camp office in the crematorium. Afraid that there would be no evidence of the scale of Nazi crimes, Marx describes how he "managed to steal two documents and secrete them on my person" (Marx 2015, 99). The documents he stole detailed the number of prisoners at the camp in March 1945, as well as the number of documented deaths that month, and were subsequently used as evidence at the Lüneberg trials in August 1945 (Stewart 2019). Erich Marx, who barely survived his ordeal at Belsen, spent several months recuperating in Leipzig prior to returning to the Roermond, Netherlands by September 1945 (Marx 2015, 100). During his convalescence he made detailed observations, knowing he was likely the only eyewitness to the inner workings of Bergen-Belsen. He ensured facts that he had been designated to document by the German authorities—and that were subsequently destroyed—survived through his own personal testimony.

The Boy Who Drew Auschwitz

Thomas Geve was a Holocaust chronicler who survived the War, even though his Holocaust-era chronicle did not. Like Erich Marx, Thomas Geve was interested in documenting the details of camp life down to the minute, ounce, and centimeter. Thomas was just 13 years old when he was deported to Auschwitz on Transport 39 (Geve 2021, 55) from Berlin on June 28, 1943.[34] During his incarceration in Auschwitz, he was appointed to the bricklaying commando. This undoubtedly saved his life, because the months spent training in the *Mauereschule* (the bricklaying school) were a reprieve from other back-breaking work like digging ditches or construction labor. Once trained, the bricklayers were part of the skilled workforce needed by the German camp authorities for their many construction projects (Auschwitz-Birkenau State Museum n.d.). It was not easy for a teenager to haul 50 kg bags of cement, but it did give him access to a precious resource—paper sacks. Thomas saved torn off pieces of paper and found a pencil to draw what he saw around him. He feverishly measured the barracks and the three-tiered bunks. He documented the precise times of roll call, breaks for lunch, the end of the working day, and curfew. He listed concentration camp terminology and illustrated what each term meant. He drew the different types of insects infesting their bunks and identified their species. Hospitals, sports, food, escapes, punishments, plans, subcamps, selections, armbands, badges, electric fences, and hunger are among the many illustrations on his cement bags (Geve 2021, 19–297).

Thomas Geve is a pseudonym. He only gave his testimony under his real name Stefan Cohn to USC Shoah Foundation in 1998 (Cohn 1998), 45 years after he started publishing. He first began to chronicle his experience through drawings while he was in Auschwitz but was not able to take his illustrations with him when forced to march from the camp in January 1945. After his liberation from Buchenwald on

April 11, 1945, Stefan was able to procure a set of index cards and pencils from the camp office. He redrew the sketches from memory, while adding new ones. The result of his effort was a set of over 80 original illustrations (79 of which survived). He had drawn the illustrations to present to his father, who had escaped to London to seek safe passage for his wife and son in August 1939, only to be separated from them during the Holocaust. Stefan, who was still just 15 years old when he was reunited with his father in 1945, wanted to tell his father precisely what had happened to him. His illustrations would be his way to tell the story to his father in detail. As further evidence of the impetus surviving victims had to "tell the world," Cohn describes the desire of the recently liberated survivors to report what had happened:

> We did not want to forget. On the contrary we felt an urge to set what we had witnessed on paper and to tell about it. I too was gripped by that desire. If we who had experienced it, I reasoned did not expose the bitter truth, people simply would not believe about the Nazi ogre.
>
> (Geve 1958, 235)

After an initial two-month period of convalescence at Buchenwald, Cohn was sent to Switzerland, where he spent the summer with a foster family before finally being reunited with his father on November 17, 1945 in London. There he learned English and obtained a degree in engineering before emigrating to Israel in 1950 (Geve 2021, 289). Cohn describes his continued desire to tell his story in the preface to his 1958 publication *Youth in Chains*:

> In 1946 when a flood of literature came out about events in war-time Europe, I looked at a stack of drawings of mine which portrayed the life of youth in German concentration camps. A year earlier they had been published by a journal in Switzerland, and now I wanted to put them to words. I tried to, but I merely produced a badly written report. Then I was sixteen. I had spent only five years in school and these, too, were restless times of persecution and war.
>
> Now I have tried again, for no one else has come forward to tell of those who grew up in concentration camps. The memoirs before you are not those of somebody famous. But of someone who was only one among thousands. I did not intend to write a bestseller. I have merely recorded the truth.
>
> (Geve 1958, Preface)

Stefan Cohn reveals that his first attempt to publish his drawings of Auschwitz was rebutted by the publisher. They informed his journalist friend, who was helping to find a publisher, that "The boy is no Picasso" and "Audiences are looking for more cheerful topics nowadays" (Geve 2021, 13). In the intervening years, Stefan published his memoirs multiple times in several languages, most notably as three English-language titles, *Youth in Chains* (1958), *Guns and Barbed Wire* (1987), and *The Boy Who Drew Auschwitz* (2021). These are essentially the same testimonial manuscript, with updates and modifications, including layout changes. The 2021 edition includes many of the original illustrations for the first time. In *Youth in Chains*, Stefan describes the origins of his sketches:

> I asked my grown-up colleagues for paper and pencil. Then armed with a stack of abandoned swastika-imprinted questionnaires of the *Nationasozialistische Deutsche Arbeiter Partei* and a few stumps of coloured pencil, I embarked on sketching camp life. Scenes of days gone by became vivid again—the arrival the selection, the punishments, the food, the diseases, the endless rows of fencing, the work, the rollcalls, the winter, the revolts, the gallows, the evacuation, the 'Kutushas' (sic). One day when I was a man, I would keep them as a souvenir.
>
> (Geve 1958, 234)

This passage is identical in *Guns and Barbed Wire* (Geve 1987, 205), but is updated in *The Boy Who Drew Auschwitz*. The "Nazi ogre" becomes "the Nazi's evil." Reference to the *Nationasozialistische Deutsche Arbeiter Partei* is anglicized to the "Nazi party." He added more specificity, too. We learn that that the questionnaires were "postcard sized" (Geve 2021, 280) and that there were now a precise number of "7 short coloured pencils." In the 2021 edition we also learn for the first time about the original drawings in Auschwitz that were lost:

> I recalled my time in Auschwitz where I first had the urge to record camp life. There using torn-off scraps from paper sacks, bits of charcoal and a pencil that I had found, I started to make lists and draw . . . When we were hastily evacuated from Auschwitz I had to leave them behind. But these images stuck in my mind and now as a free man, I started to recreate them.
>
> (Geve 2021, 280)

He makes the point that the original images had "stuck in his mind" and that the second set of images was a recreation of the first. We also learn from the footnotes in *The Boy Who Drew Auschwitz* that Geve had help from an Austrian survivor of Buchenwald. Eugen Kogon was also documenting what had happened there and was willing to share some of his findings with the convalescing teenager who was avidly sketching in his barracks (Geve 2021, 280).

Stefan Cohn, also known as Thomas Geve, has been telling virtually the same story for 75 years. In a recent conversation with him at his home in Israel, he told me. The boy who drew Auschwitz was determined as a 14-year-old to ensure the veracity of his experience was conveyed accurately, and to this day remains determined that the detail is not lost. Testimony for Stefan is not about consequence, it is about presenting facts he believes speak for themselves. The trajectory of Holocaust memory for Stefan began in Auschwitz and through his early struggle to publish in the immediate aftermath. Only now, almost 80 years later is he experiencing a surge in interest in a testimony he first published in the 1950s, and at a time in his life when he has the least amount of energy and no ability to travel to share in conversation in person.

The Theory and Practice of Hell

Eugen Kogon was a successful academic, economist, writer, and businessman living in Austria. He was also a committed anti-Nazi. Twice arrested before the March 1938 *Anschluß* of Austria, he was immediately apprehended by the Gestapo and jailed for his subversive views. Kogon spent a total of seven years in contractionary incarceration, including spending the entire Second World War as an inmate of Buchenwald. On April 16, 1945, five days after the liberation of Buchenwald, an American Intelligence Team from the Psychological Warfare Division visited the former Buchenwald Concentration Camp to prepare a comprehensive report for the SHAEF. As Buchenwald was the first main camp to fall into the hands of the Western allies, it was to be studied to understand the concentration camps system.

After an initial 400-page report was filed with Kogon's oversight, he then set to turning the findings into a book, which he wrote in the second half of 1945. The publisher's introduction to the 1960 American edition takes pains to reassure readers that "The present book is a new manuscript, although here and there sections of the original text have been used . . . at no point is there a conflict between the earlier report and the present book" (Kogon 1950, 5–9). This clarification about the similarities and differences between the two versions shows an acute awareness that such discrepancies might call these works into question. To make the point even more clear, the publisher states:

> Kogon expresses sincere gratitude to all of his friends who encouraged, advised and helped him . . . Yet Kogon alone answers for the book . . . Nor is it associated to any German or foreign agency, nor with any party or other office or other person.
>
> *(Kogon 1950, 9)*

We also learn that Kogon was so concerned that the initial report accurately reflected the experiences and knowledge of former inmates. His co-authors were all former inmates, each with at least five years' experience in Buchenwald. He also held a reading of ten of the 12 chapters of the report with 15 former inmates to ensure the veracity of the content from the perspective of those who had lived through it. Their verdict was that it was "objective and accurate" (7). If the entire panel was made up of former inmates, it is difficult to assume that they were the most objective listeners. That said, it does demonstrate that former inmates were seeking objective truth and socializing the narrative from a very early stage. The first public reading of this comprehensive and "objective" report took place just a week after the end of the Second World War.

The unidentified author of the introduction—which appears to be penned by Kogon himself—"knows that the book may be exploited for one-sided propaganda purposes or for purposes of sensationalism, both of which he despises—sensationalism more than propaganda" (11). He is also concerned that his book will "provide a blue-print for tyrants yet to come." A universal political message underpins the book, which in the immediate aftermath of the camps states that "the mirror that it holds up to mankind reflects no nameless monsters" (10). Within months of the liberation of the camps, Kogon had appropriated the Holocaust as a warning from history. He had been an anti-Nazi activist from the 1930s and had high levels of political literacy and had been curious to understand the human motivations behind the atrocities. Kogon took an interest in understanding the Nazi movement and engaged in lengthy conversations in 1937 with a member of the SS to better understand the operation of the Nazi system (13).

The Theory and Practice of Hell does not adopt the first-person voice of a "victim." Instead, Kogon attempts takes the position of historian or analyst, compiling sources of information, describing as an outsider how the SS structured and ran the system. The 23 chapters cover topics with titles as broad as "The Categories of Prisoners" (Kogon 1950, 39), "Working Conditions" (88), "Money and Mail" (125), "Scientific Experiments" (152), and "The Psychology of the Prisoners" (300). That said, it would have been difficult to compile without an intimate first-hand knowledge of the workings of the camp.

Interwoven with the detailed arm's-length account in a chapter titled "The Reprisals Against the Jews" (174), Kogon extensively quotes Jewish survivors, all of whom had been in other ghettos and camps before their final destination at Buchenwald. Kogon's secondary publishing of surviving victims of the Final Solution further illustrates how Jewish survivors were willing to speak and write down their recollections by mid-1945. Kogon provides an important clarification as a non-Jewish prisoner who was himself sentenced for liquidation in Auschwitz. He states that his report is not sufficient to describe the experience of the Jews (174). He claims that there was a clear distinction between the experience of the Jews in the concentration camp system and the rest of the population.

Kogon provides first-person eyewitness accounts only to describe the situation of the Jews in the wider concentration camp and death camp system. He reports the experience of Oskar Berger, who was deported to Treblinka from the Kielce ghetto in July 1942, making him one of the first to arrive at a camp designed for mass murder. Berger was assigned to a work detail. His account provides rare details not typically associated with the death camp, noted for its highly organized system of killing over 800,000 Jews in a little over a year (July 23, 1942—October 19, 1943). Included are scenes such as the shooting of Jews on the platform at Treblinka before the gas chambers were fully operational; workers not being fed and being left to find food from the transports; trains that arrived with all occupants already dead; and whiskey-quaffing SS guards smashing babies' heads on trees (183–184). Berger also describes his escape from Treblinka on a freight train with two others hiding in the clothes of dead Jews. In less than three pages he describes an unusual Holocaust trajectory that included deportation to and survival of Treblinka; escape and later capture as a "partisan"; the Kraków ghetto gestapo prison; Auschwitz-Birkenau; Orianienburg; Sachsenhausen; and finally the Buchenwald sub-camp of Ohrdruf.

Another of Kogon's contributors was Moshe Strigler, described as an author of *Dos Polyishe Yidntum* (Strigler 1947, 1948, 1950). Not only did he survive 12 concentration camps, he would later become editor of the New York Yiddish language paper *The Forward*. Strigler provided evidence to Kogon a year before he published in Buenos Aires. The surviving victims who provided these unique early insights also include Warsaw Ghetto resistance fighter Vladimir Blumenfeld, who provides a remarkably detailed account of a deception to assassinate SS as they came into the ghetto. He names the ghetto hero as Mordechai Nutkewicz of Ripin, who lured 25 SS into a trap. Blumenfeld reports that Nutkewicz shot the SS sergeant as a signal to his fellow resistance fighters to gun down the remaining SS trapped in the courtyard. Of interest in this account is that neither Blumenfeld nor Kogon name the death camp of Majdanek, referring to it only as "Lublin concentration camp" (191–196). It helps us understand that the emerging narrative of the resistance in Warsaw was built on particular personalities, all actions are not in Blumenthal's account, and that the nomenclature of the Holocaust itself was not yet established in early narratives.

The five brief first-person accounts included in Kogon's report were collected from survivors liberated near Buchenwald in 1945, which was their only commonality; they had otherwise had quite different experiences throughout the war. While it is not known how Kogon knew them or whether there were more reports that were not published, these brief first-person testimonial narratives constitute one of the earliest "collections" of published testimony. Despite their brevity, the 15 pages of first-person narrative—within a book published by another surviving victim—demonstrates that to understand the Jewish experience in the Holocaust it is necessary to gather accounts of surviving victims with varied experiences from multiple places. His collection is a microcosm of the vast archives that followed later, replete with data on ghettos, deportation, resistance, escape, perpetrators, family, and geography. It also underscores that, for all the information Kogon had about the workings of the camp system, only the surviving Jewish victim could provide insight about what it meant to *survive* as a Jewish person under German rule. Kogon was a seven-year alum of Buchenwald, and yet he knew that he did not have the words to describe what they had gone through. He only helped them break their silence.

Ka-Tzetnik 135633

Yehiel Feiner (later Yehiel Dinur) was placed in a British hospital in Italy for medical assistance not long after his liberation by the Soviets. His experience during the Holocaust included two years at the Auschwitz-Birkenau concentration and death camp complex. Such was his physical state and the urgent feeling that he was going to die that he asked for pen and paper "to keep my promise" (ITHL n.d.). It is not known what "the promise" he had intended to keep was, but it appeared to be a commitment to tell the world what had happened. The resulting work, *Salamandra*, is the first known novel written by a surviving victim about the Holocaust based on his own experiences. Feiner handed the manuscript to a British soldier and told him the name of the author was to be Ka-Tzetnik (a *Konzentrationslager* inmate). The full pseudonym of "Ka-Tzetnik 135633" was used when the book was published in an abridged Hebrew version, denoting the Auschwitz identity that was tattooed on his arm.

Yehiel Dinur revealed that he was Ka-Tzetnik 135633 15 years later, when he testified at the Eichmann Trial on June 7, 1961. Dinur related to the courtroom that the pseudonym replaced his original name when he was permanently tattooed. He explained that he would "carry this name for as long as the world will not awaken, after the crucifying of the nation" (USHMM 1999b, n.p.). Dinur is most remembered for fainting while addressing Adolph Eichmann during his witness statement in the courtroom in Jerusalem, and was removed from the courthouse by ambulance. It was later discovered that he had suffered a stroke while testifying. Just prior to him falling from the witness stand, Dinur had stated his commitment to fulfilling an unspecified oath:

> If I am able to stand here in this court before you . . . then I believe with all my being that this is thanks to the oath I made to them there. They gave me the strength, this power . . . that sustained me.
>
> *(USHMM 1999b, n.p.)*

FIGURE 6.1   Yehiel Dinur (Ka-Tzetnik 135633) provides witness testimony at the trial of Adolph Eichmann June 7, 1961

Source: Accessed at United States Holocaust Memorial Museum, courtesy of The Steven Spielberg Jewish Film Archives of the Hebrew University of Jerusalem.

Ka-Tzetnik 135633 became best known for his widely distributed book *House of Dolls* (1955), which describes the sexual violence experienced by women who were forced into sexual slavery in Auschwitz. Although Dinur claims the novel was based on the experience of his sister Daniella, the lines between lurid sadistic fantasy and reality become increasingly blurred in the text. *House of Dolls* has been described as, "unavoidably, Holocaust porn—written by a survivor" (Mikics 2012, n.p.). Dinur's publications, while hugely influential, have largely been consigned to being Holocaust-inspired pulp fiction. However, his first work, *Salamandra* (1946), later published in English as *Sunrise over Hell* (1977), was motivated by one reason: to tell his life story while he was still alive. Dinur survived his convalescence in Italy and went to Mandatory Palestine, where the book was published in an abridged version in Hebrew under the title *Salamandra* (Ka-Tzetnik 135633 1946).

The biography of the principal character in *Salamandra*, Harry Preleshnik, closely mirrors the Holocaust history of Yechiel Feiner. After selection at Auschwitz, Preleshnik describes the moment he receives his number:

> A peculiar scribe was posted by the last long table, a peculiar pen in his hand. He was inscribing, but not on paper; instead the newcomers, one at a time, would extend the left arm, as if letting a tailor measure its length for a sleeve, whereupon a peculiar scribe would dip his peculiar pen into peculiar ink and . . . stab the left arm's flesh and numbers would leap out: 135633. 'Get this whoreson . . . You're dead.'
>
> *(Ka-Tzetnik 135633 1977)*

To give a sense of the literary voice that Yechiel Feiner found in his hospital bed in Italy, this is the passage that describes his arrival at Birkenau:

> The train arrived on the Planet and stopped. The doors were shoved apart, and humanity drained out of the cattle trucks onto the vast platform.
>
> Night was all around, swathing the destination in black. No Screams here, no speech. The Site of Silence. . . . Night here had an essence of its own. Night here was at the beck and call of an omnipotent sovereign. . . . Night muffled, stealing inaudibly on tip toes to envelop you.
>
> The Stripees were like . . . fish . . . darting back and forth.
>
> An execution swift and silent until, from among the Demons, one approached, to move his finger right then left. . . . What was going on here? Life was nothing but a dream here- or rather, death was.
>
> . . . [A]bout fifty percent had suffocated in the cattle trucks; of the remaining percentage, forty were stood to the left, ten to the right.
>
> Harry's lot fell with the ten percent.
>
> *(Ka-Tzetnik 135633 1977)*

The common trope of the arrival at Auschwitz—the assembly of two lines, men and women inching forward to the uniformed character of Mengele, who looked handsome wagging his finger with white gloves—is not found in this raw literary description of Feiner's arrival. It is also curious whether Feiner's description of the "night" he arrived influenced the title of Elie Wiesel's *Night*, published over a decade later.

Feiner had been a poet before the Second World War. He published his first volume of Yiddish poems, *Tsveyuntsvantsik* (Twenty-Two) in 1931, which Naomi Seidman sensed had the "ready-made sighs and shadowed gravestones and bitter heart of the young poet" (Butler 2014, n.p.). Later in his life, between 1953 and 1964, Yechiel Dinur removed copies of *Tsveyuntsvantsik* from the National Library of Israel and burned them. On a third occasion in 1993, he removed a copy from the stacks in Jerusalem, cut up the volume, and returned it to the director with instructions, "I placed here the remains of the 'book.' Please, burn them as my world and everything I loved burned in Auschwitz's crematorium" (The National Library of Israel 2018). Dinur stated that he was reborn in Auschwitz after his identity as Yechiel Feiner was replaced by 135633:

> I do not regard myself as a writer and a composer of literary material. This is a chronicle of the planet of Auschwitz. . . . the inhabitants of this planet had no names, they had no parents, nor did they have children . . . they did not live- nor did they die-according to the laws of this world. . . . Theirs was a Ka-Tzetnik number.
>
> (USHMM 1999b)

Yechiel Feiner, like many of the early writers who narrated from their direct experience starting in the 1940s, were grappling with an imminent past that was still unprocessed. Those that wrote early continued to struggle with how to convey their experience for much of their lives. Ka-tzetnik 135633 published novels for the rest of his life; Kitty Hart-Moxon published several books and made four documentaries over a sixty-year period; Thomas Geve is currently publishing in many languages and editions still today. Their trajectories did not follow a typical pattern that Hass described previously. They had their own individual approach to how their memory and willingness to witness would transform itself into testimony. They were not objects of history, but subjects emerging from the horror they had endured and were willing to *be* witness. Because of who they were then, it is possible to know them now and allow them to take us into the imminence of death and survival.

Notes

1 Pinchas Gutter, email correspondence with author, November 11, 2021.
2 This was also relayed by Edith Birken in a personal conversation with the author, 2000.
3 Pinchas Gutter, personal conversation with the author, March 26, 2000.
4 Victoria Vincent, personal conversation with the author, August 1995.
5 Lisa Vincent, interview with the author, June 9, 1999. Vincent was one of the more complex *Kindertransport* stories, as she left Nüremberg on a *Kindertransport* in August 1939 bound for Holland then Harwich. Due to the outbreak of war, she was stranded in

Holland. Only in March 1940 was she, along with a small number of young transportees, brought to England on a fishing vessel.
6. Lisa Vincent, telephone interview with the author, February 6, 1999.
7. Charles Fawcett, interview with the author, September 11, 1998.
8. Paul and Corrine Oppenheimer, telephone conversation with author, February 6, 1999. The "presentation" was not a public lecture, but a class exercise in which he had chosen his "war" experience as his topic for a short oral presentation.
9. Paul and Corrine Oppenheimer, telephone conversation with author, February 6, 1999.
10. Michael Lee, telephone interview with author, February 6, 1999.
11. Kitty Hart-Moxon, email correspondence with author, November 12, 2021.
12. Although his self-imposed ten-year silence was a protest of a kind, a protest at his own lack of confidence to narrate that which he felt strongly about. That is, in the silence he imposed, he was able to wade through the ultimate protest he was to make.
13. Originally published in French in 1946. The first English edition, *A World Apart*, appeared in 1951.
14. This story was related in person to Lawrence Langer, who in turn described it in his introduction to the posthumous edition of Delbo's trilogy *Auschwitz and After*.
15. The process of psychological as well as psychiatric examination of survivors began in the 1960s when a German compensation law was designed to compensate prisoners of concentration camps whose capacity to work had been reduced. Psycho-historian George Kren notes that the process did not meet its stated preamble to be applied "in the spirit of warm hearted and generous indemnification" as it required lawyers and expert medical testimony including the advice of psychiatrists and psychoanalysts. Kren points out that an unintended outcome of the restitution law was that it brought about additional contact between survivors and psychoanalysts/psychiatrists.
16. Pinchas Gutter, personal conversation with author.
17. Jewish Care established a Holocaust Survivors Centre as a part of (or at least next door to) their Shalvata counselling center in Hendon, London, to provide daily activities and support for survivors in the London area. While "Shalvata" and the Survivors Centre are not the same thing, many survivors attending the Survivors Centre use the opportunity to take counsel as a part of their own therapeutic process.
18. As Hass himself asserts, survivors are people, not a phenomenon. Therefore, using survivors as a homogenous phenomenon in attempting to understand the psychology of "the survivor—particularly in relation to an unfolding process of witness—is bound to be unsuccessful if definitive norms are sought." However, the identification of underlying dynamics process seems valuable.
19. Documentation identifying a "Captain Batz" in Warsaw in 1939 is hard to come by. It is most likely Rudolf Batz who was later promoted to *Sturmbannführer* and appointed as one of the leaders of *Einsatzkommano* 2 responsible for the mass murder of Jews in the Baltic states. See: https://military.wikia.org/wiki/Rudolf_Batz. Retrieved, January 13, 2021.
20. It is not entirely clear how he got to New York, what papers he carried with him from the ghetto, or who sponsored him, although there is some suggestion that he was expecting to become the Polish Consul in Tel Aviv.
21. In email correspondence, Shoskes' grandson believes that Haim Shoskes may have been an early member of the Warsaw Ghetto Judenrat, although there is no clear written evidence of that.
22. Quoted in, Schwarz 2008, 185.
23. From an interview with the Imperial War Museum Oral History Collection: Leslie Hardman (IWM SR 17636). See: www.iwm.org.uk/sites/default/files/files/2018-08/Liberation_Bergen_Belsen_Transcript.pdf.
24. Waldemar Ginsburg radio interview with *BBC Home Affairs* correspondent Jon Silverrman: Interview at UK National Holocaust Memorial Centre; October 15, 1999.
25. Felix, Kitty, unpublished witness statement handed to Kitty Hart-Moxon at a function at the Imperial War Museum, by the relief team worker who had acquired it 50 years previously.

26 The Auschwitz-Birkenau State Museum indicates 1,000,000 Jews arrived to the site, of whom 900,000 were murdered on arrival, which would put the percentage who were selected to live at approximately 18%. See: www.auschwitz.org/en/history/auschwitz-and-shoah/the-unloading-ramps-and-selections/.
27 A note on the accuracy of her statement is important here. It would appear unlikely that a 16-year-old inmate would have either the capacity to obtain or ability to reconcile such figures linked to such dates. However, what is surprising is just how accurate her memory is, matching statistics from historical sources (Czech 1989; Gutman and Berenbaum 1994).
28 Anita Lasker-Wallfisch, email to author, November 12, 2021.
29 Pinchas Gutter, email to author, November 11, 2021.
30 Eva Schlposs, email to author, November 12, 2021.
31 Eva's mother Fritzi Geiringer remarried the widowed Otto Frank in 1953, after extensive searches for their missing families.
32 Sonia Warshawski, personal conversation with author, November 11, 2021.
33 Major Richard (Dick) Williams, personal conversation with author in January 2000. He confirmed to me that he had indeed been a member of a reconnaissance mission to determine the location of the camp and the conditions that were likely to have been encountered there.
34 USHMM database entry for this transport can be found here: www.ushmm.org/online/hsv/source_view.php?SourceId=7110.

References

Adelsberger, Lucie. 1997. *Auschwitz: A Doctor's Story*. London: BCA.
Aleksiun, Natalia. 2008. "The Central Jewish Historical Commission in Poland 1944–1947." In *Polin: Studies in Polish Jewry Volume 20: Making Holocaust Memory*, edited by Natalia Alesuin, Gabriel N. Finder, Antony Polonsky, and Jan Schwarz, 74–97. Liverpool: Liverpool University Press. https://doi.org/10.2307/j.ctv13qfv1t.8.
Amir, Michlean, J., and Rosemary Horowitz. 2008. "Yizkor Books in the Twenty-First Century: A History and Guide to the Genre." *Judaica Librarianship* 14: 39–56.
Ancona-Vincent, Victoria. 1995. *Beyond Imagination*. Newark, NJ: Beth Shalom.
Apenszlak, Jacob. 1943. *The Black Book of Polish Jewry: An Account on the Martyrdom of Polish Jewry Under the Nazi Occupation*. New York: The American Federation for Polish Jews.
Auschwitz-Birkenau State Museum. n.d. "The Construction of the Camp." http://auschwitz.org/en/history/auschwitz-ii/the-construction-of-the-camp.
Boder, David. 1949. *I Did Not Interview the Dead*. Urbana, IL: University of Illinois Press.
Brenner, Reeve Robert. 1980. *The Faith and Doubt of Holocaust Survivors*. New York: The Free Press.
Butler, Menachem. 2014. "The Lost Poems of Ka-Tzetnik 135633." *Tablet Magazine*. www.tabletmag.com/sections/news/articles/the-lost-poems-of-ka-tzetnik-135633.
Ceserani, David, and Eric J. Sundquist, eds. 2011. *After the Holocaust: Challenging the Myth of Silence*. Oxford: Routledge.
Cohen, Sharon Kangisser. 2014. *Testimony and Time: Holocaust Survivors Remember*. Jerusalem: Yad Vashem.
Cohn, Stefan. 1998. *Interview by USC Shoah Foundation* (Interview 48184). Los Angeles, CA: Visual History Archive.
Czech, Danuta. 1989. *Kalendarium der Ereignisse im Konzentrationslager Auschwitz-Birkenau 1939–1945*. Hamburg: Rowohlt.
Delbo, Charlotte. 1995. *Auschwitz and After*. New Haven, CT: Yale University Press.
Des Pres, Terrence. 1976. *The Survivor: An Anatomy of Life in the Death Camps*. Oxford: Oxford University Press.

Edelman, Marek. 1946. *The Ghetto Fights.* New York: American Representation of the General Jewish Workers' Union of Poland.
Einstein, Albert. 1938. "Why Do People Hate the Jews?" *Colliers* 102, no. 22.
Eitinger, Leo. 1964. *Concentration Camp Survivors in Norway and Israel.* London: Allen and Unwin.
Ezrahi, Sidra Dekoven. 1980. *By Words Alone: The Holocaust in Literature.* Chicago, IL: University of Chicago Press.
Felix, Kitty. 1946. Unpublished Manuscript. (in personal collection of Kitty Hart-Moxon)
Felman, Shoshana, and Dori Laub. 1992. *Testimony: Crises of Witnessing in Literature, Psychoanalysis and History.* London: Routledge.
Friedlander, Saul. 1994. "Trauma, Memory and Transference." In *Holocaust Remembrance: The Shapes of Memory*, edited by Geoffrey Hartman, 252–263. Oxford: Blackwell.
Geve, Thomas. 1958. *Youth in Chains.* Jerusalem: Rubin Mass.
Geve, Thomas. 1987. *Guns and Barbed Wire: A Child Survives the Holocaust.* Chicago, IL: Academy Chicago.
Geve, Thomas. 2021. *The Boy Who Drew Auschwitz.* London: Harper Colins.
Glazar, Richard. 1995. *Trap with a Green Fence: Survival in Treblinka.* Evanston, IL: Northwestern University Press.
Gutman, Yisrael, and Michael Berenbaum, eds. 1994. *Anatomy of the Auschwitz Death Camp.* Bloomington, IN: Indiana University Press.
Gutter, Pinchas. 1993. *Interview by USC Shoah Foundation* (Interview 54192). Los Angeles, CA: Visual History Archive.
Hanover, Nathan, and William B. Helmreich. 1983. *Abyss of Despair—Yeven Metzulah: The Famous 17th Century Chronicle Depicting Jewish Life in Russia and Poland During the Chmielnicki Massacres of 1648–1649.* 1st ed. London: Routledge.
Hartman, Geoffrey, ed. 1994. *Holocaust Remembrance: The Shapes of Memory.* Oxford: Blackwell.
Hart-Moxon, Kitty. 1997. *Return to Auschwitz.* Revised ed. Newark, NJ: Beth Shalom Holocaust Centre.
Hass, Aaron. 1995. *The Aftermath: Living with the Holocaust.* Cambridge: Cambridge University Press.
Hassan, Judith. 1998. "Memory and Remembrance: The Survivor of the Holocaust 50 Years After Liberation." In *Studies on the Audio-Visual Testimony of Victims of the Nazi Crimes and Genocides*, 103–110. Bruxelles: Editions du Centre d'Etudes et de Documentation Fondation Auschwitz.
Helfgott, Ben. 2013. *Interview by USC Shoah Foundation* (Interview 52910). Los Angeles, CA: Visual History Archive.
Hofmann, Edith. 2001. *Unshed Tears, A Novel . . . But Not a Fiction.* Newark, NJ: Quill Press.
Institute for the Translation of Hebrew Literature (ITHL). n.d. "Yehiel Dinur." www.ithl.org.il/page_13576.
Jewish Telegraphic Agency. 1940. "Szoszkie Honored at Dinner Here; Named Field Director of Polish Jewish Group." April 5. http://pdfs.jta.org/1940/1940-04-05_002.pdf?_ga=2.180920549.314631529.1610292466-2102934671.1610292465.
Jockusch, Laura. 2012. *Collect and Record: Jewish Holocaust Documentation in Early Postwar Europe.* Oxford: Oxford University Press.
Kahana, Boaz, Zev Harel, and Eva Kahana. 1989 "Clinical and Gerontological Issues Facing Survivors of the Nazi Holocaust." In *Healing Their Wounds: Psychotherapy with Holocaust Survivors and Their Families*, edited by Paul Marcus and Alan Rosenberg, 197–212. New York: Praeger.
Ka-Tzetnik 135633. 1946. *Salamandra.* Tela Aviv: The Dvir Co.

Ka-Tzetnik 135633. 1955. *House of Dolls*, translated by Moshe M. Kohn. New York: Simon & Schuster.
Ka-Tzetnik 135633. 1977. *Sunrise Over Hell*. London: Corgi.
Kidron, Carol A. 2012. "Breaching the Wall of Traumatic Silence: Holocaust Survivor and Descendant Person—Object Relations and the Material Transmission of the Genocidal Past." *Journal of Material Culture* 17, no. 1: 3–21.
Kogon, Eugen. 1950. *The Theory and Practice of Hell*. London: Secker and Warburg.
Kren, George. 1989. "The Holocaust Survivor and Psychoanalysis." In *Healing Their Wounds: Psychotherapy with Holocaust Survivors and Their Families*, edited by Paul Marcus and Alan Rosenberg, 3–22. New York: Praeger.
Langer, Lawrence L. 1982. *Versions of Survival: The Holocaust and the Human Spirit*. New York: New York University Press.
Langer, Lawrence L. 1991. *Holocaust Testimonies: The Ruins of Memory*. New Haven, CT: Yale University Press.
Lanzmann, Claude. 1985. *Shoah: An Oral History of the Holocaust*. New York: Pantheon Books.
Lengyel, Olga. 1947a. *Five Chimneys: The True Chronicle of a Woman Who Survived Auschwitz*. New York: Ziff Davis.
Lengyel, Olga. 1947b. *I Survived Hitler's Ovens*. New York: Avon Publications.
Levi, Primo. 1986. *Moments of Reprieve*. New York: Summit Books.
Levi, Primo. 1988. *The Drowned and the Saved*. London: Abacus Books.
Lewis, Stephen. 1984. *Art Out of Agony: The Holocaust Theme in Literature, Sculpture and Film*. Montreal: CBC Enterprises.
Lingens-Reiner, Ella. 1948. *Prisoners of Fear*. London: Victor Gollancz.
Lurie, Ido, Nehama Goldberger, Adi Gur Orr, Ziona Haklai, and Shlomo Mendlovic. 2021. "Suicide among Holocaust Survivors: A National Registry Study." *Archives of Suicide Research* (January 6): 1–12.
Maisel, Philip. 2021. *USC Shoah Foundation Interview* (Interview 58612). Los Angeles, CA: Visual History Archive.
Marx, Erich. 2015. "That's How It Was: A Report on Westerbork and Bergen Belsen (1945)." *Irish Pages* 9, no. 2: 72–101. www.jstor.org/stable/44508352.
McClafferty, Carla Killough. 2008. *In Defiance of Hitler: The Secret Mission of Varian Fry*. 1st ed. New York: Farrar Straus Giroux.
Mémorial de la Shoah. n.d. "Archives and Documentation." www.memorialdelashoah.org/en/archives-and-documentation/the-documentation-center/the-history-of-the-cdjc.html
Mikics, David. 2012. "Holocaust Pulp Fiction: The Auschwitz Survivor Known as Ka-Tzetnik 135633 Wrote Lurid Novels Derided as Pornography When They Were Published. Now He's Israel's Elie Wiesel." *Tablet Magazine*, April 19, 2021. www.tabletmag.com/sections/arts-letters/articles/ka-tzetnik.
Mitlberg, A. 1947. "Hilf durkh kultur." In *Spetsyele oysgabe gevidmet der bikher serye dos poylishe yidntum*, *XXV*. Buenos Aires: Tsentral-Farband fun Poylishe Yidn in Argentine.
Niederland, William. 1964. "Psychiatric Disorders among Persecution Victims: A Contribution to the Understanding of the Concentration Camp Pathology and Its After Effects." *Journal of Nervous and Mental Diseases* 139: 458–474.
Niewyk, Donald. 1998. *Fresh Wounds: Early Narratives of Holocaust Survival*. Chapel Hill, NC: University of North Carolina Press.
Oppenheimer, Paul. 1996a. *From Belsen to Buckingham Palace*. Newark, NJ: Beth Shalom Holocaust Centre.
Oppenheimer, Paul. 1996b. *Interview with USC Shoah Foundation* (Interview 13469). Los Angeles, CA: Visual History Archive.

Perl, Giesella. 1948. *I Was a Doctor in Auschwitz*. New York: International Universities Press.
Piper, Franciszek, and Teresa Swiebocka. 1996. *Auschwitz: Nazi Death Camp*. Owiecim: Auschwitz-Birkenau State Museum.
Reder, Rudolf. 1946. *Bełżec*. Kraków: Centralna Żydowska Komisja Historyczna.
Rosen, Alan. 2012. *The Wonder of Their Voices: The 1946 Holocaust Interviews of David Boder*. Oxford: Oxford University Press.
Rosenfeld, Alvin Hirsch. 1988. *A Double Dying: Reflections on Holocaust Literature*. Bloomington, IN: Indiana University Press.
Rossoliński-Liebe, Grzegorz. 2020a. "Introduction: Conceptualizations of the Holocaust in Germany, Poland, Lithuania, Belarus, and Ukraine: Historical Research, Public Debates, and Methodological Disputes." *East European Politics and Societies* 34, no. 1: 129–142.
Rossoliński-Liebe, Grzegorz. 2020b "Survivor Testimonies and the Coming to Terms with the Holocaust in Volhynia and Eastern Galicia: The Case of the Ukrainian Nationalists." *East European Politics and Societies* 34, no. 1: 221–240.
Rousset, David. 1951. *A World Apart (L'Univers Concentrationnaire)*. London: Secker and Warburg.
Rowe, David E., and Robert Schulmann. 2007. "Hitler's Germany and the Threat to European Jewry, 1933–1938." In *Einstein on Politics: His Private Thoughts and Public Stands on Nationalism, Zionism, War, Peace, and the Bomb*, 266–314. Princeton, NJ: Princeton University Press. www.jstor.org/stable/j.ctt46n3rd.13.
Schenderlein, Anne. 2016. "Making German History in Los Angeles: German Jewish Refugees and West German Diplomats in the 1950s and 1960s." *Jewish Culture and History* 17, no. 1–2: 133–151.
Schloss, Eva, and Evelyn Kent. 1988. *Eva's Story: A Survivors Tale*. New York: St Martin's Press.
Schwarz, Jan. 2005. *Imagining Lives: Autobiographical Fiction of Yiddish Writers*. Madison, WI: University of Wisconsin Press.
Schwarz, Jan. 2008. "A Library of Hope and Destruction: The Yiddish Book Series 'Dos Poylishe Yidntum' (Polish Jewry) 1946–1966." In *Polin: Studies in Polish Jewry Volume 20: Making Holocaust Memory*, edited by Jan Schwarz, Gabriel N. Finder, Natalia Aleksiun, and Antony Polonsky, 173–196. Liverpool: The Littman Library of Jewish Civilization; University of Liverpool Press. doi:10.2307/j.ctv13qfv1t.12
Shmulewitz, I. 1973. "Our Obligation to Remember." *Yiddish* 1, no. 3 (Winter 1973–1974): 49–59.
Shoskes, Henry. 1944. *Pages of a Ghetto-Diary: An Authentic Document on the Tragic Events in Poland, from the Invasion to the Battle of the Warsaw-Ghetto*. New York: Dr H. H. Glanz Publisher.
Shoskes, Henry. 1945. *No Traveler Returns*. New York: Doubleday.
Shoskes, Henry. 1946. *Polyn-1946: Ayndruken fun a rayze*. Buenos Aires: Tsentral-Farband fun Poylishe Yidn in Argentine.
Shoskes, Henry. 1949. *A velt vos iz farbay: Kaptilen zichroynes*. Buenos Aires: Tsentral-Farband fun Poylishe Yidn in Argentine.
Stewart, Victoria. 2019. "Crimes and War Crimes: William Hodge & Co. and the Public Understanding of the Holocaust in Post-World War II Britain." *Law and Literature* 31, no. 3: 113–127. http://dx.doi.org/10.1080/1535685X.2017.1351723.
Strigler, Mordechai. 1947. *Maydanek*. Buenos Aires: Tsentral-Farband fun Poylishe Yidn in Argentine.
Strigler, Mordechai. 1948. *In di fabrykn fun toyt*. Buenos Aires: Tsentral-Farband fun Poylishe Yidn in Argentine.
Strigler, Mordechai. 1950. *Verk "ce."* Buenos Aires: Tsentral-Farband fun Poylishe Yidn in Argentine.

The National Library of Israel. 2018. "Burn Them, as My World and Everything I Loved Burned in Auschwitz's Crematorium." July 17. https://blog.nli.org.il/en/katsetnik/?utm_source=facebook_englishpage&utm_medium=organicpage&fbclid=IwAR20FQU9USzclI268YEL5lXAFdG_sZ9NN1b_2Ih2QEGPs_1agLDBvzjUuM4.

United States Holocaust Memorial Museum (USHMM). 1999b. "Eichmann Trial—Sessions 68 and 69—Testimonies of Y. Dinur, Y. Bakon, A. Oppenheimer, A. Beilin." Film, June 7, 1961, 51:58. https://collections.ushmm.org/search/catalog/irn1001698.

Wiesel Elie. 1958a. *La Nuit*. Paris Minuit.

Wiesel, Elie. 1958b. *Night*. New York: Hill and Wang.

Wiesel, Elie. 1979. *A Jew Today*. New York: Vintage Books.

Wiesel, Elie. 1982. *One Generation After*. New York: Schocken Books.

Wiesel, Elie. 1996. *All Rivers Run to the Sea*. London: Harper Collins.

Wiesel, Eliezer. 1956. *Un di velt hot geshvign*. Buenos Aires: Union Central Israelita Polaca en la Argentina.

Williams, William. 1997. *Interview with USC Shoah Foundation* (Interview 36774). Los Angeles, CA: Visual History Archive.

Yad Vashem. n.d. "Dr. Ella Lingens." www.yadvashem.org/yv/en/exhibitions/righteous-auschwitz/lingens.asp

Yerushalmi, Yosef Hayim. 1982. *Zachor: Jewish History and Jewish Memory*. Seattle, WA: University of Washington Press.

PART III
Trajectories Beyond the Final Word

We have no right to expect from them tales of edification and redemption.
—*Christopher Browning*

7
DEEP INSIDE, I'M STILL THERE

The Holocaust Man

"I do not want to be a Holocaust Man!" In early 2016, Nimrod Ariav hadn't yet given testimony about his experiences during World War II. He seemed reluctant to become what he described as a "Holocaust Man." He used this term, which I hadn't heard before. During our initial telephone call I asked him what he meant by it. He responded that he did not want to become like "those Holocaust survivors that go memorials and light candles."[1]

There was no question that he had lived through the Holocaust. He was born Szulem Cygielman to a Jewish family that lived in Poland and remained there throughout the German occupation. His parents and twin brother, Avraham, first lived in the Lublin Ghetto, then managed to relocate to his maternal grandmother's town of Bełżyce, where Szulem found work in an electricity plant. In 1942 an "action" (deportation round up) to Majdenek death camp was carried out by the Germans, which he remembers being conducted near one of the synagogues (Ariav 2016). The family had scattered, so they were all not caught at once. In addition to the deportation of several hundred men to Majdanek (Państwowe Muzeum ne Majdanku 2020), the action led to the murder of 150 residents of Bełżyce. The dead laying around the synagogue included Lejb Cygielman, Szulem's father. The rest of the family survived the massacre. On returning to the town after the action was over, the twins and other workers were made to dig a mass grave in the Jewish cemetery and bury the dead. He described burying his own father:

> we came back [and] saw all the people who [had] died, and we brought them to the cemetery . . . there is a Jewish law that all people who die the same day should be buried together and not in separate graves . . . and my

DOI: 10.4324/9781003147220-11

brother, myself, a lot of young kids . . . buried . . . 150 people. My father was first on the right, looking down on it, on the right, the first one. This stayed with me.

(Ariav 2016, seg. # 26)

With help from a Polish family friend, Szulem and Avraham fled to Warsaw, where they assumed Christian identities. Avraham was later killed during a raid on their hiding place, at which point Szulem joined the Armija Krajova (Polish resistance army) and subsumed his Jewish identity into his adopted Polish Christian persona of Jerzy Godlewski. He fought with distinction in the Warsaw Uprising in August 1944. Although he was seriously wounded in the firefight, Nimrod "Zigi" Ariav does not consider himself a Holocaust survivor. Explaining why, he recalls that in the Lublin Ghetto he was confronted by youths he describes as *Hitler-Jugend* (Hitler Youth). Upon seeing him walking on the sidewalk wearing the mandatory Star of David armband, they attacked him. He said: "they knew that I am Jewish because I had the armband" (seg. #18). After the incident was over,

I removed that armband and I never put it back, and decided, this is how I am going to do it . . . nobody should know that I am Jewish, and maybe this way I will be able to survive all these things. [I] didn't know yet what to survive, where to survive, but I didn't want a thing like that to happen again.

(Ariav 2016, seg. #19)

Still in his early teens, Szulem Cygielman decided he would *not* be a victim of the Nazis. When the war ended, even though he had lived through almost six years of German genocidal persecution against the Jews, he never considered himself a victim. He did become a witness, however. He started to travel to Poland for business, and went to Bełżyce in search of the grave of his father, which he was unable to locate:

So later in '87 I came a few times to Warsaw [on business] and looked around [and] couldn't find [the grave]. And [I] didn't want to ask . . . I should know where I buried him. It was [in] the Jewish Cemetery. Where the hell did it disappear?

(Ariav 2016, seg. #27)

In 1988, Nimrod again returned with his two sons, and located the grave with the help of the mayor's office. They drove to where the Jewish cemetery had once been to discover that it

was a picnic ground, [a] picnic ground for the kids, with trees . . . and if that happened [in] 1942, and I was [there] in '88, that was the age of the trees.

(seg. #27)

FIGURE 7.1 Nimrod "Zigi" Ariav returns each year to Bełżyce with his sons Avi (left) and Ariel (right) and their families

Source: (Photo courtesy of Stephen D. Smith).

Nimrod Ariav restored the cemetery boundary and built a memorial to the 150 Jews who were buried there, including his father. He returned every year to Bełżyce (which he continues to this day) as an act of public witness, to pay respects to the dead. But Nimrod had never given a formal testimony.

When I spoke to him in 2016, I was intrigued by his refusal to speak about his past. But rather than turning him into an object of the past, I wanted to approach him as a subject. I traveled to Israel to learn more about why he was reluctant to speak about his history, even though he was highly committed to memorializing his father. From Nimrod Ariav, I learned that testimony only has meaning to the testifier if they are not objectified by the process.

Nimrod did not want to be made into a "Holocaust Man" (something) without fully understanding who he is as an individual (someone).

Nimrod "Zigi" Ariav was subsequently interviewed for the USC Shoah Foundation Visual history Archive in 2016. In 2017, he was the first Israeli to be interviewed for the Dimensions in Testimony interactive biography program. He answered questions for five days in English and Hebrew. In June 2018 he attended the Yad Vashem International Teachers Conference, where his interactive biography was presented to over 250 participants in the session, "A World Without Survivors: Different Approaches." After the presentation, he was given a standing ovation for his contribution to Holocaust memory and education. Ariav still maintains he is not a Holocaust survivor. After his family had spoken on camera in a 2016 interview about the significance of his recorded testimony, he stated:

> I am wiping some tears. That's . . . what I feel. It's good, [a] good feeling. Now I can say [if] somebody might call me [a] "Holocaust Man," I couldn't care less.
>
> *(Ariav 2016, seg. #189)*

Glick and Paluck found that surviving victims experience "ambivalence about remembering versus distancing themselves from the past" (Glick and Levy Paluck 2013, 201). The past affects the victim in the present because, "whether through remembrance or defensive denial . . . even the ancient past can represent a proximal cause." More recent trauma, such as the loss of family and identity through "genocidal attack" can "initiate extreme reactions" (202). Surviving victims, even those such as Nimrod who deny they were impacted, were traumatized by their experiences. As a young man, he had to lift his own father from the street and bury him in a mass grave—a highly traumatizing event in itself. If the "current interest in Holocaust survivor testimony has been stimulated in no small degree by a resurgence in interest in trauma" (Trezise 2013, 40), it does not follow automatically that the witnesses are prepared to share that pain openly. Nimrod Ariav chose to witness with his family and close friends in private, rather than to reveal his innermost secrets to the public gaze. Even so, he was a highly active witness. Not only did he annually remember, he confronted his past where the trauma had originally taken place. He made his "proximal" experience to the past in *proximity* to the geographical place in which it occurred. Nimrod's witness, which fulfilled the mandate of the dead, was his repeated silent act of memorialization at the place where it had happened.

After what appeared to be 30 years of silence from the Holocaust survivor community, the 1980s saw what Aaron Hass describes as an "explosion of material" (Hass 1991, 1) which continued into the 1990s. Surviving victims produced memoirs, oral interviews, video interviews, television documentaries, and events. Elie Wiesel suggests the silence from the surviving victims was the result of a wish to keep events concealed, and fear of being misunderstood—or worse, accused of exaggeration and seeking pity (Wiesel 1982, 9). Whatever the cause of the silence, it was the growth of public awareness of the Holocaust driven by projects such as the United States Holocaust Memorial Museum and popular media such as Schindler's List that pushed the traumatic events of the past into public consciousness. These projects and cultural developments appear to have triggered surviving victims to feel confident enough to produce new material. Surviving victims felt more comfortable sharing their testimony once it was clear that society was prepared to listen to them. Whatever the catalyst, the explosion of material has created a wealth of new content to support further study of the events of the Holocaust through the experience of those that lived it.

Reasons to Speak

To fully understand why surviving victims give video testimony (in particular), this chapter provides an insight into the USC Shoah Foundation Visual history Archive from the perspective of two phrases that serve as keywords. "Testimony-sharing motivations" applies to the section of testimony in which the witness explains why they have decided to share their life experience. "Future message" refers to the section of testimony in which the interviewee is discussing the value of their experience for future generations. "Testimony-sharing motivations" is referenced in 7841 testimonies in the Visual History Archive (at the time of writing), and "future message" is referenced in 30,412 testimonies. These keywords were originally used by the Shoah Foundation when indexers identified content related to the topic in the testimonies. The index terms are a framework to rediscover topics within testimonies that most mattered to the interviewees. The fact that nearly 15% of interviewees *chose* to speak about their motivations to give testimony (whether or not they were asked a question about their reasons to give testimony) demonstrates a high level of self-awareness about the genre of testimony itself.

As a part of my responsibility overseeing USC Shoah Foundation, I routinely made decisions about how testimonies were represented in education materials, the media, and films. I was also responsible for the mission of the institute, including the collection of testimonial interview of survivors of genocides other than the Holocaust. I received informal advice from colleagues and members of the board about whether it was appropriate to use testimony in certain ways—for example, whether to teach about tolerance or Holocaust history. Using the I-Thou framework, I decided to consult the surviving victims' testimonies in order to solicit "opinion" from the testimonies in the archive. I hoped that they would help me better understand how surviving victims perceived their own testimony, and collectively guide how the entire archive should be deployed.

The USC Shoah Foundation's "Interviewer Guidelines," which are provided to interviewers as a part of their training, suggest that "When the interviewee has finished recounting his/her experiences, it is appropriate to ask broader, reflective questions." These questions include, "What would you like to tell future generations?" (USC Shoah Foundation n.d., 44). This open question was designed to help us understand the most important personal perspectives that matter to surviving witnesses. Interviewers were given no further instructions regarding the scope of the question, or who might be included in "future generations"—potentially, family, public, governments, and students. In 2011, a random selection of 100 from 14,000 English-language testimonies that included the keyword "future message" in the Visual History Archive were analyzed. Several main themes emerged, which included:

> [the] importance of tolerance and civic engagement, and of Holocaust remembrance and education. But survivors also stressed the moral obligation

we have to be our 'brother's keeper,' and spoke of the need to strengthen Judaism, Israel, as well as our hopes for peace.

(Cohen and Beaver 2012, 3)

In 2012, a further 988 testimonies in 18 languages that contained the keyword "future message" were reviewed. An online data collection form[2] was used to flag messages within that keyword response that included 19 possible preset themes that had been encountered in the 2011 pilot study. In addition, the form used open-ended text fields to identify and track any messages not covered by the existing categories.

This content analysis was conducted in multiple languages, roughly in proportion to their incidence in Visual History Archive.[3] We used a multilingual approach to evaluate how the content of the final message changed in relation to geography and culture: English was 50%, Russian 15%, Hebrew 13% and other languages 22%, statistics consistent with the entire archive at the time. As a result of listening to over 300 hours of testimony tagged with the keyword "future message" from over 1,000 Jewish survivors, we found,

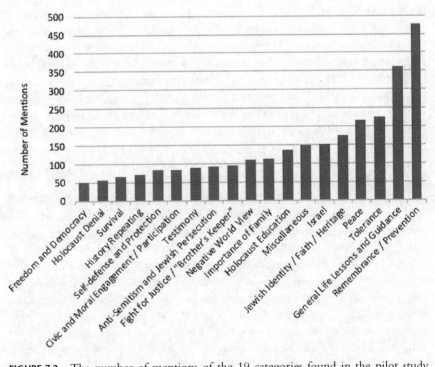

FIGURE 7.2 The number of mentions of the 19 categories found in the pilot study among the total number of testimonies analyzed (n.1088)

Source: Used with permission of USC Shoah Foundation.

a clear message for the future—remember the Holocaust so this never happens again. These survivors remind us they chose to share their memories to educate future generations, and they ask us to remember, learn, and prevent. Survivors also urge us to maintain hope for peace, harmony, and a better world. They offer guidance for a better life, telling us to be kind, generous, respectful, and tolerant. They want us to understand the importance of loved ones as well as individual identity and faith. They prompt us to get engaged, stand up, and speak out again injustices and evil. These Jewish survivors also stress the importance of Israel's existence and Jewish identity.

(Cohen and Beaver 2012)

The word cloud produced from the themes identified in the future messages lean toward "remember, learn and prevent," as illustrated in Figure 7.3.

Understanding the motivations behind the testimonies produced a secondary mandate—that *their* past is not limited to "the past." Readers of literature published by surviving victims are exhorted to guard against the possibilities of repetition. They are invited to learn and apply the lessons of the Holocaust now, before it is too late (Hartman 1994, 60). Joanne Weiner Rudof suggests that asking surviving victims "what were the lessons of the Holocaust?" will likely result in a response, "with some platitude about teaching the lessons of the Holocaust so that 'it will never happen again'" (Rudof 1998, 128). Easily digested clichés redacted for public consumption can easily turn testimony into a form of cheap social catharsis. But the surviving victim pursues a complex understanding of and healing from their own past, even when they appear to speak "platitudes." Surviving victim Trude Levi, author of *A Cat Called Adolf* (1995), states her reason for sharing testimony: "I don't want to forget about it. I want to draw conclusions from it. . . . That's why I go to schools, and I am talking about it so that to show that something must be done to prevent it."[4] Levi is determined to prevent repetition and avoids a 'never again!' cliché. Instead, she demands that "something must be done to prevent it." Her point is that a series of actions must follow her testimony for it to have any effective value.

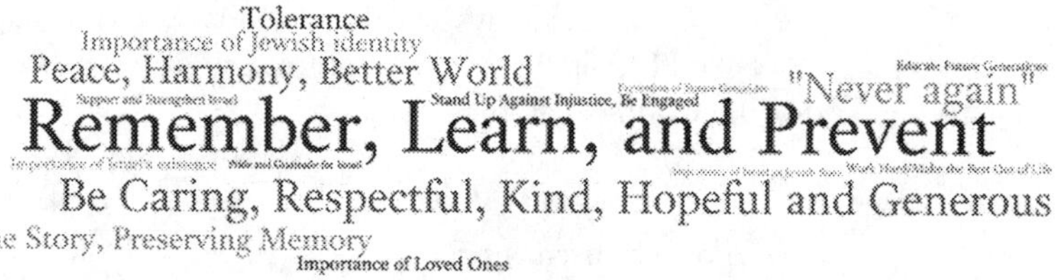

FIGURE 7.3 Word cloud derived from the keyword "future message" in the USC Shoah Foundation, Visual History Archive

Source: Used with permission of USC Shoah Foundation.

George Papanek was born in Austria on April 2, 1931 to a man who was Assistant Minister of Education. As a Jew and a Social Democrat, "he was active in political matters in the '30s, against the Nazis before it was generally understood how dangerous they were" (Papanek 1996, seg. #3). He had to "go into exile" after 1934 as the right-wing parties started to become popular. George's mother was a doctor who

> "went to medical school in Vienna in her 20s, both as a woman and as a Jew. That was remarkable" (seg. #4). George grew up in an assimilated home with no sense of Jewish identity. He only discovered he was Jewish when playing a game of "catch the Jew" with his Catholic friend and was told by his mother that he could not play that game. He describes that moment: "Suddenly I was the non-person, the, you know, the dark side . . . the demonized creature" (seg. #9). George describes his early years as, shaping "me . . . in a way that nothing else has."

(seg. #35)

In his interview, George was asked if he had a message for the future. Without instruction to do so, he looked directly into the lens of the camera and said to some unknown audience in years to come:

> I do think that there is something to be learned from these experiences. And the most important to me . . . is to take seriously what's happening now—[just] because the Nazis are gone, doesn't mean that evil is gone in this world. And there are many forms. And whoever you are, and wherever you are, you can find it. And it is very important to be part of the world in which you live, to be—as the French existentialists would say—engaged . . . in the world, and trying to do what is available to do that's useful.
>
> If you do that, you feel a lot better about . . . yourself, and you make a difference. The old saying . . . think globally, act locally is true. We all have opportunities to make a difference. And enough of us can create a critical mass so that the world can be a better place. There's no doubt about that in my mind.
>
> I think the effort is worth it. It's wonderful to make, even though sometimes it is risky. And I hope that we will continue to make this struggle and try to see that the world becomes better.

(Papanek 1996, seg. # 89)

George Papanek had not rehearsed his future message. As with all interviewees, the "future message" question was intended to illicit a spontaneous, reflective, and open response. George had thought through his philosophy since the age of seven. What he believed about the future was rooted in his past, and a constituent part of who he was as an individual in the present. It was easy for him to explain his message because it was an extension of his being. As can be seen, a word cloud

FIGURE 7.4 Word cloud generated by author from transcript of George Papanek's 'future message' in the Visual History Archive

Source: Papanek 1996 Seg. #89.

generated from his future message transcript (see earlier) makes his philosophy clear—he is hoping for a better world.

Scraps of Memory

Edith Eva Eger (née Elefant) was born in Kosice Czekoslovakia in 1927 and describes her mother as "a very wise beautiful woman who took me to a ballet school when I was very young" (Eger 1995, seg. #7). There she was taught by a "ballet master" who she describes as being "spiritual." She recalls that he told her "God built [you] in such a magnificent way that whatever happens to [you, you] always have to find the power within" (seg. #7). She then explains that this life lesson was later valuable to her in Auschwitz where she "found within what never came without" (seg. #7). In her two audio-visual testimonies (Eger 1992, 1995) Edith offers life lessons within the testimony that she derived from her experiences and her professional expertise as a therapist. Much like Viktor Frankl, who 60 years prior had applied his Auschwitz experience to his practice of Logotherapy (Frankl 1946, 1963), Edith explains her own four theories on what she describes as "The Choice Therapy."[5] She refers to these theories as: i) "learned helplessness"; ii) "thoughts create feelings and behavior"; iii) "unconditional positive self-regard"; and iv) "the worst experiences can be the best teachers" (Eger 2020, 6). She relates these therapeutic approaches to her learned experiences during the Holocaust.

Edith Eva Eger presents these reflections in two ways in her testimonial narratives. Universal *life lessons* are highlighted throughout her story, providing guidance to the inner world of her mind, rather than the external world of the perpetrators that was forced upon her. She describes her mother telling her as they sat in the cattle wagon: "No one can take away from you what you have in your mind" (Eger

1995, seg. #48). Eger's mother had no idea what fate would await her at Auschwitz or the independence her daughter would have to exert to survive. Still, she had the presence of mind to give her daughter a piece of advice that became her North Star during and after the Holocaust. The second way she navigates her past is through the professional skills she gained later in life. She uses these tools to analyse her past through *professional insights* into the psychological world she inhabited during the Holocaust. In one audio-visual testimony she analyses her own parents' marriage, which she is careful to explain she is not able to objectively diagnose because she was never their therapist. Nevertheless, she concludes that her mother saw herself "marrying, you know [down]"—the last word of which she cannot bring herself to say. In both audio-visual testimonies, she describes her father as being a "ladies' man" without saying he was unfaithful to her mother. She concludes, "they may not have had much in common . . . my mother spent a lot of time alone" (Eger 1992, seg. #19).

Unlike Victoria Vincent, who hid the meaning of the hanging scene at Auschwitz, Edith is explicit about what the events meant to her, creating a mosaic of life lessons around a rough chronological timeline. In *The Choice* (Eger 2017), her autobiographical self-help book, she explores topics such as memory, loss, and trauma. Using personal hindsight and professional insight, she creates a bridge between her own life and that encountered by her readers. Her Holocaust experience becomes the ultimate life experience—the cruel fate of human existence. She is cast as the resilient survivor who not only survived physically, but went on to master her fate by overcoming her trauma to live her life to the fullest. After surviving the Holocaust and starting a family in America, she trained in psychology. She describes the moment that she looked at her badge at William Beaumont Army Medical Center at Fort Bliss Texas, which read "Dr. Eger, Department of Psychiatry." She relates that she was treating an army veteran who was venting his rage out loud with expletives such as "Fuck America!" and "Fuck God!" She wrote that, "witnessing his fury calls out the rage in me, the need to express it, release it. *Fuck Hitler! Fuck Mengele!*" (Eger 2017, 177). She recognized in her patients that she had never taken time for her self-healing after the Holocaust. For this reason, she felt she had no right to heal others and her badge should read "imposter" (178).

At that point she concluded that she had to go back to Auschwitz to face her own past:

> I went back to Auschwitz and released the past, forgave myself. I went home and thought, "I'm done!" But closure is temporary. It's not over till it's over.
>
> *(Eger 2017, 268)*

Her confrontation with the past and continual struggle with closure creates a dialogue between her past and present. Throughout her writing, she explores the topic of memory by taking her reader back to the arrival platform at Auschwitz-Birkenau. She paints a vivid image of her standing arms linked with her mother and sister, awaiting selection. She observes these three women from the outside looking in, placing herself in line behind them, observing them from behind. With the benefit of hindsight, she knows that this is the last moment the three women will be together. However, at that moment they do not know that or "refuse to consider it" (Eger 2020, 195). She describes her mother in the middle of her two daughters who "lean inward . . . her strength the pillar that supports Magda and me." She reflects on that moment as the "threshold into the major losses of my life" to which she has "returned again and again" over the seven decades that have elapsed to "regain the life that precedes this moment, the life that precedes loss. As if there is such a thing." She explains to her reader that "childhood memories are often fragments . . . which together form the scrapbook of our life." Edith uses this analogy to explain to her readers how she will draw upon the scraps of memory at her disposal. She will compile and make sense of her past because "they are all we have left to understand the story we have come to tell ourselves about who we are."

Eger links her own trauma with her practice in a back-and-forth between her history and her therapies; "Often the patients I worked with mirrored my own discoveries about the journey to freedom" (Eger 2017, 182). Her past and present profession find commonalities in unexpected places, such as when she describes treating a teenage patient with an eating disorder as looking "like I had at Auschwitz—skeletal, pale. She was wasting away" (184). After two years of successful therapy with the patient, Edith reflects on her own restoration process and how for many years she had "housed a vacant empty place, the vast dark of the life that would never be" (191). "The vast dark" represents the things she lost, including the time and opportunity that were taken away from her that she can't get back. In her narrative, the Holocaust is transformed from being events in history into "the vast dark" which lives in her life as trauma and absence. She writes: "I couldn't let go of either piece of my truth, nor could I hold either easily" (191). In what Eger describes as "mirroring," she concludes that her patients helped her to question how she related to her past and confront how she connected with her present (195).

In *The Gift* (2020), Edith Eva Eger draws a parallel between her liberation from Gunskirchen concentration camp in May 1945 through the "Twelve Lessons to Save your Life." The opening chapter is subtitled "I learned to live at a death camp," an invocation to her readers to see the possible in the impossible, which sets the tone for the book. She sets a high bar for her readers, but also wants to make clear that her experiences give her authority to speak about the topic of her book. Her physical liberation from the Holocaust becomes a metaphor for healing and self-help; "Each moment in Auschwitz was hell on earth. It was also my best classroom" (2). In sharp contrast to Charlotte Delbo, for whom Auschwitz was a "useless knowledge," Edith puts "loss, torture, starvation and the constant threat of death" to work as a "tools for survival and freedom"—turning the "uselessness" of Auschwitz into a guide for living.

Edith does not dismiss the Holocaust for what it was or try to "undo what had been done to me." Rather, she reflects that the only way she could respond to terror and hopelessness was to find it within herself to "choose hope" (4). She is honest about her own self-healing taking many years after the moment of liberation. Her testimony of healing and self-liberation would not have been possible in the 1940s. Thomas Geve's *The Boy Who Drew Auschwitz* (Geve 2021) is almost identical to his 1958 memoir *Youth in Chains* (Geve 1958). His conviction is that his life after the Holocaust has no applicability to what happened during it. Edith, in contrast, published her first book at the age of 90, having taken time to reflect on the meaning of the Holocaust upon her life after. She unites her scraps of memory and long-term self-healing, creating a single story of her entire life—rooted in the past, reflected through the present, and mirrored through the lives of others.

Listen Then Listen Again

Audio-Visual Testimony is *not* information, although it does contain information.

Fundamentally, testimony is a relationship. It is offered by the testifier to the listener. There is an implied trust by the testifier that the listener will have the integrity to engage with the story they tell, the persona they present, and the individual they are. To "listen then listen again" to audio-visual testimony is not a theoretical concept; it is a practice that enables a closer reading of the individual behind the persona. When encountering video testimony, I typically watch the testimony twice. The first pass is to watch what is being said by the *persona* on the screen. The second pass is to try to understand who the *individual* is, and *why* they said *what* they said. Put another way, the first watching involves listening to the historical experience and engaging with the information provided. In the second and subsequent viewings, I try to understand more of the thematic meanings that the individual is conveying through their words, emotions, and intents. I apply this practice whether I am listening to the entire life history, an episode within it, or a single short clip. "Listen and listen again" is a form of empathetic listening that constitutes part of the I-Thou encounter. It starts by recognizing that the face in the frame is an individual and acknowledging their state of being—who they are, not just what they say. This practice allows the viewer to become more immersed in the individual and engage multiple senses to understand their intonation, physiognomy, emotions, and physicality.

Transcriptions—the audio video testimony redacted to the words it contains—are extremely helpful to the scholar looking for information. Transcripts are searchable and enable data—times, places, and names—to be read at many times the speed of watching video. But the transcribed text is only a fraction of the data associated with the video which contains many biometric markers which are the physical part of human encounter. The transcript provides information, the video is encounter. While the text file has utility, it affords little opportunity for empathetic listening. Roman Ferber, in his testimony, describes the difficulty of living with memory:

> The struggle has never ended—for any survivor. Look, we don't live the Holocaust. I don't live the Holocaust. I'm as far removed from it as possible. But all of a sudden, when you wake up in the middle of the night, and your head burns, and you sweat all over . . . some incidents that happened during

the war—you don't ask for it. But deep inside, it's still there. It's always going to be there till we die.

(Ferber 1998, seg. #163)

The transcribed text conveys Ferber's struggle living with the past, but as I read it, I also see Roman delivering the word, his tone, his body language, his emotion, none of which is contained in the words. From an informational perspective, we learn from the text that living with the past is ongoing. He has a life in the present no longer associated to the past, but the past still haunts him. When watching the video of Ferber relays the exact same words, we encounter a much more nuanced and animated individual than the text itself can convey. Roman uses bodily gestures, eye movements, facial expressions, intonations, and hand movements that express his lived experience. His gestures are a part of an embodied testimony, which transfers the emotions of how he feels when he is recalling his past. When I read the text I know of what happened in his post-Holocaust life. When I *encounter* him and "listen and listen again," I observe his struggle, read his emotions, and take into my own being a part of the intense reliving he conveys.

One particularly valuable aspect of audio-visual testimony that transcripts are unable to convey is silence. This emotionally laden aspect of testimony can be documented by indicating pauses between words. However, noting pauses does little to express the *feeling* of the silence, other than providing a data point about how many seconds it lasts. During an interview with Nobel Prize winner Eric Kandel in 2012, I asked him a relatively simple question about why he was telling his story. During his explanation he became emotional, which is depicted in the transcript by the pauses that document the silence:

INT: Why did you agree to do this interview for the Shoah Foundation Archive, Eric?

EK: I think it's a privilege to do it. [PAUSES FOR 13 SECONDS] I also did not realize until you told me [PAUSES FOR 4 SECONDS] how many Nobel Laureates had survived the Holocaust. [PAUSES FOR 13 SECONDS]

INT: And how does that make you feel?

EK: Pleased. [PAUSES FOR 5 SECONDS] I thought you had very few, and I'm one—one of them. [PAUSES FOR 3 SECONDS] I feel more comfortable now knowing there are others. [LAUGHS]

INT: Final question is, if there was something that you would like us to do with your story, [PAUSES FOR 3 SECONDS] what would it be?

EK: I don't think I have any special request for that. Obviously, I would like my children to have access. [PAUSES FOR 6 SECONDS] I'm worried about my crying i—in here, to be honest with you. [PAUSES FOR 4 SECONDS] Although this, this is how I feel.

INT: Why do you think you feel so deeply about this today?

EK: I'm sorry?

INT: Why do you think you feel so deeply about this during this interview?

EK: First of all, I cry easily, so this is not simply Holocaust-related. It tends in recent decades to be more Jewish-related. [PAUSES FOR 3 SECONDS] But I tear up very easily, even for other things. I'm a sentimental Jew. [LAUGHS] Look, we're speaking about the most meaningful experiences in one's life. I mean. [PAUSES FOR 33 SECONDS] No, except for my family I'm—I'm no—I don't have any specific ideas as to [PAUSES FOR 4 SECONDS] how this could be useful. [PAUSES FOR 12 SECONDS] I leave that up to you.

(Kandel 2012 Seg. #124)

During this 203-second segment of testimony there are 100 seconds when Eric is silent. About half of the interview (49%) has no narrative. Only by watching the testimony can one come close to experiencing its meaning. To reduce such a passage to text objectifies the individual, who is struggling to describe how meaningful it was for him to give testimony. Notwithstanding Eric's significant public persona, he is willing to reveal himself as an individual who is best encountered through his struggle to find words, in a time when words cannot be found.

There are public expectations that surviving victims must vividly remember everything about their ordeal and recall it on demand. But for many, their memory is vague at best. When recounting the past, it can be difficult to admit on camera that their most acute memories cannot be recalled. Mala Tribich, in her testimony about her deportation on a cattle wagon, doesn't conjure up a memory or repeat what she has heard in other testimonies about conditions in the cattle wagons:

MT: Do you know, I have no memory of the train. It's—it's blocked out. I really cannot remember. [PAUSES FOR 6 SECONDS] In fact, I have spoken to a friend that was with me, and I thought, "What was it like? Tell me!" Well she didn't tell me anything. She said it was awful. You know, we were very crowded. . . . But I don't remember any particular incident or anything. I just remembered marching to the station. And I remember people standing in the streets watching us.

(Tribich 2012, 1:50:13–1:51:02)

On listening to Mala's testimony the first time through, the data told me that the passage was about a lack of memory. Being in the cattle wagons was an experience that many surviving victims recall as being vivid, which she admits was not the case for her. The second time I watched the segment it became clear that it was not the physical conditions of the wagons, but the psychological impact of the spectators observing their misery that stuck in her memory. What follows the passage just outlined is a brief comment about the bystanders. She wonders aloud about "what they [were] thinking and why they were watching?" (1:51:15). Mala was more troubled by the attitudes of the bystanders than the abuse of the perpetrators. A passage that at first appeared to be about her *forgetfulness* of the journey in the cattle wagon is about her *remembering* the social and emotional humiliation she then felt.

There are at least 200,000 hours of audio and audio-visual Holocaust testimonies stored in archives around the world, which amounts to over 20 years of continuous content.[6] The vast amount of audio-visual testimony, along with audio and written collections, is more than a lifetime of reading, viewing, and listening. It would seem that closure to the narrative of Holocaust testimony is unlikely. Yet the demands of listening with empathy—to listen and listen again—are time-consuming. A company executive and a world leader on separate occasions both asked me to share with them the "top ten" testimony clips in the Visual History Archive. They were both busy people looking for the most compelling moments to inspire them, and to inspire others to take a greater interest in testimony. However, the need to find such a shorthand version of the past presents a danger. There is a need for society to be moved and to understand what happened during the Holocaust, when they have little time and too many competing interests to consider its complexity. The need for a shorthand version of the Holocaust is the source of creeping ossification and closure that one day could well reduce the Holocaust to myths and legends.

The Ossification of Witness

Jurek Becker, concentration camp survivor and author of *Jacob the Liar*, was asked to speak at the fiftieth anniversary of the Berlin book burning. He said of the invitation:

> [W]hat is the reason for meeting and remembering that fifty years ago the Nazis burned books? Just for remembrance? That's not enough for me. I am not interested in these memories, they are not so great—I can imagine better memories . . . The only and important good reason to remember is to ask ourselves what attitude was behind that happening, and where do we find that attitude today?
>
> (Lewis 1984, 94)

Becker insisted that even as a surviving victim he did not wish to remember for memory's sake—underscoring that the trajectory of memory is always in symbiosis with the present. Becker invites the audience to apply the memory of *that* past to *this* present. As the surviving victims have increasingly committed themselves to give testimony, those who suffered as outcasts in the past have become the "redeemers" of their own history in the present:

> Focusing on death, survivors have been depicted as silent victims—guilty, ghostly and estranged. Focusing on ongoing life—the fact of survival itself—the same survivors are celebrated as heroic witnesses, tellers of tales, redeemers of the human spirit and of hope.
>
> (Greenspan 1998, 30)

Overcoming the pain of the past to address the social fault lines that allowed genocidal ideology to succeed is laudable and necessary. However, there is a danger that the surviving victim wins the battle over memory—by providing narrative and giving it a meaning over the alternative of silence and obfuscation—but ultimately loses the war against memory (Wollaston 1996) through creeping mythologization, as society ascribes its own meaning to their past in the present. The language of dualism found in testimony—about overcoming despair with hope, failure with heroism, silence with speaking, and darkness with light—creates a quasi-theological mythology which is easy to understand, but for all its redeeming characteristics, inhibits the more demanding task of ongoing struggle with complexity. When the Holocaust becomes a mythologized world reduced to dualistic narratives of redemption, we are no longer challenged by it, because "the sanctification and ossification of memory . . . handicaps genuine ethical struggles in the present" (Ezrahi 2015, 348). Testimony needs to be read in the context of what the testifier lived through. The surviving victim of the Holocaust was not a hero or a legend from an imaginary inferno. Their life involved daily struggles in extremely hostile circumstances to survive physically, mentally, and emotionally. Testimony offers detailed insight into what it meant to live through the inhumane and lethal injustices the German authorities perpetrated on the Jews and other victims of racial authoritarianism.

The purpose of testimony is not to create redemptive legends of a mythologized past but to understand what happened to ordinary to "ordinary Jews." When Christopher Browning's introduced the concept of "ordinary men" when reviewing the actions of Police Battalion 101 (Browning 1992) he de-mythologized the Nazis as faceless monsters providing a much more human insight into how the Holocaust happened. So, too, Jews were ordinary people whose lives were turned in to a chaotic maelstrom of confusion. Faced with unprecedented circumstances, they had to make impossible choices. Those daily and at times mundane details give us insight into the unfolding of history in real time and the complexity of human nature. Their choices may be ambiguous or contradictory, and may not conform to convenient patterns of human behavior that we understand. Still, such detail gives us opportunity to continue to struggle with the implications of what we do not understand, rather than drawing convenient conclusions.

Ossification forces simplification over complexity, certainty over ambiguity. It occurs when an expected outcome—survival, love, or redemption—is demanded of testimony, even when the narrative depicts death, hate, and deprivation. The ossification of witness happens when the interpretation of the narrative becomes fixed. Such fixity limits the ability of the narrative to embrace ongoing tensions and ambiguities within the ordinariness of the Holocaust. Ossification is a demand made by the kind of listener who seeks easy answers, rather than one who is prepared to grapple with unanswerable questions. Ossification contains testimony in a form no longer in keeping with the disruptive nature of the trauma. As the corpus of testimony grows and the survivor community dies, the potential for ossification becomes more likely. Testimonial narratives risk becoming objects—redacted to versions of the past with subjective interpretations projected onto them. Creeping mythologization also provides a protective shield from the otherwise destructive nature of the unexpurgated narrative.

A friend who borrowed a book on the Holocaust from me commented that he was finding it very interesting. He then added that although it was "quite depressing" he was certain that "eventually it will come around to a message of hope." It is sometimes too difficult for a listener to hear that the Holocaust might well have been completely without hope:

> The centripetal thrust towards a mythicized terminus, which gives rise to historical absolutes, avenging spirits, and apocalyptic politics is counteracted by the "centrifugal" impulses that originate when one turn's one's back on Auschwitz and substitutes other points of departure—both into the past and into an open-ended future.
>
> (Ezrahi 2015, 348)

Dekoven Ezrahi's instructive image of Auschwitz at the centre of the Holocaust imagination, around which our memory and myth making revolve, is drawn from the physical sciences. Although collective memory is not a science that adheres to Newton's Laws of Motion, how the iconology of Auschwitz has replaced the Holocaust as a central myth can be observed. Auschwitz has become a synonym for the Holocaust in contemporary culture, a centripetal concept that pulls in language, memory, and visual culture. The image of the gate tower, railway lines, and a photograph of a tattooed number are brands of genocidal death. They evoke the unspoken meaning of the Holocaust as a whole, around which society can find mythologized meaning. I would only dispute Dekoven Ezrahi claim that a centrifugal force counteracts a centripetal force, because in science it is the same physical force experienced from different perspectives.[7] Whether we are being pulled toward the Holocaust or repelled from it, it remains at the heart of public debate; it is the same force experienced from different perspectives within the collective conscience. The fact that the Holocaust has societal "gravitational pull" means that it will remain an inescapable part of our future.

Myths and legends, such as are depicted in epic stories, do not threaten witness, provided they are sufficiently complex in their interrogation of the past and do not replace its details. The creation of symbolic figures or iconic places that summarize an otherwise overwhelming history help communicate meaning. To disinterested audiences requiring shorthand meaning, they do have real value. But contained within those myths will be heroes (such as Oskar Schindler) or villains (for example, Josef Mengele) who fulfil the need of society to see good and bad, darkness and light at the expense of many grey tones. All mythical episodes are based on a false dualism. Yet the experiences at the extremes do not represent the entirety of experience. Josef Mengele may be portrayed as evil personified through the mythological representations of his heinous acts. But to focus on him alone ignores and dilutes the actions of other doctors at Auschwitz, such as Thilo, Rhode, Köing, and Klein. An obsession with Mengele inhibits awareness of the horrifying number of doctors that practised at Auschwitz and the roles they played. Olga Lengyel, writing in 1947, did not know that later Dr. Mengele would become the mythological selector on the *rampe* (platform) at Auschwitz-Birkenau when she wrote:

> My heart thumped violently. This officer, a large dark man who wore glasses, seemed to be trying to act fairly. Later I learned that he was Dr. Fritz Klein the "Chief Selector."
>
> (Lengyel 1947a, 15)

In the mythology of Auschwitz that has evolved, Dr. Mengele has emerged as the "chief selector." Dr. Klein is virtually never mentioned in later accounts, although he spoke Hungarian and was able to communicate with the victims more readily than the German-speaking Dr. Mengele. Similarly, the reification of Oskar Schindler—as the embodiment of the idea of goodness during times of evil—deflects from other fascinatingly complex stories. Rescuers such as Varian Fry, Stefanie Podgorska, King Boris II, and Gitta Bauer acted with similar ethics, and help us envision a more multi-dimensional concept of courage. Symbols help define what we mean when we think of fear, anguish, goodness, and hope. Symbols also fix meanings.

It is all too easy to fall into mythologizing patterns. Testimony often conforms to a recognizable three-act structure, with a set-up, confrontation, and resolution. During the set-up we learn that our narrator had a beautiful childhood, surrounded by family and traditions. Life is secure, filled with hope for the future. But there is danger, as the evil of antisemitism is never far away. During the confrontation, the evil leader Hitler amasses his forces, builds a global empire, and attempts to take over the world crushing all in his pathway. Our narrator is thrown into a confusing and overwhelming situation. Small as they are in the face of armies seeking to kill them, they find ways to outwit the forces against him. The Jews are crushed by Hitler's henchmen, the SS, along with other collaborators who do his bidding without question. The smiling and handsome Dr. Mengele represents the epitome of evil. Our narrator lives through this maelstrom, and somehow does not succumb to the odds stacked against them. After epic battles, only through grit and determination, resolution finally comes. Our narrator hangs on to the bitter end, clinging to life as tanks rumble in through the gates. There is jubilation that the evil empire is gone, but sorrow at all who were lost. Finally, the Statue of Liberty comes into view, the promised land is reached. A new life can begin again.

Returning to Paul Oppenheimer's observation that "life is stranger than fiction" (1996, 24), it is sadly true that the 12 years when National Socialism ruled Germany confirmed to the utopian epic battle for world domination, which had to be overcome for there to be peace and stability. There is much in this three-act structure that helps the individual testifier give narrative shape to an otherwise debilitating and complex historical scenario. The listener also knows from the outset of the testimony that the main protagonist survives. It is a given that physically there will be a "good outcome." Only when testimony is listened to in detail is it clear that the facts of each individual life during that period cannot be contained in a ready-made narrative arc. The set-up, confrontation, and resolution do not conform to a universal meta-narrative and expected patterns. Multiple accounts, when read alongside one another, disrupt the convenience of epic narrative storytelling.

Testimonial narratives, when taken together, are counter-mythological. They struggle with the mundane, with the ordinariness and the confusion. They convey nuances at a personal level, and may even fall into tropes and over-simplify. But because each adds to what we know, they surprise us with unexpected experiences and new insights. Because they contradict one another, there can be no single narrative. Testimonies are plural and complex, so their interpretations will be similarly numerous and complex. The "facts of history are not distinct from their reflective interpretation in narrative" (Young 1990, 39). So when we interpret the facts of the Holocaust in a symbolic manner, it will by default result in the symbolization of the Holocaust. If on the other hand, we are willing to struggle with unanswered questions and grapple with their ambiguity, the Holocaust will remain an open and dynamic force within society.

During the Holocaust, victims of Nazi persecution responded with a plethora of perspectives, from optimism and the endurance of the human spirit to despair and newfound nihilism. Their emotional, spiritual, and practical experiences became confused as they were caught up in a maelstrom of unpredictability. Should not that unpredictability and confusion also be a part of our interpretation? To understand the past we learn most when we are true to it, rather than replace it with a false, convenient and less confronting version of it. It is necessary to read, recite, and confront the past for what it was, and not obfuscate the traumatic, disruptive, confusing, and ambiguous nature of all that transpired. Elie Wiesel puts the danger more bluntly:

> And so I tell you: You who have not experienced their anguish, you who do not speak their language, you who do not mourn their dead, think before you offend them, before you betray them. Think before you substitute your memory for theirs.
>
> *(Wiesel 1979, 247)*

Eva Schloss survived by hiding in Holland, as did her brother Heinz and parents. Prior to the outbreak of the Second World War, they had lived in Merwedeplein Square, in the same building as the Frank family, whom they had come to know (Schloss and Kent 1988). After the Holocaust only Otto Frank survived—his daughters Margot and Anne, and his wife Edith had all perished.

Eva's brother Heinz and her father Erich were also murdered. Only Eva and her mother Fritzie had survived. Otto and Fritzie became close and eventually married. Eva was in the kitchen when Otto Frank opened the red tartan diary of Anne Frank, which rescuer Miep Gies had found in the attic after their deportation and returned to him. Eva was there to see Anne Frank's diary published and its deceased author become famous:

> I do not like it when I am introduced as Anne Franks's stepsister. Am I not a person in my own right? Are my experiences not worthy of being listened

to also? I do not think that Anne Frank's Diary is even about the Holocaust and should not be treated as if it is.[8]

Anne Frank's diary has become an iconic representation of the loss of childhood. It has become so sacred that Eva's own contribution to witness and testimony has been devalued and her own brother ignored by history. Audiences do not come to hear her, they come to get as close to the phenomenon of Anne as they can. Eva has become objectified, and therefore silenced by her own audience, because they bring their own interpretations about the meaning of Anne's life and diary to Eva's talks:

> The irony is that Anne says that people are fundamentally good at heart and everyone clings onto that showing how insightful she is. That was before Auschwitz and Bergen Belsen. I doubt she would have said that after. My story is almost identical to hers and I can say that people are definitely *not* good at heart.[9]

By challenging what Anne wrote in her diary, Eva desacralizes the text in the present. She has unique authority to treat Anne as a co-subject in the experience they went through together. As she questions the authority of her sister's narrative, she starts a conversation in the present about the nature of good and evil. For Eva, the diary is not a sacred text and Anne is not an artefact of history. Anne is a young woman with whom she was once friends, who went through the similar experiences:

> People say to me, 'We read about the Holocaust in preparation for your talk.' I ask them what they read, and they tell me, 'The Diary of Anne Frank,' at which point I tell them that they need to start reading something that *is* about the Holocaust, because the Diary of Anne Frank certainly is not.[10]

The popularity and iconology of the Diary of Anne Frank *threatens* knowledge of the Holocaust. When it is the only book that is read about the genocidal suffering of Jews under German occupation, it gives only one small human window into the lives of those who were in hiding. It can never do more than that.

When testimony becomes a myth, it threatens the survival of testimony itself. The privileging of one testimony reduces the likelihood that the remaining ones will be fully explored. I was once asked by a prominent surviving victim of the Holocaust what would make their testimony stand out among over 50,000 testimonies in the Visual History Archive. I explained, "It would be yours." The individual did not give a testimony, because there was no guarantee it would have been the most viewed. Privileging one testimony would have been detrimental to all testimonies. So too the canonization of popular texts—*The Diary of Anne Frank*, Elie Wiesel's *Night*, and Primo Levi's *If This is a Man*—can prevent explorations of other published testimony. Their popularity means that more people understand the Holocaust than would otherwise be the case, to which the authors are owed a debt of gratitude. However, if these authors were to have the final word, the ongoing trajectory of memory will cease abruptly upon the death of the surviving victims, becoming an ossified, narrow canon of first-person literature. Alternatively, if like Eva Schloss, the surviving victim sets the framework as a *subject* in conversation and an *agent* of discourse, we can continue to learn from them, now and into the future.

Marek Edelman was the last surviving member of the high command of the Warsaw Ghetto Uprising when he delivered a talk I attended in Cape Town, South Africa.[11] Marek chose to speak in Yiddish, even though the organizers has provided a Polish translator. He began by stating to the large audience that מקנעד א זיא סא 7, גא ט לא, (this is a day of memorial). It was not a specific day of memorial. He was making the point at the outset of his talk that every day of the year is a day to remember. He also stated to the audience that speaking to them was *his* act of memorial, reinforcing that he was speaking to them as part of an unspoken mandate on behalf of the dead. Without recounting any memories from his time in the Warsaw Ghetto or the Warsaw Ghetto Uprising, he cut straight to his conclusions. He then explained to the audience about the need to learn and apply the universal lessons of the Holocaust. Within ten minutes he had completed his speech. After agreeing to take questions, the audience tried to elicit first-person witness about the Warsaw Ghetto, demanding that Marek say more about his experience. One questioner asked Marek what he was to tell his children about the ghetto after meeting him, virtually begging him to provide historical details of events in the ghetto. Marek responded to the parent that he should teach them to live as citizens of the world and never to act to others as the Germans behaved towards the Jews.[12] Marek refused to be typecast by the audience or meet their demands about what he should say to them. The audience left the auditorium without having had an encounter with him, even though he had invited them to do so by meeting him in the present. Because the *object* they had come to see did not meet their expectations of the "Warsaw Ghetto hero," they were unable to encounter him or hear his message. The audience were not engaging with the subject, they were observing the object, who in turn did not wish to be objectified. Co-fighter in the Warsaw Ghetto Uprising High Command, Antek Zuckerman, once stated, "If you could lick my heart it would poison you" (Lanzmann 1985, 196). Marek Edelman resisted such metaphors and refused to be ossified as a mythological figure of the past. He had much to say about the present that nobody was prepared to hear.

The ossification and mythologization process renders audience expectations problematic, because it puts pressure on the surviving victim to standardize their content and delivery. Each surviving victim has only one set of experiences, but there are many ways to position it in the present. Waldemar Ginsberg was an atheist (Ginsburg 1998) and would regularly discuss the source of his disregard for religion to groups at the UK National Holocaust Centre, where he regularly volunteered as a speaker. While I was director there, I noticed on the visit roster that he had been invited to be the volunteer speaker on a day that an Orthodox Jewish day school was attending the Centre. I realized that my colleagues had not thought through what would happen should Waldemar challenge the views and beliefs of the audience of believers during the question-and-answer session. I decided *not* to coach Waldemar on their sensitivities. My principle is to always to allow the surviving victim to say what they want without censure or coercion. I was also honestly curious to see how he would depict his atheism to an Orthodox group.

As the question-and-answer session started, one of the first questions was whether Waldemar believed in God after his experiences. Waldemar responded along the lines that everyone has their own way of thinking about God and that belief is very personal—without divulging his own long-held atheistic views. He urged his audience to find their own belief system, irrespective of life's difficulties that may make them question everything about both God and people. What unfolded was an I-Thou encounter that enabled two theologically opposed parties to have a rich and respectful human conversation. Waldemar yielded his direct opinion about deity in favor of an overarching insight about personal belief systems and theodicy in general. As a result of his sensitivity, the students did not have their world challenged in an environment that would not have been able to support the disruption it may have caused. Instead, they were provided with insights and foresight by a person whose life experience and views they could respect. Not all are so flexible.

Trude Levi wanted to ensure that if her testimony was ossified, she would be the one to do it. In her book, *Did You Meet Hitler Miss?* (2003) she published questions that students had sent her via mail after she had spoken at schools around the UK. She meticulously responded to them, taking pride in answering every letter she received. She wanted to ensure that the answers she gave were in print, so her views were documented and could be read by other students in future years. It was a way for her to continue encounters with students after she would not be able to meet them in person. Unlike Victoria Vincent, who subsumed the meaning of her testimony within her narrative, Trude openly discussed the moral meaning of her experience. She was aware that at some point her testimony would be fixed in time and wanted her analysis to be explicit within it. For example, she refers to two separate occasions when German individuals contributed to her survival, thus illustrating the point that not all Germans behaved in the same manner. She provided detailed account of a sabotage operation in the munitions factory. By the end of her talk, Trude raised discussion points to prompt the audience to ask questions she had deliberately left unanswered. Trude makes clear why she chose to raise these points:

> Jews were not just victims, and I think that has to be emphasized much more . . . I make a point of that because I think it is so important to show . . . I didn't go into hiding . . . but I could have gone into hiding. I think it's important to show that too, that there were decent people.[13]

Trude's self-ossification process transforms the experiencing self modality of testimony into a remembering self modality. She is not so much telling the story to recount what the Germans did to her, but to show how she responded to it in sum.

Her testimony is about maintaining agency during her lifetime by consciously making fixed points of conclusion. By way of further example, Trude was offered an opportunity to be a work leader at the Hessich Lichtenau munitions plant. She turned it down, stating in her testimony, "I refused it because I said I wanted to survive, but I did not want to survive not at any price" (Levi 1995, seg. #124).

Henry Greenspan's previously discussed concept of "recounting"—rather than the established term "testimony"—challenges the process of ossification. When "recounting" the past, testimony is a work in progress rather than an unalterable statement (Greenspan 1998, xvii). This definition fits with the trajectory of memory model, in which testimony is a product of time, place, and persona, and allows for ongoing encounter. Marek Edelman's presentation in Cape Town was a product of the moment. It was a highly performative attempt to replace testimony with an engaging challenge to his audience. What transpired was that the mythological Marek Edelmann constrained him from being an individual in the present, or for the Holocaust to be part of his ongoing recounting and engagement (Greenspan 1998). The Warsaw Ghetto Uprising mythology had become an insurmountable barrier. The audience came to meet the myth and missed out on a once in lifetime encounter with one of the truly historic figures of the Holocaust.

The Keyhole and the Clothesline

I liken testimony to a keyhole. A way to peer into a vast place that you cannot go, but that you can catch a glimpse of. The view you get is somewhat obscured, but you are nevertheless able to see the scale and scope of what is on the other side of each door. Video testimony for example "forces the viewer to personally and directly witness the process of memory recall, to listen for speech as well as silences, contradictions, gestures, and emotional expressions, and to consider the presence, in the present, of past trauma" (Hillman 2015, 217), but it never becomes your own past. It is only ever a window into it. The closer you come to the keyhole, the more you are likely to see on the other side. But you remain on the outside. In what I liken to "peering into the past" the keyhole of testimony does give us a way to see things we can never know from our own daily experiences, but we can get a glimpse when we peer hard enough. As with other aspects of the subject-subject framework it is not on the witness to provide a key, or to fully open up. The onus is on the listener to come close and peer in.

I also liken testimony to a clothesline. The clothesline is a set of facts that are pulled taut from one end to the other along the trajectory of memory. The testimonial clothesline represents the bare facts of the surviving victim's experience during the Nazi period. In many cases the surviving victim laid down those facts in the early years after their incarceration. Kitty Hart-Moxon's statement written for the Quaker relief team (see Ch. 6) was one such statement, wherein she wrote about the basic facts of her incarceration in Auschwtiz in 1946. Dario Gabbai shared a 1951 essay from his English class in which he wrote about SS perpetrator Otto Moll. Gabbai was keen to establish the facts about Moll's sadistic behavior and so used his English lesson to document what he had observed of Moll's behavior. He says of writing about the Holocaust in English class:

> This document [was written] when I came back from the camps, and I came to Los Angeles . . . the English teacher told me to write anything important from the . . . camps. And the only this I can think about [sic] was. Moll . . . the first thing that I wrote when I came cack was that he was a sadistic person.
> (Gabbai 2014, Seg #247)

Gabbai's description of Moll's behavior at Auschwitz in 1951 is almost identical to his description of the same perpetrator in his two interviews for the Visual History Archive (1995 and 2014). In 2014 he clarifies that his focus on Moll was purposeful: "I always told the story about Moll—Otto Moll. Always. I wrote about . . . everything" (Gabbai 1996 and 2014, Seg. #197). Moll is a part of a clearly definable basic text in Gabbai's narrative, which developed over time.

It might be assumed that the facts that underpin the historical veracity of a testimony drift or change. There is no doubt that testimony take a very different shape over time, which our discussion about the trajectory of what memory is has revealed is influenced by many external circumstances in the life, experience, and life cycle of the testifier. The basic facts, however, are very sticky and change very little, from an historical perspective. Kitty's initial 1946 memo of 3000 words deals solely with her incarceration in Auschwitz. Her 1961 publication *I am Alive* (Hart 1961) has 144 pages and covers much of her life under the Nazis. Her 1981 publication *Return to Auschwitz* (Hart 1981) has 240 pages, which includes more about her life after the War as well as more detailed descriptions of her period under the Germans, she makes small additions in her 1997 edition (Hart-Moxon 1997) The content of her 1946 statement is all clearly evidenced in her later volumes as an identifiable historical "clothesline" that runs through her many publications and documentaries. It does not mean that some facts do not get amended or altered, but for the main part they remain remarkably constant.

The "clothesline" is a useful analogy for how the trajectory of memory develops over time in relation to a fixed past. The facts remain constant, but from time to time there are reflections, the addition of new observations, new contextual information gathered along the way, stories told by relatives and other survivors that help make sense of what they all went through from different perspectives, stories told to children and grandchildren, visits to locations, documentaries, lectures, national and international commemorations, media appearances, social media accounts. There is a lot that is new, but that does not mean they occlude the old. Sometimes all of these are hung on the clothesline, other times just a few. But the "clothesline" is always there.

(Non)Closure

"Coming to an end, therefore, we come to no conclusion. Rather we turn to a question" (Patterson 2012, 257). Will testimony become an object of the past, or remain a dynamic subject in an ongoing dialogue about the past in future? The continued search to discover meaning in the Holocaust will continue, because "the silence that surrounds the phrase "Auschwitz was the extermination camp" is not a state of mind (*état d'âme*), it is a sign that something remains to be phrased which is not yet determined" (Lyotard 1988, 56–57). Meaning that cannot be ascribed to Auschwitz, by extension cannot be ascribed to the Holocaust. Can meaning be found when those who lived through it are no longer her here to affirm it? Eight decades have already elapsed and it is no longer the case that "Auschwitz—and Jewish Europe for that matter [are conceived as] "another planet" that had exploded and sent meteors, traces of its material existence and its total destruction into perpetual orbit" (Ezrahi 2015, 346). Meaning which began as the "dead star loaded with corpses" (Rousset 1951, 109) over time evolved to a more universalizing introspection, such as Primo Levi's "gray zone" (1988), which was a place of human ambiguity, "just this side of the "black hole" [where] all matter and all meaning are annihilated" (Ezrahi 2015, 346). As the conversation moves from what the Holocaust was in the past to what it might mean in the future, Gerda Weismann-Klein, author of *All But my Life* (1957), reflects: "Never mind giving you answers, we do not yet have the questions, nor will we in the lifetime of those who lived it. That will be down to those who follow."[14]

This book has examined how surviving victims have sought to find voice and offer meaning during their own lifetime. Each has found their own way to grapple with memory, witness, and testimony in their lives. Kitty Hart-Moxon stated:

> Everybody wanted to forget . . . I was encouraged to do it. That's the point. If it hadn't been for the Quakers . . . who constantly encouraged me to speak about it . . . I might not have done it.[15]

At 95, she hopes that 60 years of "trying to tell the world the facts" is enough to leave as her legacy. Kitty does not attempt to ascribe a meaning to her experience, she just wants to ensure that the facts are established in her own lifetime. What remains to be seen is whether the Holocaust will become a closed and canonized historical event or an open and ongoing struggle for meaning. There will come a point of closure when surviving victims cease to add to the body of testimony. It is not possible until then to know whether the discourse provoked by testimony will continue to challenge and change Western European civilization beyond the lives of those who lived through the Holocaust.

As previously discussed, Hegel (2010) provides a way to live with an idealized concept of the memory and meaning of the Holocaust—understood as *Being-in-itself*—without ossifying it through mythologization. The testimonies and sources at our disposal—understood as *something-others*—are similar to one another. However, they are also different from each other, because each is "something" and also "other" to each other. When read in context of each other, their meanings can change and even become contradictory. "Something becomes another, but the other is itself a something, hence it likewise becomes an other, and so on and so forth ad infinitum"

(149). The infinite ideality of the Holocaust contains within it the notion that all Jews were targeted for genocidal death, but this was not the reality of those who lived it. Their existences were composed of many finite experiences. Understanding "the finite" requires a constant process of comparing, juxtaposing, grappling with their contradictions, and learning from their adjacencies. Hegel has his own bottom line: "The only thing that matters is not to take as the infinite what is at once made into something particular and finite in the determination of it" (152).

Hegel's dialectic brings us back to the preface of this book. The great Jewish rabbinical sage Hillel is reported to have once described the Golden Rule of Classical Judaism to a new convert: "That which is hateful to you do not do to another. That is the entire Torah, the rest is its interpretation" (Talmud, Shabbat 31a). Hillel has an ideality about his personal meaning of the infinite Torah, but concedes the reality of what that means is found in its many finite interpretations. Rabbinic Judaism's codification of the Talmud may be a model process for Holocaust testimony to remain a dynamic and ongoing interpretative process, rather than an ossified myth of history.

The Talmud consists of two distinct parts. The first part is the Mishnah (משנה), a codified set of six tractates which explains how to practice the 613 laws (מצוות) contained in the Torah (תורה). These tractates were developed over several hundred years as an oral tradition and codified by Judah ha-Nasi in the early third century. The second part of the Talmud is the Gemara (גמרא), which is further commentary on the Mishna. The Gemara was compiled in centers of Jewish learning in Jerusalem and Babylon over several centuries following the codification of the Mishnah. The codification of the Talmud produced a religious text—the product of the lives and opinions of rabbis who grappled for centuries with questions of how to apply the laws. The rabbis, who appear by name in the Talmud much like the surviving victims of the Holocaust, are not objects of the past. Rather, the rabbis are ongoing subjects in the discussion about Jewish law. Jacob Neusner observed:

> Let us now abandon the historical mode of discourse. We have to, if we insist that the ancient rabbis [as people] *are* interesting. I do not come merely to report that they once lived and therefore should be described as objects of historical curiosity. The rabbis are interesting because they and the literature they produced constitute alternatives for people interested in how societies take shape, how life is to be lived, and, especially, how the issue of human existence may be thoughtfully analyzed and decided. Therefore, I am going to use the present tense, even though my sources derive from men dead more than sixteen centuries.
>
> *(Neusner 1984, 3–4)*

The Talmud is a "supertext"[16]—a body of work that has survived hundreds of years and influenced generations. A supertext has fundamental meaning in the society and culture to which it is associated. That ongoing association ensures texts like the Talmud remain relevant. Homer's *Illiad*, the works of Plato, the Veda, the Q'ran, and the New Testament are all supertexts. The question is whether the body of testimonial literature, art, oral history, and other eyewitness testimony of the Holocaust will become its own supertext and continue to shape society over centuries—or become a popular myth.

Historical debate will certainly rage as new archives are found, testimony translated, new stories revealed, and opinions formed. But that is not the question under review here. The question is whether there can continue to be subject-subject inquiry in the present tense—much as the rabbis remain in debate centuries after their lives ended—long after the subjects are gone. Adin Steinsaltz refers to "one of the great Talmudic commentators, the Maharsha, [who] often ended one of his commentaries with the word *vedok*, 'Continue to examine the matter'" (Steinsaltz 2006, 273). Will "the matter" of the Holocaust continue to be examined when its victims and eyewitnesses are not here?

When testimony is object, it is fixed. When it is subject it is dynamic, living dialogue with the past in the present. The analysts who are concerned that Holocaust memory is being sacralized through testimony, contribute to its mythologization. The listener who encounters testimony is open to understanding it in new ways, and never certain. When we are certain, there is closure. Alternatively, when we are prepared to live and struggle with the despair of the "Black Sun," a more "hopeful vision of the future [could be] a product of that despair, not a protection against it" (Langer 1982, 128). Johanne Baptiste Metz describes a "dangerous memory that harries the past and problematizes it, since it remembers the past in terms of a future that is still outstanding" (Metz 2007, 182). Metz's concept is compelling because, unbounded by time, it does not permit mythologization, and keeps inquiry alive. He goes on:

> This kind of remembering breaks through the spell of the ruling consciousness. It reclaims unresolved, repressed conflicts and unrequited hopes. It upholds the insights garnered from past experiences and in this way destabilizes all those things that are taken for granted in the present.
> *(Metz 2007, 182)*

Cathy Caruth makes clear that the proliferation of traumatic witness brings a "danger, as some have put it, of a 'contagion' of the traumatization of the ones who listen" (Caruth 1995, 10). It may well be traumatizing, but when memory is dangerous it also carries an imperative to stay alert to the possibilities of repetition, without resorting to clichés. The testimonies of the surviving victims are a source of such "dangerous memory" that provokes the listener to translate its meaning for the present day and future possibilities. The extreme nature of events described in testimony can lead to ossified mythologization fixed in the past. If it can also continue to live as a dangerous and living memory, demanding an ongoing reappraisal of the present.

Maurice Blanchot's carefully placed suggestion that it is necessary "to keep watch over absent meaning" (Blanchot 1986, 42) reveals that when there is an inability to comprehend it is not in itself a failure, because the attempt to understand is a fulfilment of a duty. Having permission to *not* understand everything is required to generate further curiosity. Our duty is to pursue comprehension, not to provide answers. The narrative of testimony encourages learning through asking difficult and dangerous questions, which in turn fuel further inquiry, thereby creating a virtuous cycle of discourse.

At one level closure happened during the Holocaust itself because "the majority of victims who did not survive have no narrative or personal voice" (Langer 1991, 21). Their unspoken words as the ultimate victims will remain silent and always beyond interpretation. On another level, the voices of the surviving victims are still amassing even at this late stage—a vast library of narrative that no single person will ever be able to truly know. The silence of the dead and the voices of the living are the gatekeepers of closure. When all is said that can be said, more will always be left unspoken, and unheard—demanding our silence in return.

Testimony is the last act of resistance against the debilitating erasure of Jewish life, culture, history, and memory. Those who testify do so to overcome the obfuscation and denial of their existence. When read together, testimonies are greater than the sum of their parts. Not only do they tell their own story, they add to the history of a people. It is one of the first global histories that has been written *en masse* by ordinary people who lived through it. In the tradition of Deuteronomy 25:19—in which the Children of Israel are told to "blot out the remembrance of Amalek from under heaven; thou shalt not forget it"—testimony is a reminder. It reminds us not to blot out remembrance of the German Nazis nor forget what happened in detail. Together, the surviving victims and other witnesses to the Holocaust have created their own digital supertext that will outlive the Nazi regime by hundreds of years.

Paradoxically, the memory of the Holocaust threatens its own memory. The real memory of the Holocaust is "absent memory"—that which was never spoken by the dead. The mandate from the dead that demanded the surviving victims speak might be extended to include a mandate to the next generation—the inheritors of memory—to keep watch over absent memory. Preserving the unknowability of the Holocaust may be the only means of remembering those who are forgotten. The duty to keep watch over absent memory is not to preserve the silence, but to continue to give voice to their unknowable experience.

The surviving victims who are still alive are aware that their own confrontation with their own past is perpetually in motion. Batsheva Dagan states:

> It gets new shapes and I'm . . . developing and learning and extending what I am doing . . . It is not static. The topic is developing all the time because I learn, I hear, I see. So I am not on the same spot.[17]

As a surviving victim who testifies and teaches in a professional and personal capacity, Batsheva is aware that her message changes. Closure of the interpretation of that message would constrict her teaching and discourse in the present. For the surviving victim, this does not mean that the pain lessens, as in Jean Améry's aforementioned statement: "whoever has succumbed to torture can no longer feel at home in the world. The shame of destruction cannot be erased" (Améry 1980, 40). The ability of surviving witnesses to rise above the trauma and pain to find meaning and teachable moments is fundamental to testimony in its many forms.

Academic research and public discourse about witness of the Holocaust remain anchored in interactions with surviving victims. Archives and testimony platforms give scholars and teachers access to vast amounts of digital data. Following the endpoint of the living survivor community, understanding, and representing the witness through research will be an ongoing field of study. It is important that the discipline of witness study not inadvertently supersede the act of witness itself, forcing its own form of closure. To avoid that, interdisciplinary study to testimony fits with Dominick LaCapra's methodological approach, which suggests that,

> various options may engage one another most provocatively and constructively when they incorporate an active awareness of the claims of other interpretative modes and the differential stresses and strains attendant upon any choice of interpretation. Indeed, such a field of forces may give rise to hybrid modes of thought, of delicate hue and complex configuration, that attest to the way critical thinking is positioned on thresholds, open to its own historicity, and prone to unforeseen transitions.
>
> *(LaCapra 1994, 40–41)*

"Closure" does not entail forgetting the past. If anything, it means the reverse. It is its own form of memory. Its counter memory is when the wound is left open with all of its pain. The struggle to remember is therefore never completely open or closed because the truth lies not in finding a conclusion, but in the spaces that lie between—in the quest itself.

What, therefore, does our study of witness reveal? It appears there is opportunity now, while the last surviving victims are still alive, to confront the complexities described in this book. It should be possible to create conditions in which, knowing the constraints and understanding the multiple voices that may be heard even in single text, that listening *to* surviving victims can be extended to talking *with* them. In so doing, it may be possible to accept and understand testimony for all that it can offer, with all of its polarizing messages and inherent contradictions.

Testimony is a type of history, interpretation, memory, and representation, but is never fully constrained by any of them. It is veracious, but not always accurate. Testimony is imbued with despair, but not without hope. It can be a confession of shame, while remaining proud of human dignity. The narrative of survival may thus be read and interpreted for what it is: human experience at the extreme and as such represents the paradoxes, ambivalence, and ironies that make up human experience *in extremis*. Testimony given by any individual from their memory must be accepted for what it is: a dynamic and exegetical subjective representation. In Holocaust testimony, fragments of lived experience are mediated to allow those who were not there to confront "real" events and what they have come to mean in the lives of those who have lived them.

Elie Wiesel refers in his essays and speeches to "Kafka's messenger" (Wiesel 1999, 346), who fulfils his duty to deliver the message. Wiesel models himself on the messenger, who fulfils his duty by delivering the message, whether or not it is heard.

Geoffrey Hartman would doubtless disagree with Wiesel, suggesting "heed the tale, not the teller." Yet Hartman is simultaneously aware that to hear the tale, the teller must also be heard. He goes on to say, "give the teller . . . the trust that allows a continued gathering and handing on of this legacy" (Hartman 1991, 336). The legacy is the testimony, but the testimony can never be separated from the teller.

Memory *is*, and cannot be divorced from the storyteller. Narrative gives form to memory, but the story that is told is never more than its representation—words formed from the being of memory. The encounter with memory through testimony creates an opportunity to work and re-work, listen and re-listen, read and re-read the experience—even after the teller has ceased to bear witness. This cycle of testimony brings the book full circle to the double bind of the dilemma of witness, in which "even if you understand you do not." The incompatibility of the gas chamber and human dignity, extermination and human choice, narrative, and silence—all simultaneously reveal and occlude something of testimony's true nature.

To fulfil the mandate of the dead and those who survived, there are no easy conclusions. We strain to listen and commit to understand. The surviving victims have struggled to uphold the mandate through their writing and speaking, their silence and discourse, in their living and in their dying. They have succeeded in their struggle but failed in their aim—such duty to speak has no conclusion, even when it ends. The duty remains theirs for as long as they live, since they are the only ones who can tell how it was for them. Speaking with them, listening to their thoughts, and sharing their struggle to tell leads to no conclusions, other than the disruptive, debilitating, inconclusive nature of what mass death does to the human soul.

The I-Thou encounter with testimony overcomes the dehumanizing anti-I-Thous world and the framework of forgetfulness that the Nazis created. When encountering the other as subject-subject, we enter each other's lives and a part of us is transferred. There is a concept that "the witness, to the witness, in turn becomes a witness" (Friedman 2005) but that does not quite do justice to the encounter. A witness becoming a witness is transactional—I listen and I repeat. Encounter forges a relationship. The deep listening that accompanies encounter enters the being of the testifier, as a subject and subject in exchange. When I bring myself to the encounter, I offer, not just receive. The outcome is not a new witness who points to an object (persona) in the past, but a person in the present who encounters the surviving victim (individual), thereby incorporating something of them into their own being. After several decades of being in the presence and encountering surviving victims of the Holocaust, I cannot describe what the names of the people in the acknowledgements section of this book mean to me in detail, but I can say they are not objects of history. I sense who they are, what their lives mean, and why they broke through the silence of memory, bore witness, and testified. Mostly, I am grateful that they took the time to encounter me.

Inevitably, when the last surviving victims die, whatever they wrote, spoke, sung, danced, filmed, painted, and blogged will remain their memorial to the dead. Then the responsibility to maintain the mandate will be passed to those who did not experience the original offense. As stated in the preface, this book can be summed up in a single line: listen to surviving victims with all thy heart. That is the entire book; the rest is its interpretation, because it is only a matter of time before interpretation will be all that we have:

> Somewhere in my novels I have tried to imagine being that last survivor. I do not want to be that survivor. I'm afraid of that survivor, of his vision. I'm afraid of the madness that would invade him, weigh upon him, to have so much knowledge, and to know that, with him, all this knowledge will go down, will go out.
>
> *(Wiesel in Lewis 1984, 160)*

Notes

1. Nimrod Ariav, telephone conversation with the author, 2016.
2. A preview of the online data collection form is available at: https://new.qualtrics.com/SE/?SID=SV_1Heo17IPQOGRBl2&Preview=Survey&BrandID=usccollege.
3. Language data was not collected for 91 of the 1,088 testimonies analyzed.
4. Trude Levi, audio-visual interview, September 24, 1996.
5. She described her work as "The Choice Therapy" on a video conference January 23, 2021. At this conference I was conversing with her for "Making History Alive," an international student exchange program about Holocaust history and memory. There is no reference to her therapy being called "The Choice Therapy" in her books.
6. An internal USC Shoah Foundation review of video testimonies revealed at least 85,000 interviews collected worldwide, which were an average of 2 hours and 20 in length. This is the same average as the Visual History Archive, and there are at least 195,500 hours of video testimony in repositories around the world.
7. For a non-scientist's introduction to the difference between centripetal and centrifugal forces see: https://medium.com/swlh/centripetal-vs-centrifugal-forces-whats-the-difference-4b5f848ae9bd
8. Eva Schloss, personal conversation with author, November 28, 2021.
9. Ibid.
10. Ibid.
11. Attended by the author in Cape Town, South Africa, August 5, 1998.
12. Paraphrased from memory.
13. Trude Levi, telephone interview, February 6, 1999.
14. Gerda Weismann-Klein, paraphrased from a personal conversation with the author.
15. Kitty Hart-Moxon, personal conversation with the author, November 30, 2021.
16. USC President Emeritus, C.L. Max Nikias, and USC Shoah Foundation CTO, Sam Gustman, have both referred to the Visual History Archive as a "supertext" when providing a rationale for the long-term preservation of the archive.
17. Bat Sheva Dagan, personal conversation with the author, 1999.

References

Améry, Jean. 1980. *At the Mind's Limits: Contemplations by a Survivor on Auschwitz and Its Realities*, translated by Sidney Rosenfeld and Stella Rosenfeld. Bloomington, IN: Indiana University Press.

Ariav, Nimrod. 2016. *Interview by USC Shoah Foundation* (Interview 55570). Los Angeles, CA: Visual History Archive.

Blanchot, Maurice. 1986. *The Writing of the Disaster*. Lincoln, NE: University of Nebraska Press.
Browning, Christopher R. 1992. *Ordinary Men: Reserve Police Battalion 101 and the Final Solution in Poland*. 1st ed. New York: Harper Collins.
Caruth, Cathy, ed. 1995. *Trauma: Explorations in Memory*. Baltimore, MD: John Hopkins University Press.
Cohen, Casey, and Chesley Beaver. 2012. "Future Messages." USC Shoah Foundation, unpublished report.
Eger, Edith Eva. 1992. Interview by USC Shoah Foundation (Interview 52218). Los Angeles, CA: Visual History Archive.
Eger, Edith Eva. 1995. Interview by USC Shoah Foundation (Interview 8413). Los Angeles, CA: Visual History Archive.
Eger, Edith Eva. 2017. *The Choice: Embrace the Possible*. New York: Scribner.
Eger, Edith Eva. 2020. *The Gift: Twelve Lessons to Save Your Life*. New York: Scribner.
Ezrahi, Sidra DeKoven. 2015. "A Personal Postscript." In *Marking Evil: Holocaust Memory in the Global Age*, edited by Amos Goldberg and Haim Hazan, 345–353. New York: Berghahn Books.
Ferber, Roman. 1998. Interview by USC Shoah Foundation (Interview 43707). Los Angeles, CA: Visual History Archive.
Frankl, Viktor. 1946. *Ein Psycholog erlebt das Konzentrationslager*. Wien: Verlag für Jugend und Volk.
Frankl, Viktor. 1963. *Man's Search for Meaning: An Introduction to Logotherapy*. New York: Pocket Books.
Friedman, Régine-Mihal. 2005. "Witnessing for the Witness: 'Choice and Destiny' by Tsipi Reibenbach." *Shofar* 24, no. 1: 81–93. www.jstor.org/stable/42944122.
Gabbai, Dario. 1996 and 2014. Interview by USC Shoah Foundation (Interview 142). Los Angeles, CA: Visual History Archive.
Geve, Thomas. 1958. *Youth in Chains*. Jerusalem: Rubin Mass.
Geve, Thomas. 2021. *The Boy Who Drew Auschwitz*. London: Harper Colins.
Ginsburg, Waldemar. 1998. *And Kovno Wept*. Newark, NJ: Beth Shalom Ltd.
Glick, Peter, and Elizabeth Levy Paluck. 2013. "The Aftermath of Genocide: History as a Proximal Cause." *Journal of Social Issues* 69, no. 1: 200–208.
Greenspan, Henry. 1998. *On Listening to Holocaust Survivors: Recounting and Life History*. Westport, CT: Praeger.
Hart, Kitty. 1961. *I Am Alive*. London: Corgi.
Hart, Kitty. 1981. *Return to Auschwitz*. London: Sidgwick & Jackson Ltd.
Hartman, Geoffrey. 1991. "Closing Remarks." In *Lessons and Legacies; the Meaning of the Holocaust in a Changing World*, edited by Peter Hayes. Evanston, IL: Northwestern University Press.
Hartman, Geoffrey, ed. 1994. *Holocaust Remembrance: The Shapes of Memory*. Oxford: Blackwell.
Hart-Moxon, Kitty. 1997. *Return to Auschwitz*. Revised ed. Newark, NJ: Beth Shalom Holocaust Centre.
Hass, Aaron. 1991. *In the Shadow of the Holocaust: The Second Generation*. Cambridge: Cambridge University Press.
Hegel, Georg Wilhelm Fredrich. 2010. "First Subdivision of the Logic: The Doctrine of Being §§ 84–111." In *George Willhelm Friedrich Hegel: Encyclopedia of the Philosophical Sciences in Basic Outline*, edited by Klaus Brinkmann and Daniel O. Dahlstrom. Cambridge: Cambridge University Press.

Hillman, Susanne. 2015. "'Not Living, But Going': Unheroic Survival, Trauma Performance, and Video Testimony." *Holocaust Studies* 21, no. 4: 215–235.
Kandel, Eric. 2012. *Interview by USC Shoah Foundation* (52091). Los Angeles, CA: Visual History Archive.
Klein, Gerda W. 1957. *All but My Life: A Memoir*. New York: Hill & Wang.
LaCapra, Dominick. 1994. *Representing the Holocaust: History, Theory, Trauma*. Ithaca, NY: Cornell University Press. www.jstor.org/stable/10.7591/j.ctvrf8b30.
Langer, Lawrence L. 1982. *Versions of Survival: The Holocaust and the Human Spirit*. New York: New York University Press.
Langer, Lawrence L. 1991. *Holocaust Testimonies: The Ruins of Memory*. New Haven, CT: Yale University Press.
Lanzmann, Claude. 1985. *Shoah: An Oral History of the Holocaust*. New York: Pantheon Books.
Lengyel, Olga. 1947a. *Five Chimneys: The True Chronicle of a Woman Who Survived Auschwitz*. New York: Ziff Davis.
Levi, Primo. 1988. *The Drowned and the Saved*. London: Abacus Books.
Levi, Trude. 1995. *A Cat Called Adolf*. London: Vallentine Mitchell.
Levi, Trude. 1995. *USC Shoah Foundation* (Interview 7093). Los Angeles, CA: Visual History Archive.
Levi, Trude. 2003. *Did You Ever Meet Hitler Miss?: A Holocaust Survivor Talks to Young People*. London: Valentine Mitchell.
Lewis, Stephen. 1984. *Art out of Agony: The Holocaust Theme in Literature, Sculpture and Film*. Montreal: CBC Enterprises.
Lyotard, Jean-François. 1988. *The Differend: Phrases in Dispute*. Manchester: Manchester University Press.
Metz, Johann Baptist. 2007. *Faith and History in Society; Toward a Practical Fundamental Theology*. New York: The Crossroad Publishing Company.
Neusner, Jacob. 1984. *Invitation to the Talmud: A Teaching Book*. San Francisco, CA: Harper and Row.
Oppenheimer, Paul. 1996. *From Belsen to Buckingham Palace*. Newark, NJ: Beth Shalom Holocaust Centre.
Państwowe Muzeum na Majdanku. 2020. "The Deportation of Jews to Majdanek." April 27. www.majdanek.eu/en/pow/the_deportations_of_jews_to_majdanek__1941___1944/74.
Papanek, George. 1996. *Interview with USC Shoah Foundation* (Interview 11978). Los Angeles, CA: Visual History Archive.
Patterson, David. 2012. *Open Wounds: The Crisis of Jewish Thought in the Aftermath of the Holocaust*. Seattle, WA: University of Washington Press.
Rousset, David. 1951. *A World Apart (L'Univers Concentrationnaire)*. London: Secker and Warburg.
Rudof, Joanne Weiner. 1998. "Shaping Private and Public Memory: Holocaust Testimonies, Interviews and Documentaries." *Studies on the Audio-Visual Testimony of Victims of the Nazi Crimes and Genocides* 1 (June).
Schloss, Eva, and Evelyn Kent. 1988. *Eva's Story: A Survivor's Tale*. New York: St Martin's Press.
Steinsaltz, Adin. 2006. *The Essential Talmud*. 30th anniversary ed. New York: Basic Books.
Trezise, Thomas. 2013. *Witnessing Witnessing: On the Reception of Holocaust Survivor Testimony*. New York: Fordham University Press.
Tribich, Mala. 2012. *Interview with USC Shoah Foundation* (Interview 52091). Los Angeles, CA: Visual History Archive.

USC Shoah Foundation. n.d. "Interviewer Guidelines." https://sfi.usc.edu/collecting.
Wiesel, Elie. 1979. *A Jew Today*. New York: Vintage Books.
Wiesel, Elie. 1982. *One Generation After*. New York: Schocken Books.
Wiesel, Elie. 1999. *And the Sea Is Never Full*. New York: Alfred A Knopf.
Wollaston, Isabel. 1996. *A War against Memory?: The Future of Holocaust Remembrance*. London: SPCK.
Young, James Edward. 1990. *Writing and Rewriting the Holocaust: Narrative and the Consequences of Interpretation*. Bloomington, IN: Indiana University Press.

INDEX

[Note: numbers in italics indicate a figure]

Adelsberger, Lucie 165
Adizes, Ichak Kalderon 33
Adorno, Theodore 61, 76n4, 76n5, 147
Ainsztein 137
Alterman, Nathan xiv, 87
Améry, Jean 75, 216
Ancona-Vincent, Victoria 20, *23*, 169;
    see also Vincent, Victoria
apartheid 93
Appelfeld, Aharon xv, 60–61, 75, 94, 151
Arendt, Hannah 147
Ariav, Ariel *191*
Ariav, Avi *191*
Ariav, Nimrod "Zigi" ix, 86, 189–192, *191*
Armija Krajova (Polish resistance army) 190
Arnon, Joseph 135
atrocity: Chroniclers of 130, 131, 132; German genocidal 72; Gutter's experiences of 92; Hassan's notes regarding 146; Lewin's documentation of 138; recollections of xiii; Third Reich 128; witness to 9, 25
atrocity memories 15; loss of 63; reliving of event via 64
atrocity propaganda 4
audio-visual Holocaust testimony: archived recordings of xii–xiii, xv, 203; benefit of 115; birth of (Hela Goldstein's testimony) 3, 6; collective memory and 32; cycles and chronologies as armature of 92; Eger (Edith) 197–198; Gutter (Pinchas) 79, 82; Halter (Roman), decision to use alternative forms 88; information, distinct from 200; Krausz (Donald) 96–98; Maisel's documentation of 167–168; potential hidden exegetical meaning of 26; as record of the past and object of history 31; in second or non-native language 33; Srebnik 57; transcriptions of 200–201; as vehicle of testimony 44, 87, 90–92, 200
Auschwitz: Adorno on 61, 76n5; Austrian Auschwitz Camp Survivors Association (Osterreichische Lagergemeinschaft Auschwitz) 153; "authentic voice" of 96; Bechhöfer's mother at 74–75; Birkin's novel about 144–145; *Boy Who Drew Auschwitz* 171–173, 200; bricklaying 171; as defining symbol of Holocaust 95–96; Delbo's struggle with memories of 154, 199; Eger's memories of 197–199; experiential truth of 67; Frankl's experiences at 197; Geve's deportation to and drawing of 171–173, 200; Greenman (Leon)'s deportation to 49n4; hanging execution of women at 21–26, 27, 28, 34, 169; Hart-Moxen's returns to and memories of 104–107, 150; *I Was a Doctor in Auschwitz* (Perl) 144; Janowska sub-camp 69; killing centres combined with manual labor at

Index

55; Kidron's description of 146; *Kitty: Return to Auschwitz* 87; Kogon's account of 175–176; language, insufficiency of 63–64; legal extinguishing of life at 36; Lengyal's memories of 45; Lessons From Auschwitz program 87; Levi (Primo) as survivor of 69; Lyotard on 66; multiplicity of memory at 68; Red Army liberation of xvii; returns to 104–107; Schloss (Eva)'s memory of 168; struggle of language to convey human wants and needs xiv; tattooed numbers 26, 177; "useless knowledge" of xvii; Webber on 46; Wiesel on 62
Auschwitz I: *Appel Platz* 24; *Appell* procedure 20, 24; hanging execution of women at 21–26, 27, 28, 34, 169
Auschwitz-Birkenau 71; *Anatomy of Auschwitz Death Camp* 140; Delbo's memoires of 64; Dinur/Feiner (Yehiel)'s account of 176–179; Felix (Kitty)'s report on 166–167; gas chamber and crematorium complex IV (then known as III), destruction of 20; Kanada section 69, 105; Krausz (Donald)'s memories of 96–98; Lengyel's arrival at 152m 165; Lingens-Reiner in 71, 100, 103, 164; *Love It Was Not* (documentary film) 69; *One Day in Auschwitz* (film) 105; *Sonderkommando* at 138–141; underground prisoner resistance movement 20; Union ammunitions factory 20; Victoria Vincent at 21–26, 27, 28, 34, 169; women's barracks 105; women's orchestra 73, 103
Auschwitz Death Camp album (Rozenstrauch) 21
Auschwitz Trial of 1964 153
Austrian Auschwitz Camp Survivors Association (Osterreichische Lagergemeinschaft Auschwitz) 153
Army Film and Photographic Unit (AFPU)
Aryans 67, 71, 100, 129, 136

Babi Yar 95
Bacon, Yehuda ix
Baltic countries 72, 180n19
Batz (Captain, probably Rudolf) 156–158, 180n19
Baron, Salo 147
Bauer, Gitta 206
Bauer, Yehuda 34, 41
Bauman, Janina 83–84
bayonets 128
Baum, Vicki 148

Beaver, Chesley 195
Bechhöfer, Rosa 74–75
Bechhöfer, Susi ix, 74–75
being-for-itself 83–87
Belarus 40, 72
Belsen Uncovered (Sington) 3, 109
Beniaz, Celina ix
Bergen-Belsen: British Army filming of xiii; British Movietone film crew at 3, 8; British Tanks at *110*; burial of dead at 7; diary of Anne Frank juxtaposed against 208; Felix (Kitty), report on 166–167; Goldstein (Hela), testimony of 3–9, *5*, 111; Hardman's arrival at 163; "Helen Colin" at 8; liberation of xii, 3, 7, 107, *110*; Marx (Erich), testimony of 169–171; plan (architectural) of *111*; radio broadcast from site of 6; rutabagas at 107–112; Singleton's recollections of 109; Warshawksi (Sonia), testimony of 107–109
Berg, Mary 133, 135
Berger, Oskar 175
Berney, Leonard 109, *110*
Bernstein, Sidney 4, 6
Bettelheim, Bruno 70–71
Bezwinska, Jadwiga 138–139
Binder, Janine 32–33
Birken, Edith ix, 144–145, 151, 179n2
Birkenau *see* Auschwitz-Birkenau
Birkenwalde camp 4, 17n4
Birmingham Snow Hill railway station 150
Blake, Brian 4
Blake, Naomi ix
Blanchot, Maurice 49n7: on death and dying 47, 56; "deferred death" concept of 132; "the disaster," concept of 132, 135; on the inauthentic of "authentic" 93; on the language of waiting for death 136; on "learning to think with pain" 41
Blumenfeld, Vladimir 176
Blumenthal, Ella ix
"Bolshevist Jews" 37
Boder, David 144
Boris II (King) 206
Borowski, Tadeusz 71, 150
Botton, Dolly ix
Botton, Julio ix
British Army, filming of Bergen-Belsen xiii
British Movietone, film crew at Bergen-Belsen 3, 8
British Pathé 3
British Tanks: Bergen-Belsen *110*
Bromberg, Pam 101

Browning, Christopher 30, 107; "ordinary men" concept of 204
Buber, Martin: *I-Thou* construct of 12, 48; *see also* I-It; I-Thou
Buchenwald: Bettelheim in 70; Geve/Cohn's liberation from 171–173; Heiden on 128–129; Kogon in 174–176; Rousset in 153
Bundestag 34
Burke, Peter 38

Caruth, Cathy 215
cattle wagons xvi–xvii, 21, 35, 97–98, 197–198
Celan, Paul 150
Centre of Contemporary Jewish Documentation (CJDC) (*Centre de Documentation Juive Contemporaine*) 143
Charney, Israel 62
Chełmno death camp xv, 55–60, *65*, 65–66, 88
Chmielnicki, Bohdan 168
Choice Therapy, The 197
Chronicers (of Nazi atrocities) 67, 130–137, 140
Citrom, Elisabeth ix
Citrom, George ix
Citron, Elena 69
CJDC *see* Centre of Contemporary Jewish Documentation (CJDC) (*Centre de Documentation Juive Contemporaine*)
clichés, problem with 195
Cohen, Casey 194–195
Cohn, Stefan 171–173; *see also* Geve, Thomas
concentration camp system 35
Confino, Alon 39
cookhouse 109
Cygielman, Avraham 189–190
Cygielman, Lieb 189
Cygielman, Szulem 189–190
Czechoslovakia: Kosice xvii, 197; Nazi invasion of 84
Czech, Danuta 138–139
Czerniaków, Adam xv–xvi, 132–134, 157–158

Dachau 128, 130
Dagan, Bat-Sheva or Batsheva ix, 216
Dawidowicz, Lucy S. 137
death: Blanchot on 47, 56; denial of 42, 46
death camps: Bettelheim's misunderstanding of 70; liberation of xii; Srebrnik's survival of 57–58; *see also* cattle wagons; Chełmno death camp; Majdanek
death march 20, 75
Death's Head SS Unit 74
deep listening 16
Defonseca, Misha 114–120
Delbo, Charlotte xvii; Auschwitz as described by 64–65, 99, 199; *Auschwitz and After* 153–154, 180n14
Desbois, Patrick 72
Des Pres, Terrence 42, 46, 62, 70; *Survivor, The* 46, 93, 152
dialogical context 85
dialogical process 91
dialogic encounter 11, 16
Dinur, Benzion 93
Dinur, Yehiel 176–179, *177*
Dos Polyishe Yidntum series 162
Drix, Samuel: *Witness* 46
Dunicz-Niwinska, Helena 103, 121
Dzierżoniów 104

Ebert, Lily ix, 44
Edelmann, Marek 209, 211
Eger, Edith Eva ix, xvii, 197–199
Eichmann, Adolph: trial of 1961 57, *58*, 72, 144, 156, 177, *177*
Einsatzkommando 2 180n19
Einsatzgruppen killing squads 35, 72, 88, 148; Subsequent Nuremberg Proceedings #9, the Einsatzgruppen Case of September 1946 74
Einstein, Albert 152
Eisenhower, Dwight D. 6
Eisen, Max ix
Eisler, Riane ix
Elefant, Eva *see* Eger, Edith Eva
Eliach, Yaffe 69
Elster, Aaron ix
encounter, definition of 11; as means of resolving dilemma between *witness* and *mandate* 42–48; *see also* dialogical encounter
epistemology of the historical sciences 9
Endölsung der Jüdishe Frage, der ("the Final Solution of the Jewish Question") 68; *see also* Final Solution
Erdman, Lisa 95
escapees 6
Esther, Book of 168
Ezrahi, Sidra DeKoven 76n5, 166, 205

false testimony 120; *see also* Defonseca; hoaxers; Wilkomirski
faschschaft (Nazi professional union) 129

226 Index

Fawcett, Charles 147
Feiner, Yechiel 176–179
Feldman, Gisella ix
Felix, Kitty 166–167; *see also* Hart-Moxon, Kitty
Felman, Shoshana 15, 67, 91
Fénelon, Fania 73, 103
Ferencz, Benjamin 74
Feuchtwanger, Lion 148
Final Solution 40; *Endölsung der Jüdishe Frage* ("the Final Solution of the Jewish Question") 68
Firestone, Renee ix
Fossoli 28
Frank, Anne: *Diary of a Young Girl* 135, 207
Frankl, Viktor xvii, 197
Frank, Otto 168, 181n31, 207
Frank, Steven ix
Fransman, John ix
Fried, Heidi ix, 88
Friedlander, Saul 41, 147, 149
Friedman, Philip 143
Fritzschal, Fritzie ix
Fry, Varian 147

Gabbai, Dario ix, 63, 211–212
Ganzfried, Daniel 112, 121n17
Garbarini, Alexa 127, 131
Geiringer, Fritzi 181n31, 207
Gertner, Ala 20
Gestapo 101, 158, 174; prison 175
Geve, Thomas (Stefan Cohn) ix, 151, 179; *Boy Who Drew Auschwitz* 171–173, 200; *Youth in Chains* 172–173, 200
ghettos (WWII Jewish): escapees as witness-authors 6; Kogon's collection of first-person accounts from 175, 176; purpose of 35; USC Shoah Foundation data on xiv, 90; writing by victims trapped in 127, 130, 136–138; *see also* Riga ghetto; Warsaw Ghetto
Gies, Miep 207
Gill, Anton 75
Ginburg, Ibi ix
Ginsburg, Waldemar ix, 164, 209–210
Glazar, Richard ix, 150
Glick, Peter 192
Goebbels, Josef 118
Golden Rule of Classical Judaism xi, 214
Goldstein, Hela 3–9, 5, 111
Gotz, Ely ix
Gradowski, Salmen 138–140
gravestone 162, 179
Greenman, Leon ix, 49

Greenspan, Henry x, 16, 65, 94, 99, 203; "recounting," concept of 91, 211
Gross Rosen Concentration Camp 106
Grunberg, Bernard ix
Gunskirchen concentration camp 199
Gutter, Helena 80
Gutter, Mendel 80
Gutter, Pinchas ix, xv, 79–82, 92–93, 145, 155, 168; twin sister of 80, 82
Gutter, Sabina 82

Habermas, Jürgen 46
Halbwachs, Maurice 39, 49n5
Halter, Roman ix, 88, *89*
Haft, Harry 69
Haman 168
Hass, Aaron 155–156, 179, 180n18, 192
Hassan, Judith 146
Harel, Zev 155
Hartman, Geoffrey 40–41, 218
Hart-Moxon, Kitty ix, xv, 64, 83; arrival in England 149–150; documentaries made by 104–107; *I am Alive* 87; *Kitty: Return to Auschwitz* (film) 87; memories of 106–107; *One Day in Auschwitz* (film) 105; report (unpublished) for Quaker relief team at Bergen-Belsen 166–167, 211, 213; Stockholm Forum, speech to 87–88
Hardman, Leslie (Chaplain) 163
Hass, Aaron 155–156, 179, 180n18, 192
Hassan, Judith 146, 154–155
Hegel, Georg Wilhelm Fredrich: *being-in-itself* of 84, 213; dialectics of 84, 100, 214
Heiden, Konrad 128–129
Helfgott, Ben ix, 88
Herman, Judith 25
hermeneutics of memory 42–43
Hersch, Arek ix, 76n3
Hersonski, Yael 6
Hessich Lichtenau munitions plant 211
HET *see* Holocaust Educational Trust
Hilberg, Raul 113, 137
Himmler, Heinrich 30–31, 137
Hippler, Fritz 118, *119*
Hirsch, Marianne 13
historiographical defiance 136–140
historiography: determining what is of value to 161; memory and 29, 30, 31, 40; process of 41; testimony and 26
Hitler, Adolf 7, 35, 59; *I Survived Hitler's Ovens* (Lengyel) 152; *I was Hitler's Prisoner* (Lorant) 129; mythologizing of 206; "war against memory" 101
Hitler-Jugend (Hitler Youth) 190

hoaxers and hoax testimony 114–115, 118, 120; *see also* Defonseca; Wilkomirski
Holland, Luke 74
Holocaust: absence of names and dates of Jews murdered during 35; Auschwitz as defining symbol of 95–96; Being-in-itself and 84; crisis of witness of 36, 42–45; anti I-Thou relationship created by 67; documentation of 143; *encounter* as means of resolving dilemma of witness and mandate 42–48; France 143; Friedlander's avoidance of 147; International Holocaust Remembrance Alliance (IHRA) 39–40; lived experience of 66; mandate of witnessing 45–47; memoirs about 93, 144; Poland 156, 161; popular culture and 28, 120; rehumanization of Jews via testimonies of 38; role of Vatican 38; sites of 104
Holocaust denial 103
Holocaust Education and Archive Research Team 56–57
Holocaust Educational Trust (HET) 87
Holocaust literature 41, 100
Holocaust Man, The 189–193
Holocaust memory: symptoms of 15; trajectory of 163, 173; typologies of 13
Holocaust museums and centres 11; Cape Town Holocaust and Genocide Centre 79; Houston 8; UK National Holocaust Centre 20, 21, 26, 28, 29, 34; US Holocaust Memorial Museum 57, 58, 59
Holocaust porn 178
Holocaust scholars 113
Holocaust survivors 114, 144, 146, 151; *see also* individuals by name
Holocaust witness: defining 66–73; impossibility of forgetting and 73–75; origins of 125–136
Holocaust witnessing 41; imperative of 164
Horowitzova, Katerina (Lustig) 47
Horowitz, Richard ix

IHRA *see* International Holocaust Remembrance Alliance
I-It (Buber) 48
International Holocaust Remembrance Alliance (IHRA) 39–40
I-Thou (Buber): anti-I-Thou relationship created by Holocaust 67–68, 218; Chroniclers read according to 132, 140; critical analysis based on 102; Czerniaków reading according to 134; deficit in comprehension reduced by 63; dehumanization overcome by 218; dissonance between surviving victim and listener recognized by 66; *Dos Polyishe Yidntum* read according to 161; empathy with the past facilitated by 44; encounter with visual testimony (Halter) 88; Ginsberg (Waldemar)'s engagement with session according to 210; Hass' congruence with 156; I-It (Buber) contrasted to 48; Gutter's relationship with his audience 93; Lewin reading according to 138; "listen and listen again" 200; memory encountered and confronted through 75; new testimonial modality based on 12–13, 120; ontological reading of testimony according to 85, 87; onus placed on listener by 96, 98; overview and summary of positional frame of 48; relationship trust within 85; Riess and Schoskes establishing a relationship according to 158; subjectification at heart of 161; surviving victims' testimonies consulted according to 193; three modes of memory experienced via 61; trust as foundational to 112

Janowska camp 46, 69
Jehovah's Witness 69
Jewish Historical Commission (*Centralna Żdowska Komisja Historzcyna*), Lublin, Poland 143–144
Jewish memory, modern dilemma of 162
Jockusch, Laura 143–144
Johnston, Jennifer 84
Josephs, Jeremy 74
Jungblut, Karen 17n5
Jung, Carl 14; concept of the individual and the persona 12, 15

Kahana, Boaz 155
Kahana, Eva 155
Kahneman, Daniel: concepts of "experiencing self" and "remembering self" xiii, 12, 15, 24, 91
Kandel, Denise ix
Kandel, Eric R. ix, 201–202
Kant, Immanuel 36, 48
Kantrowitz (judge) 118
Kaplan, Chaim 133, 136
Kaplan, Israel 143
Karpf, Anne 114
Katin, Miriam ix
Katz, Ruben ix, 76n3
Kaufmann, Joshua ix

Ka-Tzetnik 135633 176–179
Kent, Roman ix
Kessel, Sim 101
Kidron, Carol A. 146
Kielce ghetto 175
Kindertransports 74, 147–148, 179n5
Kirschenbaum, Izik 33
Kirschenbaum, Jeremiah 33
Kleinau, Klaus 74
Klein, Fritz 206
Kogon, Eugen 173–176
Korczak, Janusz 133–135
Korets ghetto 96
Kor, Eva ix
Krausz, Donald 96–98
Kren, George 180n15
Kulmhof 57
Kuznetsov, Anatoly 94–95
Kwiet, Konrad 120

LaCapra, Dominick 217
Ladino language 33
Langer, Lawrence: "double bind" identified by 42; "choiceless choice" of 152; falsification as understood by 103; on life and death merging in metaphor 27; on Lingens-Reiner's moral choices 153; Magda F. interviewed by 42, 44–45; memory strata identified by 75; testimony as understood by 90
Lanzmann, Claude: *Shoah* (film) xiv–xv, 54–58, *59*
Lasker-Wallfisch, Anita ix, 103, 168
Laub, Dori 15, 67, 91
Lax, Sonia ix
Lebovics, Paula ix
Lee, Michael ix, 149
Lee, Vera 114
Lengyel, Olga: *Five Chimneys* 45, 144, 151–152, 165; *I Survived Hitler's Ovens* 152; on Mengele 205–206
Lesser, Ben ix
Levi, Primo 73–74, 145–146; *Drowned and the Saved* 69; "gray zone" 69, 213; *If This is a Man* 208; memory and forgetting as described by 98–99, 101
Levi, Trude 120n2, 195, 210
Lewin, Abraham 137–138
Lewis, Helen 84
Lewis, Mike 7
Lewis, Stephen 95
Lichten, Joseph 134
Lichterman, Miriam ix
Lincolnwood, Illinois 32
life lessons 197–199

Lingens-Reiner, Ella ix; as "Aryan" in a concentration camp 71; complexity as "witness" 99–103; *Prisoners of Fear* 144, 151–153, 164
Lipok, Karl-Heinz 74
Lithuania 40, 69, 86
Łodz 79; District Court 56
Łodz ghetto 145
Logotherapy 197
Lorant, Stefan 129
Love It Was Not (film) 69
Lublin 80, 176
Lüneberg trials 1946 67
Lustig, Arnost 47
Lwów Ghetto 46
Lyotard, Jean François 42; on Auschwitz 66; "differend" of 62–63; on testimony and truthfulness 85

Maharsha, the 215
Maisel, Philip ix, 100–101, 167–168
Majdanek 55, 80, 92, 161, 176, 189; two women about to be hanged, final words of 169
mandate 46; *encounter* as means of resolving dilemma between witness and 42–48
mandate of witnessing 45–47
Maniker, Edith ix
manikins 64
Mann, Grace 74
Mann, Heinrich 147
Mann, Erika 129–130; *School for Barbarians* 129
Mann, Thomas 129–130, 148
Marx, Erich: *So war es* 169–171
matseyeve (gravestone) 162
matzevah (memorial stone) 131
Maydanek (Strigler) 161
McDonagh, Francis 61
Megilah, The 168
Mémorial de la Shoah 143
memorial stone 131
memory, definition of 10; *see also* Holocaust memory
Mendelsohn, Steven ix
mental health professionals 154–155
Metz, Johanne Baptiste 215
Milan, city of 20, 23, 24, 145
Milan, Johanna ix
Miller, Daisy ix
Miłosz, Czeslaw 45
misery: "unity of" 94
Moll, Otto 211–212
Moore, Barrington 94

Mosberg, Ed ix
munitions plant 211

National Relief Committee for Deportees 144
Nelson, David 104, 107
Neuberger Holocaust Centre, Toronto Canada 79
Neumann-Neurode, General von 158
Neusner, Jacob 214
Niederland, William 154
Nora, Pierre 27
Novick, Peter 39
Nutkewicz, Mordecai 176

Oberrotman, Janine 32–33
Ohrdruf sub-camp 175
Oneg Shabbat team of historians137–138, 143
Oppenheimer, Corinne 180n8
Oppenheimer, Eve ix
Oppenheimer, Paul ix, xiv, xv, 83, 99, 148, 180n8; life or fact as "stranger than fiction" 61, 206
Oppenheimer, Rudi ix
"ordinary men", Browning's concept of 204
Orianienburg 175
ossification 204
Osterreichische Lagergemeinschaft Auschwitz (Austrian Auschwitz Camp Survivors Association) 153
Ozick, Cynthia 113

Panzer Training School 3
Papanek, George xvii, 196, *197*
Pathé News 4
Pearce, Andrew 29
Perl, Gisella 46, 151, 165–166
Pisar, Samuel ix
Pivnik, Nathan ix
Pivnik, Sam ix
Plato 214
Podchlebnik, Michael xv, 58, 60, 98
Poland 38
Police Battalion no. 101 204
Podchlebnik, Michael 60
Pollak, Susan ix
precious stones 105
professional expertise of survivors as therapists and teachers xvii, 197, 198, 216
professional fantasist 103
professional historian 42, 103, 161
professional insight 198
professional union (Nazi) 129

Purcell, Steven: *One Day in Auschwitz* (film) 105

Ravensbrück 71, 97
"recounting," Greenspan's concept of 91, 211
Reder, Rudolf 96
Reichenbach 104
Ricoeur, Pau 9, 29–31, 39–40
Riess, Curt 156–159
Riga ghetto 136
Ringelblum, Emmanuel 133, 138
Robota, Roza 20
Rosenblat, Herman 120
Rosenblat, Rosa 120
Rosenfeld, Alvin Hirsch 45, 61–62, 150, 164
Rosenstrauch, Zofia *21*
Rossoliński-Liebe, Grzegorz 38, 40
Rousset, David 153
Routier, Marcel 73
Rubenstein, Richard 36
Rudof, Joanne Weiner 195
Rwanda xiii

Sachsenhausen 96, 97, 128, 175
Safirsztayn, Regina
Salt, Renee ix
Scharf, Rafael Felix 113
Schindler, Max ix
Schindler, Oskar 205–207
Schindler, Rose ix
Schindler's List (film) 28
Schloss, Eva ix, 168, 207–208
Schneersohn, Isaac 143
Schneidrman, S.L. 135
Schwartz, Dana ix
Schwartz, Jan 160–163
Schwartzmann, Gina ix
Schwartzmann, Roy 9
Schwartz, Jan 160–163
Shachnow, Sid ix
SHAEF *see* Section at the Supreme Headquarters Allied Expeditionary Forces
Shandler, Jeffrey 33
Shapiro, Sara ix, 96
Shenker, Noah 35, 44
Shmulewitz, I. 162
Shoah Foundation Archive 201
Shoah (Lanzmann) 150
Shoskes, Haim 180n21
Shoskes, Henry (Henryk Szoszkes) 156–161
Silman, Trudy ix

Sington, Derrick (Lt.) 3, 109, *110, 111,* 112
Smith, Stephen D. xii–xix
Sobibor 97
something-other 83–87
Sonderkommando 57, 96, 131, 137–140; Gabbai 73
Sonnenburg camp 127–128
Sophie's Choice (book and film) 28
South Africa: apartheid 93; Cape Town 79, 92, 209; Gutter residing in 92–93, 155; Truth and Reconciliation Commission in South Africa 25, 76n8
South American Federation of Polish Jews 160
Srebrnik, Szymon xv, 54–61, 65–66
SS: Belsen 109; Death's Head SS Unit 74; in *Final Account* (film) 74; lured into trap by Mordechai Nutkewicz; Otto Moll 211–212; Podchlebnik (Michael)'s memories of 60; Sonnenburg camp 127; Wünsch 69
SS women 169
social catharsis 195
Steiner, George 94, 156
Steinsaltz, Adin 215
Stern, Martin ix
Stevens, Andrew ix
Stier, Oren Baruch 30
Stocken, Grace 74
Stone, Dan 30
Strigler, Moshe 176
Stutthof 96
suicide: attempts at Sonnenberg camp 128; Czerniaków xvi, 133–134; gas chambers as 70; Hitler 7; Lengyel's "mental ripeness" for 165; Lewis (Helen)'s relatives 84; of surviving victims 150
Section at the Supreme Headquarters Allied Expeditionary Forces (SHAEF) 6
'surviving victim' as term 17n3
survivor *see* 'surviving victim' as term
Survivor, The (film, about Harry Haft) 69
Szoszkes, Henryk *see* Shoskes, Henry

Telefunken factory 104
testimony: concept of 16–17; definition of 11; variations of 87–91; *see also* audio-visual testimony; USC Shoah Foundation
Third Reich 38, 68, 72, 128, 147, 157
"thirst" "hunger" "cold" xiv, 63, 64
Thomas, D. M. 95

torture xvii, 35, 199; considering the possibility of 165; memory of 75, 101, 216; succumbing to 216
Treblinka 97, 133, 134, 150, 159–160, 175
Tribich, Mala ix, xvi, 202
Truth and Reconciliation Commission in South Africa 25, 76n8
Tumblety, Joan 99
Turgel, Gina ix
Turski, Marian ix, 40

UK National Holocaust Centre 20, 21, 26, 28, *29*, 34
Ukraine 38, 40, 72, 86
Ukrainians xiv, 87
untermenschen 72
USC Institute of Creative Technologies 32
USC Shoah Foundation: 19 categories in testimonies analyzed from *194*; Defonseca 115–118, 120; De Wael 118; "Dimensions in Testimony" 32; Eger xvii; "experience groups" 115; Geve/Cohn 171; Goldstein 8; Gutter 79, 82; Halter 88; Hart-Moxon 87; Krausz 97; life history methodology used by xiv, 90; Maisel 168; policies 114; Smith at xiii–xvii; Oberrotman 32–33; Oppenheimer 148; Srebrnik 57, *59*; Visual History Archive 8, 33, 37, 44, 88, 114, 193; verification protocols 120; Visual History Foundation 28; Warshawski 108; word cloud from keyword "future message" 193, *195*
USHMM 177, 179
US Holocaust Memorial Museum 57, *58, 59*

Vatican 38
Verolme, Hetty (née Werkendam) 6
Vincent, Albert 20
Vincent, Lisa ix, 147
Vincent, Victoria (Victoria Ancona-Vincent) ix, *29*; *Beyond Imagination* 27; hanging scene at Auschwitz recounted by 20–29, 75, 98, 169, 198; identity disguised by 145; *Kindertransport* story of 179n4; paper diary hidden by *23*; Levi (Trude)'s approach to narrating her experiences of the camps compared to 210; smells of burning flesh described by 64; unexpected death of 26, 49n3
Viterbi, Erna ix

Wael, Monique de 115, 117; *see also* Defonseca
Wajcblum, Ester 20
Walker, Patrick Gordon 6
Wandering Jew (film) 119
"Wandering Jew," stereotype of 118
Wannsee Conference 36
Warsaw: Cygielman family in 190
Warsaw Ghetto 6; Batz (Captain, probably Rudolf) 156–158, 180n19; Berg as child in 133, 135; Defonseca's claims regarding 115, 120; German propaganda footage compiled in 6; Gutter (Pinchas)'s avoidance of describing 92; Jewish Council xv, 132; Judenrat 180n21; Korczak's diary 134; *Oneg Shabbat* team of historians meeting in 137–138, 143; resistance fighter Blumenfeld 176; Shoskes' warnings regarding 156–160
Warsaw Ghetto Uprising 80, 156, 190; Marek Edelman 209, 211
Warshawksi, Sonia ix; testimony of 107–109, 169
water 5, 97
watercolors *21*, 88, 90
Watt, Donald 120
Waxman, Zoë 30
Webber, Jonathan x, 46
Webb, Max ix
Wehrmacht 38
Weimar Republic 69
Weinreich, Max 161
Weismann-Klein, Gerda 213, 219n14
Weiss, George ix
Werfel, Franz 148
Werzberg, Benno 150
Westerbork 169
Westheimer, Ruth ix
white, color as symbol 55
White Hotel, The (Thomas) 95
white person in South Africa 93
white racial persecution 93
"White Raven, The" (Marx, Erich) 170

White, Hayden 61
Wiesel, Eli 73, 88, 207; on being the last survivor 219; Dubow quoted by 137; Hartman's differing perspective from 218; Himmler, counter to 31; "Kafka's messenger" referenced by 217–218; *Night* 161, 162, 179, 208; on power of giving witness in numbers 44, 47; Rosenfeld (Alvin)'s quoting of 62–63; self-imposed silence of 151; on silence or speaking out 65, 149, 192; on *Sonderkommandos* 131, 137; on surviving victims' decision to kill themselves 150
Wiesenthal, Simon ix
Wilkomirski, Binjamin 112–114, 120: *Fragments* 112–114
Williams, Bill 102, 121n7
Williams, Richard (Dick) 181n33
Wineman, Frieda ix
Winston, Simon ix
witness, definition of 10–11
Wulf, Joseph 150
Wünsch (SS officer) 69
Wyland, Paul 4

Yad Vashem 44; 1947 conference 143; Righteous Among Nations 153; Video Testimony Resource Centre 57; World Holocaust Memorial 144
Yahad in Unum archive 72
Yale Fortunoff Archive 44
Yerushalmi, Yosef Hayim 30, 162, 168
Yiddish culture 162–163
Yiddish language 33, 57, 160, 209
Yiddish literature 161–162; poetry 179
Yiddish newspaper: *Forward, The* 176; *Jewish Journal* 156
Yizkor Books 144, 162
Young, James 41
Yudkowsky, Naomi *21*

Zuckerman, Antek 209

Printed in the United States
by Baker & Taylor Publisher Services